International Comparisons in
Human Resource Management

International Comparisons in Human Resource Management

Edited by C. Brewster and S. Tyson

Pitman

Pitman Publishing
128 Long Acre, London WC2E 9AN

A Division of Longman Group UK Limited

First published in 1991

British Library Cataloguing in Publication Data

International comparisons of human resource management.
  1. Personnel management
  I. Brewster, Chris   II. Tyson, S.
  658.3

ISBN 0 273 03316 6

Typeset by Medcalf Type Ltd, Bicester, Oxon
Printed and bound in Singapore

Contents

List of figures

List of figures

List of tables

List of tables

List of contributors

Professor D. Akinnusi — University of Lagos

Professor F. Bournois — ESC Lyon

Dr C. Brewster — Cranfield Institute of Technology

Dr P. Briggs — City of London Polytechnic

Mr J. Grahl — Queen Mary and Westfield College, University of London

Dr L. Haiven — University of Saskatchewan

Professor A. Kakabadse — Cranfield Institute of Technology

Professor P. Kirkbride — Hatfield Polytechnic Business School

Mr A. Lai — Topic Development Limited, Hong Kong

Dr P. Lawrence — Loughborough University of Technology

Mr C. Leggett — City Polytechnic of Hong Kong

Ms P. Metcalfe — Price Waterhouse Consultants

Dr N. Papalexandris — Athens School of Economics and Business

Professor M. Roomkin — Kellogg School of Management

Professor B. Sharma — University of New Brunswick

Professor B. Springer — American Graduate School of International Management, Arizona

Dr M. Tayeb — Heriot-Watt University

Dr P. Teague — University of Ulster

Professor K. Thurley — LSE, University of London

Professor S. Tyson — Cranfield Institute of Technology

Acknowledgements

The papers collected in this volume were mostly selected from those presented at a Conference held in 1988 at Cranfield, which was jointly sponsored by the International Institute for Labour Studies of the International Labour Office, and the Cranfield School of Management, England.

We would like to express our thanks to all those who attended the Conference, whose many suggestions have been incorporated in revised versions of the papers published here. We would also like to thank Rosemarie Greve of the ILO and our publisher Penelope Woolf for their advice and encouragement.

Any errors or omissions remain our responsibility.

Chris Brewster and Shaun Tyson
Cranfield 1990

1
Introduction

CHRIS BREWSTER AND SHAUN TYSON

In the twentieth century there has emerged the concept of the 'global market': a trading system based on the interdependencies which arise from the internationalisation of trade and business. There is now 24-hour-a-day trading via London, New York and Tokyo stock exchanges, information is spread through satellite, computer and television, customers and suppliers cross national boundaries, there are international marketing and manufacturing.

Every political movement seems to have an international dimension. The collapse of the Soviet empire and the reunification of Germany have reverberated throughout Europe at a time when economic union among the European Community has raised the question of cultural differences and similarities. Japanese export strengths have dramatically affected the economies of Europe and America. Third World debt has shaken financial confidence around the world. Ecological disasters such as global warming are seen as international problems. There are few distinctions now between the realm of what is national and what is international.

This book is about how people are managed in different countries and different cultures. It focuses on the main variables which we should consider when making comparative studies. We use the phrase 'human resource management', itself a successful North American export, to describe the range of policies which have strategic significance in an organisation. These may be designed 'to maximise organisational integration, employee commitment, flexibility and quality of work' (Guest, 1987, p. 503), or they may have broader business goals, encompassing change to the organisational values, to organisation structure and changing productivity, from outsourcing to franchise operations. Whatever the brand of human resource management, in the context of this book we have taken it to include subjects which have traditionally been the concerns of personnel management and industrial relations scholars, as well as the topics which cover more innovative and strategic approaches to people management.

Why take a comparative approach?

Our reasons for taking a comparative approach to human resource management can be explained by reference to the managerial and social scientific purposes behind our thinking.

For managers, already battered by the 'waves of change', coping with technical innovation and economic shifts; there is a need to develop the competencies necessary to manage their working futures (Morgan, 1988). Not only do they need to understand the nature of these changes, but they need also to take on an international perspective in order to manage in different cultures and with different customs.

As common technologies spread globally, there is a growing recognition that the solutions to most technical problems are now possible. What we do not find easy is solving the people problems: how to change behaviour, how to improve performance, how to predict future performance, and how to make the best use of the talents available. Human resource management is concerned with how people are managed. Along with technical advance has come an awareness that people are resources, which, if managed effectively, will bring a competitive advantage to any organisation. Interest is growing in how people can be managed in order to maximise that competitive advantage (Storey, 1989). For many years there has been a widespread interest in the different production systems and management strategies adopted in Japan, the USA and Europe, increasingly now attention is also focused on the people management systems, attempting to explain the differences in terms of culture, but also to discover differences in management techniques and policies (Taira, 1973; Dore, 1973; Jacobs *et al.*, 1978; Mansfield and Poole, 1981).

There is therefore a need to understand how different cultures undertake human resource management for what Doeringer (1981) calls 'pragmatic' reasons. That is, because there are lessons to be learned from other cultures and we need to control for cultural influences when examining solutions. To this can be added the further pragmatic and urgent reason that managers must now practise their skills and techniques in multicultural contexts, and achieve objectives internationally.

In contrast to the managerial purposes behind our book, there are social scientific reasons for international comparisons of human resource management. Broadly, these are to discover the causes and effects of social action. The analytical techniques are similar to those found in the study of industrial relations. Poole (1986), for example, takes a 'strategic choice of action' model, an action frame of reference which he combines with Dunlop's idea that industrial relations can be viewed as a system. He examines the 'meanings' of the actors in the system – government, trade unions and employers – and looks at how these meanings interact with structures and cultures. The forces for divergence and convergence are thus described by reference to cultures, ideologies, environments and institutions.

Such a framework is valuable in classifying knowledge for comparative analysis, but it does lead us to view societies as 'wholes'. This is convenient for comparative analysis but also dangerous, since we can make assumptions about the differences *between* societies without asking whether these differences also exist *within* the society. Some of these difficulties can be overcome if we use comparative studies to analyse the differences: 'Comparative industrial relations is a systematic method of investigation relating to two or more countries which has analytic rather than descriptive implications' (Bean, 1985, p. 3).

One of the crucial issues in comparative studies must therefore be the level of analysis. Here we may see a coincidence of managerial and sociological purposes. Neither the nation state nor the employing organisation can be taken as the appropriate level of analysis without oversimplifying the data.

Political and economic changes in the 1980s in the Eastern Bloc and the European Community have heightened awareness of human resource issues: for example in labour markets, participation structures, the impact of supranational laws, differences in rewards, recruitment patterns and the harmonisation of qualifications. These changes exemplified by Europeanisation have brought out the opportunities for re-evaluating human resource management in a broader, regional rather than national context.

Western values have spread through the influence of colonial power, through trade and through multinational corporations (Jaeger, 1983; Beamish, 1988; Martinez and Ricks, 1989). They have often been accepted as the received wisdom by developing nations in Africa, the Middle East, Far East and in South America. Against the assumption of Western-style notions of efficiency and effectiveness must be placed a growing awareness that religious, cultural and national characteristics may be opposed to European and North American values and styles. The role of multinational corporations in transferring expertise is of interest here. Similarly, new-found wealth and economic growth among developing nations impose strains on local economies, on existing institutions and on traditional relationships. Comparative studies which reveal patterns or signs can be used to adduce whether dependency relationships are changing, and how this affects the management of people and their personal development.

Issues raised by comparative studies

There is an argument, then, and we believe a strong argument, to be made for the value of comparative studies. Such studies are not, however, unproblematic: they raise both conceptual and methodological concerns. This section addresses some of these conceptual issues and the next section considers some of the methodological problems. The two are not distinct; but it is useful here to separate them out for the purpose of discussion.

The convergence thesis

One major area of dispute concerns the extent to which the facts support a thesis of convergence. There is a line of argument from such authors as Harbison and Myers (1959) to Pugh (1990) that developments in technology and economics are creating a world which is less differentiated – few societies now have no automobiles, or watches, or radios and televisions. In almost all cases the numbers, although they vary markedly throughout the world, are increasing. The multinational corporation and international trading both benefit from and increase the extent of such similarities. Therefore, the thesis runs, as societies become more alike, businesses will become more alike. They will all need such things as profit and loss accounts, marketing, effective management information systems. Protagonists of this view can point to successful multinationals which make a point of operating in the same way in many different nations: they can point to developments in management in the People's Republic of China and the USSR which indicate a move towards Western-style management techniques. There are many educators and specialists who believe that what is in origin American managerial philosophy has been successfully transplanted around the world – and, indeed, should be so transplanted.

Many of these educators and specialists will argue that there are universal truths about the management of human resources which can be applied in the same way as the truths in any other area of management. Effective manpower planning, recruiting, training and development, work allocation, motivation and control of the workforce are requirements for any successful organisation and, while they will of course need to be adapted, for example, to local labour markets, the basic principles hold true in any country.

The convergence thesis is not unchallenged. In the human resource management area in particular there has developed a small but increasingly visible line of authorities who argue that a developing equivalence of technology does not lead to a similar convergence of managerial approaches. (See, for example, Laurent, 1983; Hofstede, 1980.) While none of these authors would argue for an independence of human resource management from economic and technological developments, they all consider that there are deep-rooted cultural differences between societies which are not susceptible to rapid change. The effects of these cultural distinctions can be seen in the way that management styles within a relatively small area with a long history of development, like Europe, remain obstinately national. They can be seen in the way that newly developing societies adopt certain Western practices, adapt others and reject some.

Protagonists of the power of cultural factors point to the way in which ideas such as quality circles have been adopted, adapted, developed and then retransmitted by particular nationalities.

It would be presumptuous to draw conclusions about this debate. Undoubtedly, there are elements of, particularly, economic and business life which are now less disparate than they were. It is equally true that the deep-rooted and 'sticky' nature of cultural differences must not be overlooked and is likely to mediate the effects of convergence. In general terms it is clear that researchers who focus on the content of management tend to find similarities; researchers who focus on process tend to identify cultural variations. Our ability to agree on terminology and the paucity of our evidence make any better summary impossible.

Common themes

One conceptual issue that can be addressed with rather more clarity concerns the subject matter of international and cross-national studies of human resource management. The focus here is only incidentally on nation states. It is the employing organisation (and sometimes the employee-representing organisation) that the studies in this book take as their material. The concern to locate such organisations, and related issues, in the nation in which they operate is seen as a means of challenging assumptions and drawing lessons which are not nationally determined, rather than as a means of illuminating national differences. That they may also perform the latter function is a bonus, not a purpose.

Within such an approach the themes identified for study are remarkable only for their universality: the role of a specialist personnel department, the role of women in employing organisations, disputes and conciliation, the development and training of managers. Only the theme which considers fundamental cultural differences on such issues as training opportunities, commitment to the organisation and work-related attitudes and organisational structures would be unusual in a single-nation textbook.

It may be somewhat obvious to conclude that employment organisations in all countries have to address the same human resource management issues: how to obtain and keep people to perform relevant tasks; how to develop them to be able to fulfil such tasks; how to resolve the dilemma of control and commitment. It would appear sometimes to be less obvious that the means found in each country to resolve these issues will be, to a degree at least, based upon and be part of the culture of that country.

Interpretation of data

It is usual in the field of comparative research to find unremarkable statements like those above leading to a labyrinth of both conceptual and methodological problems. We will mention briefly here, to identify rather than explore, five of the theoretical issues before we discuss some of the major methodological ones.

First, there is the question of levels of analysis. Social phenomena are by nature interdependent. It is impossible to understand any single social action in isolation. It makes sense only within a particular context. We live our lives in specific social contexts and imbue a series of assumptions about how simple actions and use of words relate to the rest of the context so that we can say we understand them – shaking one's head from side to side means agreement in some cultures, disagreement in others. At more complex levels of interaction we understand by drawing more generalised assumptions. In the context of the studies presented here this provides the authors with a choice of levels: they must investigate simple phenomena with as detailed an understanding of the context as they can muster – or more complex behaviours, with a consequent loss of detailed surrounding contexts. There are obvious advantages and disadvantages in each choice.

A further refinement of the question of levels of analysis concerns the nature of the conclusions that can be drawn. A simple example would be the question of reward structures within two organisations in different countries. A comparison of pay rates is uninformative without detailed knowledge of purchasing power, lifestyles, cultural issues, state social security provisions, working hours and working lifetime details and so on, for each country. Comparisons of pay structures – to what extent are performance-linked systems used, or what is the differential from top to bottom of the organisation – while still flawed, may be more valid.

Second, and to some extent independent of the choice of levels of analysis, there is the question of subject matter. This is intrinsically related to the nationality issue: certain issues will be 'live' and controversial in some societies, unacknowledged or unremarkable in others. Studies of industrial relations, for example, might focus on strikes and disputes in a cross-Atlantic context; but on dispute resolution and conciliation in a Pacific Basin analysis. Researchers deal with this problem in a variety of ways. Some choose to compare societies which may be said to have broad cultural similarities; others undertake joint research programmes; and some choose to stand outside the cultural context, comparing societies which are beyond their own cultural upbringing.

This problem too has an associated dimension. Does the subject matter lend itself to 'hard' or 'soft' data? 'Soft' data, where individuals are asked for their views or perceptions of reality, is a traditional and powerful approach to social enquiry. There is, however, in all cases a temptation to read back from soft data to hard reality. This becomes much more of a problem when the soft data is mediated by perhaps different languages, different customs and styles or different cultural assumptions.

Third, and closely related, is the question of choice of countries to compare. There are arguments for choosing countries which are, in as many ways as possible, as similar as can be. If the distorting effects of very different population sizes, industrial segmentation, wealth, infrastructure and cultural values can be diminished, then genuine differences in national human resource management style can be more clearly identified. The counter-argument suggests that it is precisely the differences between societies which illuminate and challenge the unacknowledged assumptions in the way organisations obtain and deal with their human resources. On this argument the most powerful research is that which compares organisations in very different countries.

Fourth, the role of the researcher is problematic. Each particular researcher will bring to the task of comparative study a particular set of cultural assumptions and a particular degree of knowledge and expertise. The cultural assumptions will not only give the researcher easier access to understanding of his or her own society – and make understanding of other societies more difficult – but they are also likely to affect the researcher's choice of subject matter and 'intellectual style'. The degree of knowledge of societies is fundamental to understanding the behaviour of people within employing organisations in those societies. Joint research is clearly one way to try to handle this issue. In most, but not all, cases in this volume authors are comparing human resource management in societies in which they originate with that in societies that they have lived in or know through other means.

Fifth, there is the question of dynamism. This underlies almost all of the points made above and takes us, at least partly, back to the issue of convergence. We are still far enough from a detailed understanding of the concept of culture as a stochastic problematic to have explored in any depth the concept of culture as a dynamic phenomenon. The point is recognised, but not yet explored. Societies and cultures are dynamic, in process of change. There are undoubtedly elements of the Chinese and Arabian cultures, to take two examples, which have remained substantially unchanged over the last half-century. But those two areas of the world have seen changes in economy, technology, infrastructure, communications, government and lifestyle which were inconceivable to their inhabitants 50 years ago. Cultural values may be slower to change than other aspects of society; but, with these dramatic developments, change they will. The implication is that in this area, as in other aspects of social science research, the search for universal truths is a fruitless one. All we can do – and a very important task it is – is to extend our understanding incrementally.

Methodological problems

The conceptual issues surrounding comparative research are accompanied by methodological problems. The task of all social science research is to develop understanding of the reality of social phenomena. It is trite, but true, to point out the need to distinguish this from appearance. The collection of data provides outward manifestations of reality, the appearance, and is itself complicated by cross-national comparison. It is, however, the analysis of the data which provides the understanding of reality. Our discussion so far of the conceptual issues involved raises many of the analytical difficulties. This section focuses on the methodological problems.

In broad terms we can characterise the methodological problems into two kinds: those which arise by the nature of the comparative exercise, and those which arise through the process of conducting fieldwork in two or more countries.

National differences which create problems in the nature of the comparative exercise revolve around the issue of accessibility. Governmental statistics, to take one obvious feature, show considerable differences even within a small area like Europe. Different information is collected and published, different definitions are used, different degrees of reliability can be placed on the published figures. The more different countries are in other respects the less comparable are their national statistics. The same holds true at the employing organisation level. This provides the researcher with considerable problems, even beyond the obvious ones. For example, questions of sampling and representativeness, which may be relatively simple to articulate (if not, sometimes, to solve) at national level become active problems in cross-national research.

Accessibility also involves the propensity of people within organisations to answer enquiries. Some societies are more open than others − some societies have certain topics which are deemed to be almost taboo while they are much freer to discuss other subjects. The family circumstances of employees, for instance, would be seen as a perfectly normal line of enquiry in the USA, as somewhat unusual or strange in many Pacific countries, and as quite inappropriate in the Middle East. Even between, say, the USA and Great Britain enquiries about a manager's financial reward package would need to be handled differently, with the British likely to be less open. Subsidiaries of the same company in different countries will deem different information to be confidential.

This leads to queries about the nature of international research design. Should the researcher insist on identical information being gathered − at the risk of losing or misunderstanding data; or should the researcher adapt the design to take account of these national differences − and put at risk the comparability of the study?

The issue is seen most clearly in analysing cross-national questionnaires. There is, first, the question of translation: processes of retranslation and test questioning can ensure, to a considerable degree, the maintenance of an identical list of questions. Whether, however, response rates are nationally determined, whether the answers mean the same thing, and the kinds of conclusions that can be drawn, may be less certain. In some cases, clearly, answers to identical questions may simply not be comparable. For the researcher these facts are compounded, often, by the impossibility of controlling for response rates or of following up the questionnaire in a country which may be many thousands of miles away.

Beyond this question of accessibility there are practical fieldwork difficulties surrounding this form of research. If researchers are working with partners in the other country or countries there are the difficulties of liaison, of language and of the amount of time that can be spent on the origination phases of the project (usually considerably longer and more important than the fieldwork).

If the researcher is working independently questions about the amount of time spent in each country and the financial constraints become important. Without considerable time spent in a country, and where necessary considerable fluency in relevant languages, it is difficult for the researcher to absorb local cultures, to understand the way organisations operate and the people within them behave, and to gain the credibility needed for access to undertake certain kinds of fieldwork.

Opportunities provided by comparative study

Although there are problems and methodological difficulties, there are many opportunities to advance our knowledge of human resource management through comparative research. Comparative studies challenge many of the taken-for-granted assumptions found in the literature, where too often the class-bound values and the working relationships of particular societies are built into a debate on general principles. Most texts on personnel management and industrial relations from British or North American authors rely on their own institutional frameworks, which are historically determined.

Such a broadening of the research agenda is essential. Western dominant economic paradigms are currently under re-evaluation from within Western societies (Handy, 1984; Thurley and Wirdenhius, 1989). Unrestrained growth brings inflation and eventually unemployment, income growth is not evenly distributed, questions about how to restructure industry in the post-industrial and post-arms-race era are as yet unanswered. Prompted by these issues and by demographic change, human resource managers have a new agenda, centring on employee commitment, new technology and occupation change, education and skills development, changing relations with trade unions, flexible employment practices, health and the environment (Brewster and Connock, 1985; Leighton and Syrett, 1989). This is an appropriate time, we feel, to review human resource management, and comparative study sheds new light on these issues by revealing what is different and what is the same under varying economic, social and political circumstances.

The coincidence of sociological and pragmatic reasons for comparative studies provides an opportunity to research corporate cultures. The study of corporate cultures compared to the countervailing power of national cultures reveals how human resource management and corporate cultures are adapted and modified at the organisational level. National cultures affect organisation structures, and policies, as well as the work-related values and attitudes of employees (Tayeb, 1988). National cultures also influence the process of organisation decision-making, and the relationships between people in organisations (Hofstede, 1980; Schneider, 1989). Since organisation cultures are often powerful mechanisms for establishing structures, values and relations (Deal and Kennedy, 1982) the questions we explore in this book are of direct relevance to the management of human resources in the emerging international context.

The structure of the book

The book is divided into five parts. We begin by taking up the debate on cultural differences which is central to comparative study. We then make a distinction between human resource practices and strategies (the subject of Part two); roles and structures, in Part three; and human resource policies in Parts four and five.

Human resource practices and strategies derive from the broad social, cultural and economic conditions in which organisations operate. The role and structure of the human resource specialist function are also major determinants of how human resources are conducted at the organisational level of analysis. Comparative studies of human resource policies are then examined, taking the two extremes of human resource management as examples: the 'hard' industrial relations end, where conflict resolution and negotiation policies are deployed; and the 'soft' developmental end, where management development and executive management policies are adopted. Such policies ultimately influence roles, structures, practices and strategies. The application of these practices and strategies is influential on societal cultures, thus completing the circle.

While we hope this circular flow of ideas will help the reader to make sense of the many different socially derived meanings analysed in the book, the chapters that follow are intended not to have a unifying but a diversifying effect. That from such diversity patterns do emerge encourages us to think that these research studies will contribute to the debate about the nature and purpose of human resource management.

References

Beamish, P. W. (1988) *Multinational Joint Ventures in Developing Countries*, Routledge, London.

Bean, R. (1985) *Comparative Industrial Relations. An Introduction to Cross National Perspectives*, Croom Helm, Beckenham.

Brewster, C. and Connock, S. (1985) *Industrial Relations. Cost Effective Strategies*, Hutchinson, London.

Deal, T. E. and Kennedy, A. A. (1982) *Corporate Cultures*, Addison-Wesley, Wokingham.

Doeringer, P. B. (Ed.) (1981) *Industrial Relations in International Perspective*, Macmillan, London.

Dore, R. (1973) *British Factory – Japanese Factory, the origins of national diversity in industrial relations*, University of California Press, Berkeley.

Guest, D. E. (1987) 'Human Resource Management and Industrial Relations', *Journal of Management Studies*, Vol. 24, No. 5, pp. 503–21.

Handy, C. (1984) *The Future of Work*, Blackwell, Oxford.

Harbison, F. H and Myers, C. A. (1959) *Management in the Industrial World: An International Analysis,* McGraw-Hill, New York.

Hofstede, G. (1980) *Culture's Consequences. International Differences in Work-Related Values,* Sage, Beverly Hills.

Jacobs, E., Orwell, S., Paterson, P. and Weitz, F. (1978) *The Approach to Industrial Change in Britain and West Germany,* The Anglo German Foundation.

Jaeger, A. M. (1983) 'Transfer of Organisational Culture Overseas', *Journal of International Business Studies,* Fall, pp. 91–114.

Laurent, A. (1983) 'That Cultural Diversity of Western Conceptions of Management', *International Studies of Management and Organisation,* Vol. XIII, No. 1–2, pp. 75–96.

Leighton, P. and Syrett, M. (1989) *New Work Patterns,* Pitman, London.

Mansfield, R. and Poole, M. (Eds) (1981) *International Perspectives in Management and Organisations,* Gower, Aldershot.

Martinez, Z. L. and Ricks, D. A. (1989) 'Multinational Parent Companies' Influence over Human Resource Decision of Affiliates. US Firms in Mexico', *Journal of International Business Studies,* Fall, pp. 465–87.

Morgan, G. (1988) *Riding the Waves of Change,* Jossey-Bass, San Francisco.

Poole, M. (1986) *Industrial Relations: Origins and Patterns of National Diversity,* Routledge, London.

Pugh, D. S. (1990) *Organisation Theory,* 3rd edition, Penguin, Harmondsworth.

Schneider, S. C. (1987) 'Strategy Formulation: The Impact of National Culture', *Organisation Studies,* 10/2 pp. 149–68.

Storey, J. (Ed.) (1989) *New Perspectives on Human Resource Management,* Routledge, London.

Taira, K. (1973) 'Labour Markets, Unions and Employees in inter-war Japan', in A. Sturmthal and J. G. Scoville (Eds) *The International Labour Movement in Transition,* University of Illinois Press, Urbana.

Tayeb, M. (1988) *Organisations and National Culture,* Sage, London.

Thurley, K. and Wirdenius, H. (1989) *Towards European Management,* Pitman, London.

Part one
Aspects of cultural differences in human resource management

The three chapters in this section address a fundamental issue in international comparisons of human resource management: the issue of culture. The concept has been considered in the introductory chapter and it is not necessary here to re-examine the definitional points made there. It was argued in that chapter that culture is indeed more than a 'dustbin' category: that it has real meaning and importance whatever the definitional difficulties. These three chapters take the argument one step further, applying the concept, *inter alia*, to particular subjects and nations and thereby allowing its value to be expressed.

Each author writes from a distinctive personal perspective and from his or her own cultural background. Thurley is an Englishman with a deep knowledge and understanding of the Japanese environment. His thesis can be read as an attempt to persuade Westerners of the value of typically Japanese concepts. Briggs, by contrast, takes a European look at Japan: and the chapter is European in its quizzical rather than its idealistic mode. Tayeb's chapter is a nicely judged exercise in cultural neutrality. The author compares the English and Indian employee relations environment; but is herself neither English nor Indian.

Thurley addresses the issue of skill shortages and the utilisation of human resources. He draws upon the ideal implicit in much Japanese thinking, that anyone can do anything: if they do not appear capable it is because they do not wish to, or they have not had the training or opportunity. He examines the Western notion that few people have the ability to perform well, and then only if they are motivated, trained and have opportunities. Thurley examines notions developed from within the Western culture to explain why the full utilisation of human resources is so stifled and, implicity, argues for a move towards the Japanese ideal.

Briggs addresses the Japanese employment situation more directly. Unlike many who have written about Japan, Briggs takes a view that is far from starry eyed: she writes, she says, in a 'more cynical vein'. The chapter sets out to answer the question posed by the contrast between the widely noted outward signs of commitment of the Japanese worker and the continuing research evidence that the Japanese worker shows low employee commitment. A detailed analysis of the human resource management techniques of the larger Japanese companies leads Briggs to conclude that there are only two possibilities. One, which is rejected, is that the Japanese workforce is subjugated. Instead, Briggs offers a cultural solution: finding elements in the Japanese culture to account for the apparent paradox.

Tayeb addresses the issue of culture more directly, testing for that and for work-related attitudes and organisational structures and systems. She finds that the impact of culture is considerable and influences both work-related attitudes and the organisation. Her work enables her, however, also to indicate the limitations of a total focus on culture. Other aspects such as hierarchy and status mediate the influence of culture.

The three chapters provide further perspectives on some of the issues raised in the introductory chapter. They emphasise the limitations of a single-culture perspective and the power of a multicultural view. Aspects of human resource management can be understood much better by contrast between societies. They also raise, however, some questions about the ways in which such issues can be explored. It is necessary to have a deep knowledge of, and analytical frameworks for investigating, societies before the complex of behaviours and interactions that constitute employing organisations can be fully understood. These chapters indicate that the informed outsider is often well placed to provide explanations.

2

The utilisation of human resources
A proposed approach

KEITH THURLEY

The utilisation of human resources in work organisations

Any discussion of the question of how far human talents and skills are 'utilised' at work has to start with the observation that the majority of educationalists as well as that of commentators on the industrial scene clearly believe there to be an enormous wastage of individual potential. Industrial society is seen as depending on the execution of jobs which mainly comprise a set of narrowly defined tasks, easily learned in a short time. Such jobs may be acceptable to those employed in them; job satisfaction may be fairly high and workers may resist schemes for giving them greater responsibility or 'enriched' tasks. Nevertheless, considering the huge variety of skills and knowledge acquired in mass full-time education and in family and community life in advanced societies, there are few who would argue that work roles typically 'utilise' more than a fraction of the potential capacity of the average employee. In a study of 275 jobs of male and non-craft workers in nine firms in Peterborough, England, Blackburn and Mann (1979, p. 280) reported that: 'Eighty-seven per cent of our workers exercise less skill at work than they would if they drove to work. Indeed, most of them expend more mental effort and resourcefulness in getting to work than in doing their jobs.'

Of course, it is obvious there are jobs that demand great effort and judgement to perform well and these typically include technical, administrative and risk-taking roles as well as senior managerial positions, but the sense of a general wastage of human resources and of the mismatch of job demands and human capacity is usually applied to a large sector of blue- and white-collar work.

This judgement is the basis of the 'utilisation' problem. In order to proceed further we need to define our terms.

'Utilisation' itself implies measures both of human capacity and of the performance demanded from the individual. Human capacity is generally analysed in terms of skills and knowledge acquired by the individual, considered as a stock available at any one point in time. 'Skill' is a highly ambiguous term in that it is used to mean both a learned sequence of activities involved in performing a particular task (by trainers, for example) and the recognised capacity to respond 'to the unexpected and the unpredictable' (as used by sociologists) (Asanuma, 1982). In this chapter, 'skill' will be used in the most general sense of 'learnt capacity to respond to particular situations and problems' and therefore covers the activities involved in 'programmed' tasks, in Simon's (1960) sense, as well as unprogrammed tasks. Performance demanded is conventionally related to the work or employment contract and to the tasks which are required by custom and practice in a given role. It is essential to see that such standards of performance are socially determined and will vary plant by plant, organisation by organisation and society by society. 'Utilisation', therefore, on these definitions, is a relative matter which has to be investigated in a precise historical and economic/social context.

Classical and neo-classical economic theory

From the viewpoint of market equilibrium economics, there is no structural problem of the lack of utilisation of human resources, only a set of conditions which are temporarily preventing a full match of capacity and demand for that capacity. Adam Smith did, it is true, give some emphasis to the concept of differing skill levels and the role of training and education in explaining the levels of actual wages. Ricardo and his followers, however, used the idea of homogeneous labour inputs, without any quality dimension, and this eliminates all problems of utilisation (Ziderman, 1978). Becker's (1964) human capital model, however, reviewed the importance of on-the-job training as an economic investment process. Such investment is rational for firms only if the training is 'specific', i.e. it raises the productivity of trainees in the firm but not the potential productivity in other firms. This formulation was made under the assumption of perfect competition. Yet it is in the context of labour market restrictions, in particular dual-labour market theory, that the Becker theory has been used successfully to explain investment in training (Doeringer and Piore, 1971). Even in the reformulation, however, there is a very limited explanation of the 'utilisation' issue. Essentially, 'human capital' is a very simplistic concept of the development of specific skills which are necessary for a particular production system. There is little or no treatment of the possibility of a continuous substitution of 'technical capital' for 'human capital' as seems to be suggested by those studying the impact of technology on employment. The dual-labour market theory, of course, pinpoints the under-privileged position of those who cannot break into the sheltered world of the internal labour market of the large firm, with its possibilities of upgrading and promotion. The explanation of this, however, is institutional rather than economic. The theory is still dealing with market imperfections, which restricts the rationale of training and development. We have to go beyond both classical and neo-classical economics in finding an adequate theoretical framework to deal with the 'utilisation' question.

Moral criticisms of individual and social 'waste'

From a completely different source of ideas, European moral philosophers and psychologists have emphasised the unique potential of individuals. There is a clear connection between such an idea and the Christian thesis about the perfectibility of human beings. For Aquinas this is expressed as the achievement of the Divine Essence, but is possible only by the grace of God, not by the exercise of talents and skill. The implication is that 'potential' is gradually unfolded throughout the life span of the individual and is only half understood by that individual at any point of time. When the idea was expressed by secular thinkers in the nineteenth century we find that the emphasis is on the endowment of every individual with talents which, if allowed to be expressed, will show their intelligence and aptitude in all realms of life. Rousseau, for example, argued that the temperaments of individuals were inherited genetically and this determined character. Life could provide 'training', which would allow character to be developed to perfection. The emphasis on this development process for all individuals, in this century, has been largely expressed by psychologists. Piaget is perhaps the best example. In the industrial psychology field, Maslow's 'levels of motivation' theory also assures the possibility of moving upwards from 'lower' to 'higher' needs of self-enhancement.

What is important here is the sense of individual significance and of what might be achieved through it. Such an approach leads to condemnation of the barriers to full self-fulfilment. Human 'waste' is a moral crime given what might have been achieved by those who are not given the opportunities to develop. Educationists, greatly influenced by such ideas, have therefore tended to be bitter critics of the lack of training opportunities for the young (Williams, 1959). It is no surprise that conflicts have arisen between those following the doctrine of economic rationalisation, in the market or within the firm, who assume human resources as given and concentrate on the best arrangements for using them, and moral critics who can only see the potential of individuals going to waste in those markets. For our purposes here, however, neither view is adequate. The strength and weakness of the moral critics are that the doctrine of 'potential' is asserted as a basic value. It is easy for economic rationalists to attack such ideas as leading to 'do-gooding', as too often the actual beliefs and aptitudes of those defended by the critics are ignored. There is no proof here of 'under-utilisation', only a vision of what might be achieved under different social and economic conditions.

Sociological theories of social deprivation

Sociologists have attempted to fill this gap by proposing various theories which explain the nature and extent of social deprivation in different societies. There is insufficient space to deal with such theories adequately here, but most theories have developed from a Marxian critique of European capitalism and emphasise social class as a basic dimension of economic inequality. Three main arguments are in fact used by sociologists in explaining the cause and extent of social deprivation.

(a) The argument that inequalities in income and opportunities for jobs, education, work and consumption prevent a large section of lower strata in the class system from experiencing or even desiring the possibilities of a more creative life (Parkin, 1971). There is considerable agreement on the argument, but disagreement on the proportion caught in such inequality and on how far it results in consciousness of class exploitation (Westergaard and Resler, 1975).

(b) The argument that economic decline, exacerbated by the current recession, has created whole areas of the 'inner city' were jobs are scarce and the population suffers from poor housing and social services and drifts into becoming 'marginal' to the main society. This particularly applies to immigrant groups and leads to ethnic conflict and high rates of crime and conflict with the police.

> What makes the inner city zones of great conurbations stand out from other urban and rural areas is that the burden of restructuring the economy is falling with disproportionate weight on the working class of the older urban areas. As this has occurred, so sections of the inner city working class have been marginalised from the dominant sectors of the economy and either become dependent on social security or found themselves obliged to work in the worst paid reaches of the economy.
>
> (Friend and Metcalf, 1981, p. 22)

Again the facts here are widely recognised; what is in dispute are the precise causes and the effects on 'consciousness' and attitudes.

(c) The argument that among the unqualified working class, their labour market experience emphasises powerlessness and uncertainty and this inhibits the possibilities of any successful action to 'escape'. 'The human reality of the labour market has been distorted for long enough. It is not natural; it wastes human resources, it stunts, alienates and dehumanises – all in the good times of full employment' (Blackburn and Mann, 1979, p. 304).

All these arguments deny the contention that current social and economic institutions 'rationally' allow a match between the demands for skilled performance and the capacities available in the working communities that are available. Some writers emphasise the interconnection between the three arguments, especially those following the Marxist tradition with its emphasis on alienation. Other writers may take a less comprehensive view of 'under-utilisation' of capacity and judge the important issue to be that of the *degree* to which such problems arise in different social structures and under different political and economic management. Clearly the causes of 'under-utilisation' may be laid at the door of the whole type of 'political economy' or it may be argued to be due to more specific causes.

Technology and the 'deskilling' controversy

One particular cause of importance here is the effect of automation and of the adoption of advanced technology. The dehumanising effect of new technology is a familiar theme among industrial sociologists and psychologists, which has been expressed since the advent of the industrial revolution. What is important in contemporary debate on this issue has been the assertion by Braverman (1974) that there is a long-term trend towards production rationalisation enforced by managements dominated by the ideas of 'Taylorism' so that the range of occupations required by new technology is fundamentally 'deskilled'. Actual task demands on workers therefore become routine, alienative, standardised and trivial. The papers of a recent conference on this subject have been collected by Wood (1982b), and this volume reveals very considerable disagreement among different sociologists as to the validity of the Braverman argument and the extent of 'deskilling'. The argument indeed for many French and German sociologists is a very long-standing one as research has long concentrated on the changing nature of the occupational structures and the skill content of jobs. As Wood (1982b, p. 15) argues, the 'problems of Braverman's work arise from his use of Taylor. For he takes the logic of Taylorism to be the logic of capitalism, which in Braverman's terms is the necessity of ensuring that control over the labour process passes into the hands of management.' This assures that management have to follow such a strategy and that they are bound to be successful. There is much empirical evidence against both these propositions. Lee, in particular (1982, p. 162), is convinced that craft labour persists as 'a stable and enduring component of the British working class' and that there is no real evidence of a general decline in net skills.

It can be argued that the attempt to provide a global and comprehensive account of 'deskilling' as a general tendency has distracted from the examination of the effects of particular types of new technology on the skills demanded. In any particular case there is nothing inevitable about the decline of skills; basically it depends on decisions taken by managers and others as to the most appropriate new roles that should be created given labour market shortages, pay rates, the need for controls, etc. The current 'office automation' boom is a good case in point. Word processors and electronic typewriters can be operated by typists either individually or in teams. There is much opportunity here for decentralisation and grafting new responsibilities on to the technical skills required by the operators.

In the automobile industry, the major technological changes taking place are the use of robots for routine semi-skilled tasks (for example paint spraying) and the use of on-line computers for controlling the flow of materials, checking faults, etc. Process labour is replaced by machinery and there is an expansion of maintenance and technician tasks. In certain processes the reduction of process line labour is very dramatic; in other processes little change has really taken place. The 'utilisation' argument really applies not merely to the roles actually carried out by workers, but is more applicable to the sequence of tasks and roles available through job rotation and promotion.

The impact of enterprise recruitment and selection policies

The issue of job rotation and promotion raises the question of the system of division of skills between workers at different status levels, i.e. the meaning of the term 'occupational skill system'. In any society the traditional occupational divisions (between trades for example) have been regulated by union policies and state intervention (for example defining qualification levels, the length of apprenticeship, etc.) as well as by the demand for skills, which is determined by the technology used by firms and the personnel policies of such firms. The meaning and value placed on particular skills can be conceptualised as an exchange relationship in a market situation as suggested by Asanuma (1982) (see Fig. 2.1).

This model is useful in depicting the survival of occupational systems of skill division as dependent *both* on institutional and 'political' factors as well as on managerial policies and the type of technology utilised. Economic factors are constrained by the institutional and 'political' influences of interest groups.

Asanuma (1982), in a pioneering paper, used the model to examine the realities of two sharply contrasting societies in the way that skill is defined in the traditional world of the construction industry in Japan and the UK. In the latter the clear distinction between craftsman and labourer which has existed since the late Middle Ages has survived into the late twentieth century. Craftsmen are defined as 'tradesmen' and typically still serve apprenticeships before becoming qualified to earn the adult 'craft' rate. In 1966 a Building Research Station report (BRS, 1966) reported that 92 per cent of operatives graded as craftsmen under 30 years of age had served an apprenticeship and 77 per cent had studied at a further education college in connection with this (although not all gained the appropriate City and Guilds Certificate). This system has been gradually breaking down over the past 15 years in spite of the efforts of trade unions and the Construction Industry Training Board to regulate and stimulate the number of apprenticeships. The growth of mechanisation on sites has involved an increasing number of 'semi-skilled' operatives operating plant and carrying out tasks which were not included in the traditional trades, for example steel fixing. Numbers of unskilled labourers have shown a constant decline, due to the collapse of the 'mate' or 'craftsmen assistant' system.

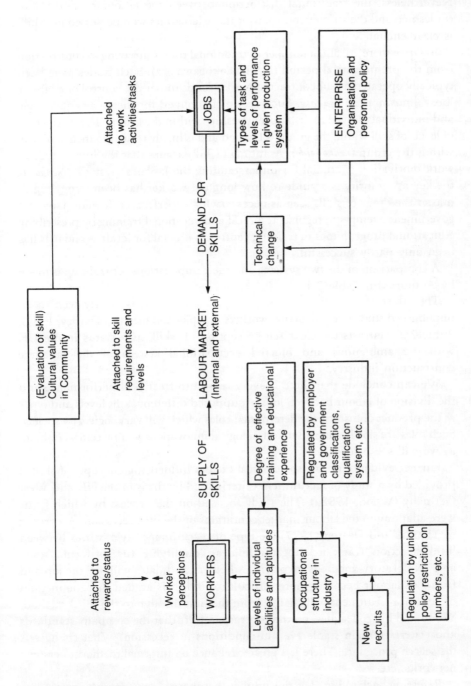

Fig. 2.1 An exchange model of skill
Source: Asanuma (1982)

Nevertheless, the traditional distinction between the autonomy granted to tradesmen and the stricter control over those labourers who possessed no 'skill' is clear enough.

In Japan there are also a number of traditional trades surviving in construction from the pre-industrial period (in the Tokugawa era). Such trades have been typically operated as subcontracted work groups under the control of a labour 'boss' known as an *oyakata*. Such groups bargained for their pay collectively and individuals served their 'apprenticeship' within the group. The distinction of levels of skill within the group is blurred and is highly related to their seniority within the group (*nenko seido*). Asanuma (1982) argues that the importance of work motivation is crucial for understanding the Japanese system. *'Nenko'* is the key as seniority is a guide to how long the worker has been struggling to master the range of skills seen as necessary for a 'perfect' craftsman. Japanese government attempts to regulate technical and vocational training by prescribing educational programmes in training centres as crucial for 'craft' standards has been only partly successful.

A comparison of the two systems and their implications for training is made by Asanuma in Table 2.1.

The effect of such systems on perceptions of 'skill' is clearly seen in an unpublished study of construction workers in Japan and the UK (Thurley, 1977). Table 2.2 contrasts the clear self-perception of 'skill' as a status in the UK with the ambiguous and blurred occupational system of the Japanese construction industry.

We can conclude that there is every reason to treat skill performance and the division of labour between jobs of supposed different skills levels and types as the product of historically determined roles which will vary society by society. Such roles are slowly adapted to technological innovations in a piecemeal fashion, as we will see below.

Further evidence on the sociological factors influencing concepts of skill is provided by a study of recruitment criteria used by firms in the UK and West Germany (Wood, 1982a). The study focused on the process by which firms were adapting to the labour market conditions of the then recession. According to Thomas and Deaton (1977) the type of recruitment 'style' varies between 'rank selection' (rank-ordering candidates), 'qualifying' (use of formal tests) and 'exploratory' methods (exploring whether candidates will 'fit' the job and firm). As labour becomes more difficult to find, it is argued that the method or style of recruitment will change from the first through to the third method. Wood and his colleagues, on the contrary, report that the company standards and criteria remain stable even in conditions of recession. What changes is the search procedure. There is a greater reliance on informal methods, personal networks, etc.

Referring back to Fig. 2.1, this implies that there is considerable importance in the formal and informal expectations by companies of the meaning of 'skill' (enterprise organisation and personnel policy). Utilisation is therefore affected by the standards expected in the occupations being recruited. Personnel policy and strategy thus become of key importance.

Table 2.1 Differences in concepts of skill and its implications on training

United Kingdom	Japan
Concept of skill	
Attribute of individual capacity to perform certain tasks learnt by initial occupational experience, backed by formal educational courses and recognised by formal status/wage/union distinctions to belong to skilled craftsmen class (as distinct from semi-skilled).	Atrribute of individuals within an occupational work group; capacity to perform certain tasks learnt by long-term work experience and formal off-the-job and on-the-job in-company training. Recognition of individual capacity by length of service and merit pay, status within the group, but no clear distinction of the class of 'skilled' from 'semi-skilled'.
Implications	
● Skill is the basic criterion for labour market evaluation.	● Labour market categories defined by educational/social categories (especially age, length of service, initial entry point to work organisation).
● Skill is the basic criterion for wage classification.	● Remuneration decided by personal criteria as above plus group performance.
● Skill is the justification for task autonomy by worker/employer.	● No theoretical basis for autonomy.
● Skill is the basis for occupational identity for workers/employees/ managers.	● Identity based on organisational membership (including work gangs for subcontractors).
● Skill is the framework for defining task performance and stimulating work motivation to achieve it.	● Motivation based on organisational membership and need for organisational performance.
Implications for training	
● Training is where workers learn the required skill.	● Traditional training is where workers are taught the required 'skill' including submissiveness, etc. to be 'proper'.
● Training is where workers acquire qualification to be in skilled status/jobs/market.	● No basis for qualification.
● Emphasis on technical competence, which is the basis of autonomy/boundaries to other tasks.	● Emphasis on motivational force, which is the basis of attaining the perfect images required by superiors. Technical skills regarded as secondary, but necessary.
● Acquisition of certain levels of skill regarded by workers to be in the market.	● Number of years regarded to be a proper craftsman.

Table 2.2 Perception of skill: occupational groups and the percentages rating themselves as skilled

	UNITED KINGDOM			JAPAN		
	% of occupational groups perceiving themselves as:					
	Skilled	Semi-skilled	Unskilled	Skilled	Semi-skilled	Unskilled
Traditional trades						
Carpenters	100	0	0	46	49	5
Bricklayers/masons	100	0	0	61	17	22
Plasterers	n.a.	n.a.	n.a.	67	17	16
Modern trades						
Steel erectors		n.a.		60	20	20
Fitters	100	0	0	88	12	0
Electricians	100	0	0		n.a.	
Pipe fitters/plumbers	96	4	0	40	50	10
Semi-skilled	24	72	4	63	37	0
Unskilled	7	6	87	15	39	46

Note: data compiled from a 1969 survey of five English and ten Japanese sites.

Source: Thurley (1977), Table 3

A model of skill utilisation

Summarising the argument so far, we have seen that the difficulties facing previous attempts at building a theoretical social science framework for understanding the problem of utilising skills include:

(a) equilibrium theory, which focuses on the constraints preventing a 'natural' balance of skills demanded and supplied;

(b) ethical/psychological theory, which denounces waste on a priori grounds without detailed evidence of the actual processes by which capacity is unused in job demands;

(c) sociological theory, which argues generally that lower strata are caught in situations in which opportunities are minimal or declining due to decreased needs of new technology, but again without (in most cases) detailed evidence of the process by which workers are frustrated by the lack of use of their capacity and explanations of why the situation is sometimes accepted and sometimes rejected.

The problem lies with the assumption that 'capacity' is an objective phenomenon and that the difficulties rest with the matching process of finding appropriate jobs at the right level for fulfilling the varying capacities of individuals. In reality 'capacity' needs to be regarded as a relative matter, directly affected by the demands for skilled performance made on individuals and on the expectations and perceptions of others and the individual self as to what his or her limits really are. There is a considerable literature in industrial sociology and psychology dealing with expectations and self-definitions of identities among different occupations. Socialisation requires interpretations by actors as to the roles and behaviour which are seen as relevent and practical in the social situations expected to be encountered. Subjectively, at least, those without qualifications or experience of performing a 'skilled' role will tend to perceive themselves over time as unable to perform such roles. In crisis situations, such as war, it is easy to find examples of individuals performing roles of which neither they nor anyone else believed them capable. The use of women in wartime skilled occupations is a very clear case in point.

If we start our analysis, then, with the process by which individuals come to perceive their occupational or work identity, it is obvious that the first set of influences on this stems from the family and local community in which the individual grows up. Expectations are clearly moulded by the examples of parents and siblings in their work roles. The literature on occupational choice makes this very explicit. What is more problematic is the effect of formal schooling and higher education on such self-identities. On the one hand, school 'success' may lead to perceptions of an academic career which may lead further either to a 'professional' career (in Anglo-Saxon countries particularly) or to admission to organisations at certain status levels according to the formal qualification held. An 'organisational' identity may be easily fostered when some organisations, such as the Civil Service, provide clear career structures for entrants with given educational qualifications. On the other hand, school 'failure' may drive individuals into the belief that they are of low competence generally. There is much evidence that 'streaming' of talent in schools and highly selective systems of education, as typically found in Western Europe, have precisely this effect on the 'C' streams and drop-outs from school competition. Of course, motivation for school performance will itself reflect family values, as the contrast between Asian and West Indian immigrant families itself shows in the present-day UK school system.

The technical and vocational education system is even more difficult to analyse from this perspective. In the British case, this has been built up as a set of *ad hoc* qualification systems for various 'levels' of skill with the emphasis placed on craft and professional courses. In recent years, as discussed by the OECD project, The Training of Middle-Level Skilled Manpower (SME/ET/81-18), professional organisations, colleges and governments have sponsored special 'accelerated training' for particular skills and technician courses for those between craft and professional status. Elaborate 'ladder' plans have been made by educationists to allow transfer of individuals from one stream of vocational training to another or higher stream. What is clear is that such courses, 'ladders' and schemes rarely provide an adequate self-identity for the individuals concerned. Technician status is notorious for its inherent frustration as a middle-level role which may be acceptable for a young adult only as a temporary expedient.

The crucial factors affecting the way that vocational education is perceived by trainees and 'graduates' from its courses lie with the nature of the internal labour market of organisations and the use of the qualification gained for obtaining entry to an organisation at a particular status level. A plethora of new courses which are unrecognised by firms in their selection and promotion criteria will lead to confusion, lack of identity and frustration. It is fairly obvious that bureaucratised organisations, particularly in the public sector, are more likely to use technical qualifications for organisational decisions on selection and promotion, and the vocational training system tends to feed these organisations rather than the private sector.

The other, again fairly obvious, influence of the educational system on self-identity relates to the numbers of 'graduates' produced relative to demand. In a recession, with cut-backs on recruitment easier to enforce than redundancy, it may happen that large numbers of vocational and general academic courses are devalued in the eyes of the participants by the prospect of unemployment at the end of the course. The many attempts at providing special technical training for the unemployed now being tried in European countries are obviously at risk from this viewpoint.

The fourth and more fundamental set of factors influencing identity lies at the micro-level of custom and practice in actual 'production systems'. This term is used to describe *all* operational work systems, covering services as well as manufacturing and primary production. As indicated by Wood (1982a), above, such systems carry with them expectations of a set of roles with given stereotyped task demands. These systems are, of course, affected by technical change and new roles and titles may be created for such situations. The experience of working in a new and experimental system will be very different from working in a long-established system. The most fundamental influences on perceptions of capacity undoubtedly occur from the actual work experience encountered by individuals as part of their life career. Subjective standards used by supervisors, managers and personnel officers also stem from *their* experience of the reactions of employees to such work experience. There is much evidence, too, that senior management will carry over to their decision-making the assumptions and expectations of human behaviour gained in their own early work experience within production systems. This particularly applies to assumptions about 'learning capacity' and the possible capacity of individuals to tackle entirely new tasks.

In the British example it can be argued without too much exaggeration that family, educational, vocational training and production system experience all operate within a framework which perceives talent and motivation to be scarce commodities. There are few individuals of exceptional talent and each hurdle 'filters out' those who clearly do not qualify. An effective system should, it follows, be successful in identifying high fliers and in persuading the others that they should be happy to live with their lack of talent. IQ tests in the school system may easily be used for this purpose. If it is also assumed that new technology increases the predictability of tasks, then the importance of selecting the exceptional person and 'cooling off' the remainder is evident.

It should be recognised that the reality of many production systems is starkly contrasted with this view of ever greater predictability. Studies of supervision and middle management (Thurley and Wirdenius, 1973) show that dealing with crises and breakdowns are common tasks for this group; and ones in which they exercise considerable autonomy. The problem here lies with the lack of recognition of the importance of the discretion being used, both by senior management, because of communication blockages, and often by the supervisors themselves. In this case we can conclude that the actual experience of tackling new problems is not enough to build up perceptions of capacity unless it is openly recognised and rewarded. Too often the discretion used is actually secret and against the formal rules of the organisation.

Our proposed model for the analysis of 'utilisation' therefore starts from the analysis of the targets, standards and performance levels demanded from a given production system (and the logic behind this). This avoids starting either from individual capacity *per se* or from some model of the social system. This 'demanded performance' is translated into roles with their own individual sets of expectations, usually by reference to traditional occupational stereotypes or company practice.

The second point of analysis therefore has to be the beliefs, expectations about skills, work norms, etc. which are held by workers, supervisors, shop stewards and managers and are seen as fair or reasonable in the actual situation ('feasible performance'). Clearly there may be differences in such expectations from the various groups involved and a description of these norms would have to take account of the whole range. It is also assumed that 'fairness' and 'reasonableness' mean 'given the perceived constraints of the situation'. If trains are always late, timekeeping norms will be adjusted to that fact. Such beliefs are therefore grounded in the experience of the actors in actually trying to carry out these roles.

A third point of analysis would focus more on 'learning capacity' as imputed to each actor (and as perceived by him or her). 'Learning capacity' is a judgement on the potential and relative efficiency of individuals to undertake new tasks in a given period. Such judgements are made constantly by those in authority and reflect the motivational patterns and related behaviour which have been learnt in the family and school training systems as well as in previous work experience. It is the *perceived limitations* to 'learning capacity' which are of the greatest importance.

'Utilisation' therefore is a relative and ambiguous concept which reflects three types of 'gap' of perception:

(*a*) The difference between the levels of 'feasible performance' perceived by the employees actually working in a production system and the levels of 'feasible performance' seen by managers in charge of the system. (Quality standards, for example, can often be *higher* among workers than among the staff of quality control departments.)

(*b*) The difference between levels of 'feasible performance' perceived by employees and the actual technical capacity of the system (as judged by management). There may be many reasons for running a system below capacity, particularly the short-term problem of over-production for other linked systems, but such reasons are often not explained to employees by managers.

(*c*) The difference between employees' self-perceived 'learning capacity' and the view of management on the potential 'learning capacity' of those individuals. If self-appraisal systems are used, this 'gap' may be openly discussed, but this is rare among blue- and white-collar employees in Western Europe.

Figure 2.2 expresses these relationships in a formal model. It will be noted that the utilisation problem arises basically from the interaction between three major factors:

(*a*) design decisions on technology and production arrangements;

(*b*) company business strategy and personnel strategy on human resource development;

(*c*) the effect of actual work experience in current production systems on perceptions of 'potential' and standards of 'feasible performance' by employees and managers.

None of these factors are immutable and all could be changed.

Implications for policy choice

The argument implicit in the model in Fig. 2.2 has a number of critical implications for policies designed to promote economic restructuring and the raising of productivity and quality levels among private and public sector organisations in OECD countries. It may be useful finally to outline these implications for public debate.

(*a*) It is assumed, first, that current levels of unemployment among OECD countries are the result of government monetary policies designed to fight inflation, declining levels of international competitiveness among European and North American export industries and of the results of technological rationalisation and automation policies used in firms to meet this situation. Low or zero-growth policies stem from the collapse of international confidence that world trade will continue to expand.

(*b*) This economic situation has arrived after several decades of social policies in which secondary and tertiary education in OECD countries has continually

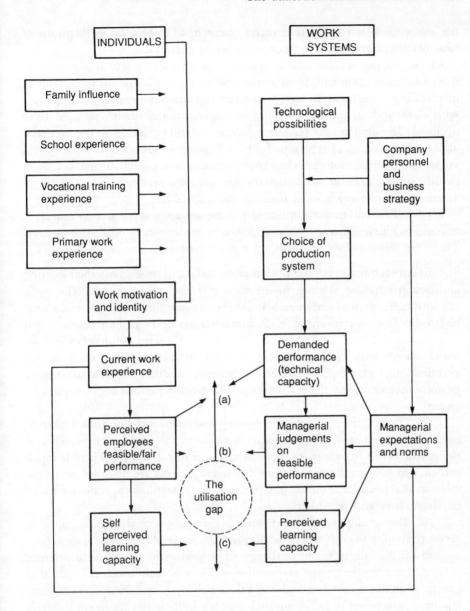

Fig. 2.2 A model of utilisation of skill

expanded. The result of this collision between social policies which assume growth and innovation and the recession is that a whole generation of leavers from the educational system are faced with job prospects which lower their expectations of a work career at the same time as their self-image of what they might be capable of performing has been expanded. It is an empirical question, not really answered by current social research, as to how far perceptions of 'feasible performance' have been changed by these factors.

(c) The impact of robotisation, information technology and automation on this situation is again hard to determine. What is clear is that the uncertainties of planning a work career have increased and the numbers of young people with clear and stable occupational or organisational identities must have declined. The demand for tertiary education is still probably on the increase, although the results of trying to find a job without educational or technical vocational qualifications are clear to most entrants to the labour market. Such qualifications, however, do not guarantee jobs, and students are increasingly aware of this – which must increase their anxieties.

(d) The first and major implication of the situation is *the need for enterprises to attempt to plan and develop a more comprehensive human resource development strategy.* There are three elements to this:

(i) An examination of the work that organisations need to run their existing and new production systems in the most effective ways possible. The work of consultants, such as Christian Schumacher's project in a major international electronics firm, is relevant here. (Schumacher has developed an 'organisation restructuring' approach based on an (implied) combination of scientific management with 'socio-technical systems' thinking.) The need is for examination of what type of roles are really needed at different levels, to improve performance and raise the standards of 'demanded performance', system by system.

(ii) The use of better self-, peer-group and managerial appraisal systems to ascertain what type of talent actually exists in the workers employed and to provide better information about actual 'learning capacity'. There is much evidence to support the proposition that managements are ignorant about the talent available and that managerial perceptions of 'learning capacity' are based on stereotypes and prejudice.

(iii) The development of a long-term programme of clearly defined possible career routes for all employees and of training and development activities, both on and off the job, to try to challenge employees to be prepared to attempt new roles and to take greater responsibility. There is again much evidence that managers do not demand enough from their employees and the success of some Japanese enterprises in following such a policy in their European subsidiaries is highly significant (Reitsperger, 1982).

(e) The second implication of this analysis *is the need for the State to provide a new framework for supporting individuals in developing their technical skills and job competence throughout their work careers.* This framework has to include facilities for part-time and full-time study for adults, new qualification systems attached to such courses and grants and loans to enable these facilities to be used. As discussed by Chris Hayes and colleagues (Hayes *et al.,* 1982), all this requires a proper foundation training of a broad comprehensive nature to give entrants to the labour market a wide range of preliminary technical and social skills. Continuous adult education will be unsuccessful unless there is a broad basis for initial job competence, which is not provided by the existing educational system. A change in the priorities in tertiary education is also implied by this argument. Resources will have to be diverted from those courses centred on the full-time education and qualification process for the young adult going into specialist and professional occupations, to supporting part-time study for those in early middle and late middle age. Educational institutions and professional bodies will clearly resist this policy, but the misuse of current resources is clear. Induction training and qualification training are very useful for professional regulation of entrants to the labour market, but the task of developing and utilising human talent over a longer period of a work career is far more important.

(f) The third and final implication of this approach relates to ideology rather than institutional practices *per se*. The model makes it clear that the major problem of utilisation is the perception by individuals and groups that they are limited in talent and are of only marginal use to society. These perceptions and self-images are grounded on actual work experience and are clearly difficult to change. Basically the problem lies with the individualism assumed both by 'progressive' education and by traditionalists arguing for a return to simple competence in reading, writing and arithmetic. Clearly, individuals will respond to greater demands on their skills and capacity if a clear social need and purpose are implied in such a demand. The problem goes to the heart of the economic malaise in advanced technological countries. What social policy could inspire a new determination to work and develop every possible skill and talent which might be available? Patriotism, belief in social progress or the future of the 'company' all seem to be discredited in the eyes of many Europeans. What new substitute is possible?

It is hard to avoid the implication that ultimately a new set of political purposes has to be created, which must include the development of work organisations which would offer a genuinely creative life. Such organisations might have to be restricted in terms of democratic control and ownership, before enthusiastic participation in a work career was released. What *is* certain is that *belief in the infinite possibilities of human adaptation and development has to be recreated – on a mass scale.* Each person needs to raise his or her own horizons in terms of what he or she might be capable of achieving. Self-learning, however, requires the stimulus of an accepted collective purpose. We may all have to reassess the argument of Professor Higgins in Bernard Shaw's *Pygmalion* that, with training based on careful scientific knowledge, there is nothing that cannot be achieved; even the conversion of a flower-girl into a lady in six months.

References

Asanuma, K. (1982) 'The Social Context of Industrial Skill and its Training Implications' (unpublished paper), University of Sussex, Brighton.

Becker, G. S. (1964) *Human Capital: A Theoretical and Empirical Analysis,* National Bureau of Economic Research, New York.

Blackburn, R. M. and Mann, M. (1979) *The Working Class in the Labour Market,* Macmillan, London.

Braverman, H. (1974) *Labor and Monopoly Capital,* Monthly Review Press, New York.

Building Research Station (1966) *Building Operatives Work,* Vol. 1, HMSO, London.

Doeringer, P. S. and Piore, M. (1971) *Internal Labor Markets and Manpower Analysis,* D. C. Heath, Lexington, Mass.

Friend, A. and Metcalf, A. (1981) *Slump City: The Politics of Mass Unemployment,* Pluto Press, London.

Hayes, C., Izatt, A., Morrison, J., Smith, H. and Townsend, C. (1982) *Foundation Training Issues,* Report No. 39, Institute of Manpower Services, University of Sussex, Brighton.

Lee, D. (1982) 'Beyond Deskilling; Skill, Craft and Class', in Wood (1982a), pp. 146–62.

Parkin, F. (1971) *Class Inequality and Political Order,* MacGibbon and Kee, London.

Reitsperger, W. (1982) 'The "Secret" of Japan's Success: Plain Managerial Competence', *Financial Times,* 26 May, London.

Simon, H. A. (1960) *The New Science of Management Decision,* Harper and Row, New York.

Thomas and Deaton (1977) *Labour Shortages and Economic Analysis,* Blackwell, Oxford.

Thurley, K. E. (1977) 'A Deviant Case; Construction Workers in Japan and Britain', unpublished paper given to the Mitsui Conference on Industrial Japan, School of Oriental and African Studies, University of London.

Thurley, K. E. and Wirdenius, H. (1973) *Supervision: A Reappraisal,* Heinemann, London.

Westergaard, J. and Resler, H. (1975) *Class in a Capitalist Society,* Heinemann, London.

Williams, G. (1959) *Recruitment to the Skilled Trades,* Routledge, London.

Wood, S. (1982a) 'The Flexibility of Recruitment Systems' (unpublished paper), Industrial Relations Department, London School of Economics and Political Science.

Wood, S. (Ed.) (1982b) *The Degradation of Work? Skill, Deskilling and the Labour Process,* Hutchinson, London.

Ziderman, A. (1978) *Manpower Training: Theory and Policy,* Macmillan, London.

3

Organisational commitment
The key to Japanese success?

PAMELA BRIGGS

Introduction

Although many factors are responsible for the Japanese 'economic miracle', a great deal of emphasis has been placed on their methods of human resource management. Particularly intriguing is the relationship between 'paternalistic' styles of management and workforce commitment, since the latter is commonly held to be the real secret of Japanese success. A typical analysis would be as follows:

> What then is the nature of the advantage which Japanese employment practices have been supposed to confer? It consists of a stable work-force with a high level of commitment to the company: extremely co-operative in accepting change, extremely unwilling to enter into strikes or other forms of conflict, and generally putting the company's interests level with or even ahead of its own. The outcome is a high and rising level of productivity, and an altogether easier climate in which management can plan for change in products and processes. These results, it is argued, are produced by employment practices which emphasise the commitment of the company to its employees, which give them security, status and material benefits, and which develop their potential in a systematic, long-term manner. Another feature which is often stressed is the way in which group cohesiveness and co-operation are fostered, rather than individualism and personal initiative.
>
> (White and Trevor, 1983, p. 5)

The outward signs of Japanese commitment are undoubtedly a source of envy to the average British manager: we hear that most Japanese workers are reluctant to take their allotted holiday entitlement; we read that they work longer hours than their British or American colleagues, often unpaid; we learn that their contribution to their company's success is not only in terms of high-quality production, but also in the form of frequent suggestions for improvements. And yet there is something of a paradox in the literature: away from the journalistic reports of the Japanese success story, we find evidence that the Japanese show less job satisfaction than their British or American counterparts (Azumi and McMillan, 1976; Cole, 1979; Lincoln, Hanada and Olsen, 1981; Naoi and Schooler, 1985); they are more discontented with their jobs following technology-induced change (Yuchtman-Yaar and Gottlieb, 1985); they feel their jobs to be less of an accomplishment (Naoi and Schooler, 1985); they are less likely to report that they work hard because of a feeling of responsibility to the company and to co-workers; they show less pride in their firm than their American counterparts (Lincoln and Kalleberg, 1985; Naoi and Schooler, 1985); and overall show lower levels of organisational commitment as measured by Porter's Organisational Commitment Questionnaire (Lincoln and Kalleberg, 1985; Luthens, McCaul and Dodd, 1985).

These research findings tell a very different story from the one we have become accustomed to, and yet they show a certain internal consistency: given the other indices (low job satisfaction, etc.), one would reasonably expect employee commitment to be low. What is interesting is that these results, sprinkled throughout the literature, have not really changed the 'received view' that commitment is the cornerstone of Japanese success. Why not? One factor concerns the reporting of these results – in many cases researchers who have found evidence of low commitment in the Japanese population simply dismiss or distort their findings. Thus Cole (1979), having found Japanese work commitment to be lower than anticipated, casually argued that, in Japan, commitment is focused on the company rather than the work *per se*; while Lincoln and Kalleberg (1985), at a loss to explain their findings of low organisational commitment with a Japanese population, were forced to question the validity of their cross-cultural methods, especially perceptual measures, (Lincoln and Kalleberg, 1985).

It seems rather rash to dismiss these findings so easily. A better alternative would be to consider the extent to which Japanese human resource management (HRM) techniques are likely to foster commitment, in order to try to pin down the inconsistency with which we view the subject. As a starting point, let us consider one of the more popular stereotypes of Japanese human resource management.

Consider the Japanese method, as represented by Ouchi's (1981) Theory Z (see Fig. 3.1). Here, emphasis is laid on the major incentives each individual employee is offered upon commencing work with the major corporations: lifetime employment and the associated benefits of subsidised housing and company welfare; extensive in-house training and the various pay incentives (seniority-based salary and bi-annual bonus tied to company profit). Ouchi also stresses the importance of good working relationships between colleagues. High levels of intimacy and shared decision-making are believed to underlie improved job satisfaction; greater autonomy; a greater concern for quality; and greater pride in the firm.

It is hard to see how such a system would fail to engender high levels of employee commitment. However, it is possible to take a somewhat more cynical view of Japanese HRM practices (e.g. Sullivan, 1983; Sethi, Namiki and Swanson, 1984; Briggs, 1988). In this more cynical vein, let us review the major

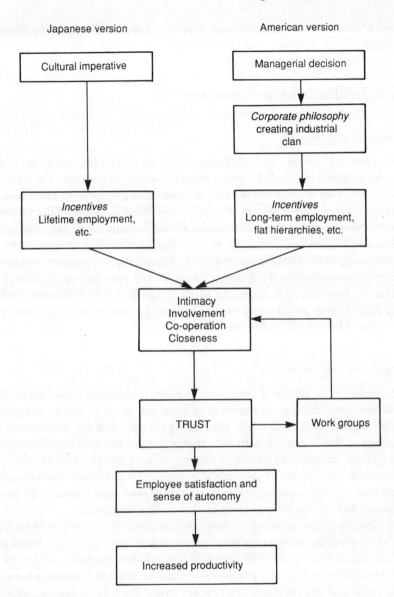

Fig. 3.1 Theory Z
Source: Sullivan (1983), p.133

components of the Japanese method, and see just what kind of employee commitment they might foster.

Looking at Fig. 3.1, it is possible to isolate two areas of human resource management. The first concerns the individual and his or her career development; the second involves the day-to-day interaction between colleagues and the ways in which teams operate. It is useful to consider these two factors separately.

The individual's career structure

Lifetime employment

The number of Japanese offered lifetime employment with the major companies is steadily diminishing, and at present stands at about 30 per cent. The situation for other workers is often bleak, and so considering only those embraced by the lifetime employment system creates a very distorted view of the Japanese at work. Nevertheless, given our concern with commitment, the practice of lifetime employment is important, since it has far-reaching consequences for both the employee and the corporation. Essentially, it ensures a 'captive workforce', necessarily willing and able to fill any role they are assigned. In this manner Japanese companies can easily create the kind of 'flexible rigidity' which allows them to adapt to economic change; and to respond swiftly to innovation. How is this achieved?

Recruitment and selection

The first step is to recruit a very high number of university graduates. This is relatively easy, since large numbers of Japanese go on to higher education. The recruitment process is made simpler by the fact that the institutions are themselves so clearly graded: with the national universities, and most prestigious of the private universities sitting at the top of the pile. The aim at this stage is to capture the interest of the very able, irrespective of their specialisation. To this end, the top students are occasionally offered employment with prime companies before the official start of the recruitment season.

For university applicants the season begins towards the end of their final year, when students are given a month in which to visit any of the firms they find interesting. Having done their homework, Japanese students are then faced with a very difficult decision, and this point marks a major divergence between the Japanese and British systems; since, for many of the Japanese, recruitment requires total commitment to the firm rather than being perceived as a contract. (Sasaki, 1980).

Furthermore, the choice must be made decisively: applicants cannot apply to more than one company, hoping to take pot luck, since the selection procedure for all the major companies is held on the same day. Naturally, in making this decision, students consider the company, but not the job. They cannot afford to see themselves as specialists, with professional loyalties, when they are about to become company men.

Training

With such a recruitment and selection policy, the training needs of each new employee will be high. The Japanese favour on-the-job training; and in keeping with their preference for generalists, they encourage job rotation. A typical in-company career profile is shown in Fig. 3.2.

- 1954–61, at a local plant:
  1954–7: as a foreman
  1957–60: in the quality control section
  1960–1: as an open hearth section chief

- 1961–6, at the Tokyo head office
  1961–3: in Sohmu-Bu (a general affairs department)
       Duty: to study the possibility of technological co-operation with foreign companies in collaboration with a specialist in law
  1963–6: section chief in technology development

- 1966–9, at a major plant:
  1966–7: director of a factory employing 600 workers in steel manufacture
  1967–9: manager of the technology department

- 1969–72, at the Tokyo head office:
  1967–70: a member of the organisation committee
  1970–2: a manager in the research and development department

- 1972–, manager of the technology department, International Iron and Steel Institute

---

Fig. 3.2 Job rotation of Mr K (Nippon Steel)
Source: Sasaki (1980)

From the company viewpoint, there are a number of advantages to this system: first, it means that each manager can build up a wide network of contacts, which facilitates the *ringi*, or widespread consultation method of decision-making. Second, it ensures that each manager has had wide experience of the kind of work being conducted by his or her subordinates. This in turn helps to bind work teams together, since it is not uncommon for managers to step in to help a subordinate if required. This contrasts markedly with the management/labour division so commonly encountered in Britain. Third, it ensures workforce flexibility. This is essential when we consider that large companies might find themselves burdened with too large a workforce. They can adapt to market changes, not by resorting to large-scale redundancy – but by large-scale re-training. In this manner, the Japanese find little opposition to the introduction of new technology.

From the worker's point of view, things are a little less rosy. Job rotation schemes mean that they have little control over the work they do, and indeed over where they live. It is quite common for Japanese workers to be regularly transferred to distant sites; and their families are naturally expected to uproot themselves at very little notice. Workers cannot cling on to jobs or places they find particularly stimulating; and job satisfaction often suffers as a result. As stated earlier, the Japanese rate lower than their Western counterparts in measures of job satisfaction (Cole, 1979; Lincoln, Hanada and Olsen, 1981); and are often tense and nervous at work (Hofstede, 1980). This situation is exacerbated when workers are faced with the job changes resulting from the introduction of new technology: whereas most countries have reported fairly positive consequences of technological change (e.g. more responsibility, less physical strain, greater cleanliness), the Japanese are more likely to associate technological change with greater monotony, and greater difficulty on the job (Yuchtman-Yaar and Gottlieb, 1985).

Seniority-based pay

Associated with the practice of lifetime employment, and naturally resulting from Japanese training practices, is the system of seniority-based pay. For most workers in Japan the key determinant of salary is the length of service with the company. For many this simply means that their years of experience are amply rewarded; but for any who seek a new employment contract late in life, experience and expertise count for little. Table 3.1 plots the relationship between salary and years of experience with the firm. In contrast to the British the Japanese are severely penalised by inter-company job transfer. The situation is made worse by employees' heavy reliance upon company housing subsidies, and in-company welfare schemes: the loss of these benefits can prove financially crippling to a small family.

Table 3.1 The first wage of the 'non-standard' worker

Age	The ratio of the first wage to the wage of 'standard' worker			
	1967	1970	1972	1973
25–29	81	83	81	81
30–34	74	76	73	75
35–39	67	71	70	71
40–49	56	60	59	59
50–59	52	56	54	55

Standard worker: a worker who enters a firm immediately after graduating at school and continues working in the firm.
Non-standard worker: a worker who enters a firm not immediately after graduating at school and who has not worked over a year in the firm.

Source: Wage Census, Rodo Horei Kyokai, Tokyo, 1973

Would the policies we have considered in this section (i.e. lifetime employment and the associated recruitment and selection practices; in-house training and seniority-based pay) be likely to foster high levels of commitment in the Japanese? From what we have discussed so far, it is easy to see why Japanese workers seldom contemplate leaving the company. Not only have they been offered a job for life, but they are qualified to work really only within one company; and besides, their pay (and other benefits) would suffer should they contemplate transfer. They are clearly a captive workforce – but we have seen little to suggest that they are a contented, far less a committed, workforce. Perhaps the commitment comes from the second of the cycles listed in Ouchi's Theory Z, i.e. from team spirit and good working relationships with other colleagues. Certainly the 'team factor' as manifested in group decision-making and quality circle programmes is held to contribute greatly to the Japanese success. We go on to discuss this possibility in the next section, by considering worker co-operation under the headings of organisational structure, participation and integration.

Co-operation between colleagues

Organisational structure

As a starting point, we should note that the factors which determine the nature of an individual's contract with the firm also affect the company's overall organisational structure, and this in turn affects the kinds of interaction typically found between colleagues. Japanese firms tend to possess tall, vertical structures – i.e. they promote finely graded status hierarchies. This is hardly surprising when we consider the respect for seniority bred in the culture and reflected most obviously in the seniority-based pay (Lincoln, Hanada and McBride, 1986) – years of experience must count for something, hence the abundance of small promotions available to each individual. Note that a change in formal status does not always reflect a change in real responsibility. Thus the spans of control of Japanese managers are not necessarily smaller than their British or US counterparts (Lincoln, Hanada and McBride, 1986).

Participation

A related issue concerns the operation of consensus decision-making. The popular view has it that decision-making is spread throughout the company, and that employees at all levels actively participate in the process. Given that the Japanese hierarchies are many-levelled, it is surprising that a decision can be reached at all. However, a number of authors have pointed out that the work structure differs from the decision-making structure. The reality is that not all employees wield real power, and that promotion does not necessarily entail increased responsibility; nevertheless, a 'show' of joint decision-making is necessary to save face. In fact, the system does ensure that the question (as opposed to the answer) is defined and redefined in the process – a valuable activity in itself (Drucker, 1971); nevertheless, when it comes to making the decision, workers feel under great pressure to agree with supervisors (Klauss and Bass, 1974); and unpopular group 'decisions' are simply ignored (Naoi and Schooler, 1985).

Integration

With status so finely graded within the large Japanese corporations, one might anticipate an increase in the prevalence of formal communications, with correspondingly less integration between collegues. However, the popular view holds that the opposite is true, and that the usual alienation between superior and subordinate, management and workforce, is absent in most Japanese companies. Proponents of this view focus upon the Japanese avoidance of overt displays of status: management often dress in the same overalls as the shop floor workers and will usually eat in the same canteens (White and Trevor, 1983). However, since status is so clearly marked in other ways (Briggs, 1988), it is more realistic to assume that the formal structure is in operation, although invisible to the Western eye. The research literature supports this assessment: for example, Hofstede (1980) found that Japanese rate low on their desire for a good working relationship with their managers; a result confirmed by Henderson and Argyle (1986), who note that the Japanese rules of work prohibit intimacy. Both in their attitude to superiors and in their attitude to subordinates, Japanese rated high on an 'avoidance of intimacy' measure. Also, in their relationships with subordinates they showed greater endorsement of formal behaviour than workers in any other country.

In general the research literature is fairly consistent on this point. However, there is ambiguity concerning the nature of Japanese relationships with their immediate co-workers. For example, in one Japanese–American comparison we find evidence that Japanese have more close relationships at work than their American counterparts (Lincoln and Kalleberg, 1985); while in another the evidence suggests that Japanese and Americans do not differ at all in this dimension (Lincoln, Hanada and Olsen, 1981). The Henderson and Argyle (1986) study would support this latter finding, to a certain extent, since Japanese workers were equal to British, Hong Kong and Italian workers in terms of the amount of support and disclosure they received from their colleagues. Nevertheless, in the same study the Japanese showed much greater inhibition of emotional expression. We return later to the reluctance of the Japanese to show personal feeling, as it has some bearing on the commitment issue.

One final point, which bridges the issues of participation and integration, concerns the 'quality circle' (QC). QCs have been one of the more prominent imports from Japan (although they were formerly present in America under a different guise, and they are not too dissimilar to European autonomous work groups). In Japan QCs have registered phenomenal success (Munchus, 1983), although their reputation abroad is rather more dubious. However, even in Japan the quality circle is seen less as a tool capable of nurturing support and mutual trust within a work team and more as an instrument of management (Cole, 1979).

At the interpersonal level, then, there is no obvious reason why a Japanese worker should show more commitment to his or her company than a British or American collegue. In only one study of the many cited is there any indication that the Japanese system is saturated in harmony, intimacy and trust between fellow workers. At this stage, it begins to look as though we must accept the results of Cole (1979), Lincoln and Kalleberg (1985) and Luthens, McCaul and Dodd (1985) at face value: Japanese show lower organisational commitment than Americans; and, what is more, there seems to be every reason why this should be so.

Conclusion: commitment and culture

Of course, the real paradox concerns the split between opinion and behaviour. The Japanese rate themselves low on job satisfaction, pride in their firm, organisational commitment, etc., but nevertheless they do work much longer hours than their British or American counterparts, and for less reward. Why? One solution is to assume that the cost of rebellion is simply too great; and that the Japanese are a cruelly subjugated workforce. Although there certainly are coercive elements to the Japanese method, this conclusion is not really tenable. The Japanese do have many long-standing unions; and although they tend to be organised around the major corporations, they do, nevertheless wield a certain influence. Also, as stated earlier, only 30 per cent of Japanese are offered lifetime employment and so there are alternatives (albeit poor ones).

It is much easier, and more realistic, to seek a cultural solution to this problem, and one is readily available. It concerns the Japanese deep-felt desire to keep the realm of duty separate from the realm of personal feeling. A number of writers have discussed this issue – although the classic work is Ruth Benedict (1946). Basically, for the Japanese, duty – in the form of work – must come first; and must exist totally separate from the domain of 'personal feelings'. Dissatisfaction, lack of motivation, unhappiness at work are typically brushed to one side, while the work continues. This capacity for endurance, coupled with a reluctance to reveal true feeling, is not something we have only just learnt about the Japanese – after all, we have been using the term 'inscrutable' for a long time now. Yet we have been slow to understand the implications of this reluctance to act upon emotion or personal feeling. It is not commitment in the Western sense that binds a Japanese worker to his or her company: loyalty is not fostered by any sense of obligation or by any specific employment practice. The young student makes his or her choice, and is simply prepared to stick by it, irrespective of personal satisfaction. It is a form of commitment we could choose to admire or dislike, but it is probably not the kind of commitment that could be imported.

References

Azumi, K. and McMillan, C. J. (1976) 'Worker Sentiment in the Japanese Factory: Its Organisational Determinants', in L. Austin (Ed.) *Japan: The Paradox of Progress*, Yale University Press, New Haven.

Benedict, R. (1946) *The Chrysanthemum and the Sword*, Charles E. Tuttle, Tokyo.

Briggs, P. (1988) 'The Japanese at Work: Illusions of the Ideal', *Industrial Relations Journal*, Vol. 19, No. 1, pp. 24–30.

Cole, R. E. (1979) *Work, Mobility and Participation: A Comparative Study of Japanese and American Industry*, University of California Press, Los Angeles.

Drucker, P. F. (1971) 'What We Can Learn from Japanese Business', *Harvard Business Review*, Vol. 49, No. 2, pp. 110–22.

Henderson, M. and Argyle, M. (1986) 'The Informal Rules of Working Relationships', *Journal of Occupational Behaviour*, Vol. 7, pp. 259–75.

Hofstede, G. (1980) *Culture's Consequences: International Differences in Work Related Values*, Sage, Beverly Hills.

Klauss, R. and Bass, B. M. (1974) 'Group Influence on Individual Behaviour Across Cultures', *Journal of Cross-Cultural Psychology*, Vol. 5, pp. 236–46.

Lincoln, J. R., Hanada, M., and McBride, K. (1986) 'Organizational Structures in Japanese and U.S. Manufacturing', *Administrative Science Quarterly*, Vol. 31, pp. 338–64.

Lincoln, J. R., Hanada, M. and Olsen, J. (1981) 'Cultural Orientations and Individual Reactions to Organizations: A Study of Employees in Japanese-Owned Firms', *Administrative Science Quarterly*, Vol. 26, pp. 93–115.

Lincoln, J. R. and Kalleberg, A. L. (1985) 'Work Organization and Workforce Commitment: A Study of Plants and Employees in the U.S. and Japan', *American Sociological Review*, Vol. 50, pp. 738–847.

Luthens, F., McCaul, H. S. and Dodd, N. G. (1985) 'Organisational Commitment: A Comparison of American, Japanese and Korean Employees', *Academy of Management Journal*, Vol. 28, No. 1, pp. 213–19.

Munchus, G. (1983) 'Employer–Employee Based Quality Circles in Japan: Human Resource Policy Implications for American Firms', *Academy of Management Review*, Vol. 8, No. 2, pp. 255–61.

Naoi, A. and Schooler, C. (1985) 'Occupational Conditions and Psychological Functioning in Japan', *American Journal of Sociology*, Vol. 90, No. 4, pp. 729–52.

Ouchi, W. G. (1981) *Theory Z: How American Business Can Meet the Japanese Challenge*, Addison-Wesley, Reading, Mass.

Sasaki, N. (1980) *Management and Industrial Structure in Japan*, Pergamon Press, Oxford.

Sethi, S. P., Namiki, N. and Swanson, C. L. (1984) *The False Promise of the Japanese Miracle*, Pitman, Boston.

Sullivan, J. (1983) 'A Critique of Theory Z', *Academy of Management Review*, Vol. 8, No. 1, pp. 132–42.

White, M. and Trevor, M. (1983) *Under Japanese Management: The Experience of British Workers*, Heinemann, London.

Yuchtman-Yaar, E. and Gottlieb, A. (1985) 'Technological Development, and the Meaning of Work: A Cross-Cultural Perspective', *Human Relations*, Vol. 38, No. 7, pp. 603–21.

4

Socio-political environment and management – employee relationships
An empirical study of England and India

MONIR TAYEB

Introduction

Research studies have pointed to considerable diversities as well as similarities in the forms and shapes of the structures and management systems of organisations within and between nations. Of various explanations offered by organisational theorists those put forward by the advocates of three major perspectives in organisation study – contingency, political economy and culturalist perspectives – are more closely relevant to the purposes of this chapter.

Contingency perspective suggests that factors such as technology, size, industry and environmental uncertainty play a crucial role in shaping organisational structure and behaviour (Woodward, 1958; Lawrence and Lorsch, 1967; Marsh and Mannari, 1981). Although the studies which concentrated on contingency – structure relationships arrived at contradictory conclusions, many of these contradictions appear to have arisen by the inconsistencies and inadequacies in the research methodologies employed, rather than the 'true' nature of the relationships *per se.* These relationships cannot, therefore, be ruled out or accepted without further examination.

In the past very little attention has been paid to the implications of *political economic* factors, such as economic system, labour movement, political regime and other national institutions, for organisations, especially in cross-national comparative studies (Child and Tayeb, 1983). My own experience, both as a manager and a student of management and organisations, in an Asian country with political economic institutions totally different from those in the Western countries (Tayeb, 1981), has led me to believe that these institutions and their priorities have significant implications for organisations. These implications are more pronounced in such areas as objective setting, planning, recruitment policies and the role of trade unions in organisations.

Studies conducted within the *culturalist perspective* have been successful in drawing attention to the significance of cultural institutions in shaping organisational structures and systems. The conclusions arrived at by the researchers vary from a complete denial of the influence of culture (Hickson *et al.*, 1974) to its over-arching role (Hofstede, 1980) in determining organisational structure. However, the methodological inadequacies employed in most of these studies make it unwarranted to accept or reject the influence of culture on organisations without a more comprehensive study of the subject.

The studies conducted within these three perspectives, although they make valuable contributions to our understanding of organisations in their own way, have been only partly successful in finding an answer to the question of what determines organisation and its structure. The reason for this partial success is that they have been confined to the boundaries of their respective framework, and hence failed to recognise the credits due to the others. There is clearly a need for a multi-perspective approach to the study of organisations, in which the views expressed within these perspectives are recognised and integrated.

The present study was yet another attempt at understanding organisations. The main objectives of the research were to examine systematically the degree to which there was a consistency between Indian and English cultures and the structures and management styles of organisations operating within them, and the degree to which non-cultural factors played a role in organisations.

The study to be reported consisted of a cultural phase, in which a sample of the general public in England and India was surveyed; a work-related attitudes phase, in which a sample of employees of seven carefully matched pairs of manufacturing firms in England and India was surveyed; and the organisational phase, in which the structural charcteristics and management styles of the same 14 firms were studied. English data were collected between October 1981 and June 1982, and the Indian data between February and June 1983. The English organisations were situated in various parts of England, and the Indian firms in the state of Maharashtra.

The study

The cultural surveys

Since the role of social institutions in people's cultural traits is an important one, the present section begins with a brief description of the salient characteristics of these institutions in India and England compared with one another.

Primary institutions

The family is much more extended in India than in England. A traditional Indian family normally includes three to four generations; whereas an English family generally consists of parents and children, and the children normally leave their home even before they set up their own families. The structure of family is less hierarchical and more egalitarian in England than in India, and the members' roles are less rigidly defined in the former than in the latter.

Religions in both countries are tolerant of other religious beliefs and practices, but more so in England than in India, as expressed in violent clashes between different religious communities in the latter. In England religious tolerance is manifested in the many different Christian sects, Catholicism and Protestant denominations. In India Hinduism, the main religion, consists of numerous forms of worship and religious practice. Hinduism emphasises reincarnation, and is, as far as this life is concerned, a more fatalistic religion than Protestantism (the religion of the majority of the English). The latter emphasises free will and encourages individual action and individualism.

The teaching prctices in Indian educational institutions are based on a one-way power relationship between teachers and pupils, and learning is generally through passive acceptance of 'facts' and memorising textbooks. In England learning is largely based on self-discovery, experimentation and games, and the system encourages challenge, discussion and argument.

Secondary institutions

The economic systems in both countries are based on a capitalistic mode of production with both public and private enterprises. However, Indian capitalism is much more protectionist and the government is involved in direct intervention in the economy to a larger extent. Local industries are protected against foreign competition through strict import policies. English capitalism, especially under the present Conservative government, is rooted in the concept of reduced direct government intervention and on the stimulation of industry through monetary policies which aim to facilitate the free play and interaction of market forces. In pursuit of this aim, import controls have been dismantled and, in consequence, manufacturing companies face fierce competition from foreign firms.

Trade unions in England have lost much of their power in recent years because of job insecurity under the conditions of high unemployment (caused by economic recession), loss of membership (due to mass redundancies), and 'anti-union' legislation. In India the organised sector is very small compared to the total workforce but the government's industrial relations Acts are 'pro' workers and the unions are more powerful than are their English counterparts. A fairly typical comment made by one of the Indian managers who participated in the research demonstrates the extent of the legal protection that the organised manual workers enjoy:

> There is nothing much that we can do about the shopfloor people if they are late or do not do their job properly. We cannot sack them because of the government's employment policies. We cannot decrease or deduct from their wages, again because the government forbids us. And also because they are unionised and the unions are very powerful as far as these matters are concerned. These people can get away with murder.

The political regime in both countries is based on parliamentary democracy. Freedom of expression and other collective and individual civil rights are respected in both systems. However, in practice Indian democracy is less 'democratic' and more centralised than the English democracy. Opposition parties are weaker and much more fragmented in India. Since independence, except for a brief period in the late 1970s, only one party (Congress) has been in power. Frequent irregularities during elections have also led the cynics to have reservations about the extent to which democracy is practised in India (*Sunday Observer*, 20 March 1983).

Social stratification in England is based, primarily, on economic factors such as occupation, ownership and control of means of production, wealth, etc. The society is divided into two large middle and working classes with a relatively small 'upper' class at one end of the social hierarchy, and an 'under' class of low-paid women and unemployed at the other. In India social stratification is based, primarily, on caste. The caste system is sanctioned by Hindu religious precepts and caste membership is determined by birth and, in turn, determines to a large extent a person's occupation as well as social standing. Class membership in England has a 'subjective' aspect, and the system is much more fluid and flexible than is the Indian caste system. In England a former member of the working class can consider himself or herself as a member of the middle class once his or her occupation and economic conditions change from a working-class category (e.g. manual work) to a middle-class category and type (e.g. managerial work). In India social stratification is very rigid: a person is born into a caste, and no matter what professional and economic position he or she comes to occupy later in life, he or she will remain a member of the caste of his or her birth.

This brief description of the two societies shows that Indian and English people are exposed to different socialisation processes. Consequently one would expect them to differ from one another in the extent to which they hold certain attitudes and values, such as their attitude to power and authority, individual independence, and fatalism. The following section examines some of the characteristics that have in the past been attributed to Indian and English people, and then presents the findings of the surveys carried out by the present author to verify the presence of these traits among a sample of people in the two countries.

English and Indian cultural attitudes and values
Terry (1979), summarising the views of numerous English and foreign observers of the English over the centuries, attributed to his fellow countrymen and women the following: conservatism, tenacity, compromise, rural focus, liberty and individualism, violence and aggression, class consciousness, love of sport and

fair play, pragmatism, reserve, lack of ambition, chauvinism, and orderliness and discipline.

Indian culture admittedly is far from being homogeneous, but a close examination of findings of various studies of the culture of different regions and religious communities of the sub-continent indicates that there are many characteristics which are more or less common to the people as a whole, such as familial relationships, attitudes to seniors and caste consciousness. Moreover, it seems that regional cultural differences are more visible in such matters as religious and community rituals, eating habits and marriage ceremonies. The traits which are more saliently attributed to the Indians in general by Indian and non-Indian writers are: respect for and obedience to authority (Kakar, 1971), public expression of emotions (Parekh, 1974), group morality and community-orientation (Sega, 1971; Prekh, 1974), dependence on others (Koestler, 1966), caste consciousness (Beteille, 1969), and selfishness and lack of concern for others (Mother Teresa of Calcutta, in an interview with *India Today*, 31 May 1983).

There are very few studies which have attempted to compare Indian and English people. Parekh's (1974) and Child's (1982) works are the nearest to the purpose of the present study.

Parekh compared Indian and English people and concluded that the English are more individualistic, less emotional, more concerned about other people, more self-contained, more rule-governed and spatial, more resourceful, and more disciplined than the Indians.

Child, in a comparative study of play behaviour among English and Asian (Indian and Pakistani) children living in England found that English children were more independent, more aggressive, had less respect for people in authority, and maintained more physical distance between themselves and others compared with the Asian children.

The present surveys

This stage of the research was based on the past literature on English and Indian societies, and on the author's participant and non-participant observations. It was complemented by the administration of cultural questionnaire surveys among a small sample of the population in each country.

These surveys were an exercise in the verification of attitudes and values attributed to Indian and English people on the basis of which the consistency between culture and work-related attitudes could later be examined. The surveys were carried out with the help of a brief questionnaire. Its main body consisted of 35 pairs of opposing characteristics placed on seven-point scales. The respondents in each country were asked to rate their compatriots on the scale against each pair. The items had been selected on the basis of their salience in the literature. They were also indirectly related to the issues and relationships involved in work organisations and among their members. The areas covered in the questionnaire were: acceptance of responsibility, honesty and trust, obedience to and respect for senior people, independence, trustworthiness, corruption, group-orientation, individualism, ability to cope with ambiguity and uncertainty, self-confidence and resourcefulness, discipline and self-control, tolerance, friendliness, fair play, interest in community affairs, fatalism, and social stratification.

In India both English and Hindi versions of the questionnaire were used where appropriate; and where necessary, bilingual Indian friends of the author interpreted the questionnaire orally for those who spoke other Indian languages and/or who could not read at all. The questionnaire was first piloted in the two countries. The main English study was conducted between August 1981 and February 1982, the Indian between February and June 1983.

The samples

It was decided to study in each country a sample of 100 whose occupational mix matched that of their respective country as a whole. In England the ratio was 47 middle-class professions to 53 manual occupations (1971 census). In India, because there was no reliable information about the breakdown of various occupations, the dividing line was arbitrarily drawn at the 50/50 point.

In England 140 copies of the questionnaire had to be completed by the poeple who were approached at random up and down the country in order to achieve the occupationally representative sample of 100. In India, the sample ws drawn from (1) the urban working population, (2) people from Maharashtra and nearby states living in Bombay, and (3) mainly Hindus. One hundred and thirty copies of the questionnaire were completed before the required sample was achieved.

Although the size of the samples is small, the findings of the surveys are remarkably consistent with the socio-cultural backgrounds of each sample and are supported by similar conclusions arrived at by many other writers about the salient traits of English and Indian peoples in general.

The results

Table 4.1 summarises the comparison between English and Indian samples.

As the table shows the two samples are different from each other with respect to some of these characteristics. The Indians are more obedient to their seniors, are more afraid of and respectful to powerful people, and hate less to be told what to do compared to the English. These appear to be consistent with Indian and English people's respective upbringing, familial relationships and structure, and educational practices.

The Indians are more dependent on their parents, more emotional, less

Table 4.1 Comparison of English and Indian cultural characteristics

Cultural characteristics	English sample (mean) N = 100	Indian sample (mean) N = 100	Value of 't'**	Level of confidence p
Independent of their parents	2.72	3.92	4.60	.000
Not afraid of powerful people	3.01	4.40	5.74	.000
Do not believe in fate	3.94	5.25	5.55	.000
Hate to be told what to do	3.41	4.47	4.64	.000
Prefer to work on their own	2.83	3.80	3.82	.000
See things through	2.36	3.49	5.35	.000
Prefer to be on their own	4.27	5.14	3.70	.000
Unemotional	4.01	4.49	4.32	.000
Respect powerful people	3.82	2.54	− 5.78	.000
Aggressive	3.56	4.29	3.45	.001
Not open to bribery	2.96	3.80	3.51	.001
Believe in sharing fairly	3.31	4.10	3.44	.001
Have a strong sense of responsibility	2.25	2.83	2.88	.004
Cope well with setbacks	2.45	3.02	2.69	.008
Obedient to their seniors	3.08	2.54	− 2.45	.015
Honest	2.43	2.88	2.40	.017
Trustworthy	2.34	2.81	2.38	.018
Disciplined	2.76	3.26	2.29	.023
Modest	3.77	3.26	− 2.28	.024
Reserved	3.80	4.35	2.21	.028
Able to cope with new and uncertain situations	2.88	3.34	1.85	.065
Possess self-control	2.66	3.00	1.62	.106
Interested in community affairs	3.24	2.89	− 1.56	.122
Law-abiding	2.60	2.92	1.47	.144
Class/caste conscious	3.84	3.48	− 1.41	.161
Self-confidence	2.71	2.96	1.15	.253
Respect the law to the letter	3.38	3.14	− 1.04	.302
Have trust in others	3.14	3.37	0.96	.340
Prefer to stand on their own	4.01	4.24	0.88	.381
Tolerant	3.00	2.82	− 0.79	.432
Friendly	2.68	2.83	0.69	.490
Willing to take account of others' opinions	3.77	3.82	0.24	.810
Rational	3.10	3.15	0.21	.832
Opposed to change	4.17	4.21	0.61	.876
Play safe	3.83	3.81	− 0.08	.937

Note: The lower the score, the more the characteristic is present in the culture. The higher the score, the more the opposite is present.

*Tests of statistical significance

disciplined, less tenacious (see things through less), and are less able to cope with setbacks and new and uncertain situations than are the English. This, again, is consistent with the child-rearing practices and teaching methods at schools in their respective countries.

The English prefer more to be and work on their own, and are more reserved than the Indians. This seems to reflect the English people's love of privacy and emphasis on individualism and independence, and the Indian people's emphasis on conformity, extended family and dependent emotional relationships among family members.

The English believe less in fate compared to the Indians. This is consistent with their respective religious doctrines and practices.

English people are more honest and are less open to bribery. This is consistent with a relatively low level of corruption in the public administration in England and much higher and more pervasive corruption in the Indian government bureaucracies.

The Indians believe less in sharing fairly than do the English, which is consistent with the former's communitarianism and the latter's belief in 'fair play'.

The surveys showed no significant differences between the two samples with respect to such characteristics as self-control and self-confidence, friendliness, tolerance, and attitudes toward the law, social stratification and change.

As can be seen, there is a high degree of consistency between the values and attitudes that English and Indian people hold, on the one hand, and the socialisation processes to which they are exposed in their respective social institutions, on the other. The next step in the research was to examine whether or not these values and attitudes were held by organisational members to similar degrees.

The work attitude surveys

The respondents

The participants in this phase of the study worked in 14 manufacturing organisations in which the author conducted an investigation into their management style and structural characteristics as the third phase of the research project.

Seven hundred copies of the questionnaire were distributed among the sample of employees of the English companies (100 in each), of which 376 copies were completed and returned to the author – a response rate of 53.7 per cent; 475 copies were distributed among a similar sample of employees of the Indian organisations operating in the state of Maharashtra, of which 341 copies were completed and returned – a response rate of 71.8 per cent. In the Indian study Hindi and English versions of the questionnaire were used where appropriate. Trusted interpreters in some companies helped the participants who could not read or write at all.

The occupational composition of the sample in each organisation consisted of a cross-section of jobs and the respondents fell within one of the following categories:

(a) directors and other senior managers;
(b) superintendants, supervisors, foremen, and section heads;
(c) technicians, engineers, inspectors, controllers;
(d) specialists (e.g. chemists, computer programmers, accountants);
(e) office workers, receptionists and telephonists; and
(f) shopfloor manual workers.

The educational levels of the respondents ranged from primary school qualifications to the highest university degrees. The age groups varied from just under 20 to over 60 years old.

In order to maintain some degree of cultural homogeneity, those respondents who were not of English/Indian origins (three generations at least) in the respective samples were excluded from the study. It was also decided to exclude from the analyses the responses of those who had lived and/or received education abroad for longer than a year on the grounds of the influence of the host country's culture on their attitudes and values. This process led to the exclusion of 33 respondents from the English sample and four from the Indian sample.

A vast majority of the two samples represents the dominant religion of its respective country. Of the 343 English respondents, 259 adhered to Protestant denominations. In the Indian sample 266 were Hindus. For the Indian respondents a further question concerning their caste had also been included in the questionnaire but a very few people answered it.

The questionnaire

Eighty-seven items were included in the main body of the questionnaire, of which 71 are relevant to the present discussion. The issues and relationships they covered were: perceived power, tolerance for ambiguity, individualism, job satisfaction, commitment, trust, expectations from job, and attitudes towards management practices. Some of these items were devised by the present author and others were selected from among the available measures designed and tested by other researchers (see Tayeb, 1988, for details).

The results

Table 4.2 illustrates a summary of the results of this phase of the study.

On the basis of the findings of the first phase of the project, the cultural surveys, Indian employees were expected to perceive a larger power distance between themselves and their managers (lower perception of power) compared to the English employees. This indeed was the case: Indian employees perceived themselves to have far less power at work.

English employees avoided uncertainty less and tolerated ambiguity to a greater extent than did the Indian employees. The direction of the differences

Table 4.2 Comparison of English and Indian work-related values and attitudes

Work-related attitudes and values	English sample (N = 341)	Indian sample (N = 337)	Value of t*	Level of confidence p
Perceived power	32	28	13.28	.000
Tolerance of ambiguity	36	34	6.41	.000
Individualism	18	18	0.57	.569
Commitment	34	35	– 1.31	.190
Trust	34	34	– 0.69	.489
Expectations from a job:				
job security	3.92	3.67	3.49	.001
get to know others	3.56	3.62	– 0.76	.445
good pay	4.04	3.86	2.75	.006
belong to a group	2.36	3.09	– 8.89	.000
autonomy	3.88	4.01	– 1.80	.072
learn new things	4.06	4.40	– 5.94	.000
status and prestige	3.44	4.00	– 7.75	.000
initiative and creativity	4.06	4.28	– 3.49	.001
Management philosophy:				
attitude to others	3.05	2.93	1.76	.078
sharing information	3.16	2.46	10.05	.000
attitude to participation	3.13	3.19	– 1.02	.306
attitude to control	3.14	3.03	1.86	.063

*Tests of statistical significance

between the two samples is consistent with their respective cultural backgrounds.

Indian people are more fatalistic than are the English. One would expect Indian employees to have lower expectations from their organisation and, as a consequence, to be more easily motivated. This, in turn, would be reflected in their greater satisfaction with their company, compared with the English employees. Table 4.2 shows that this was the case and the Indian employees expressed a higher degree of satisfaction with their work organisation.

If Indian employees carried their collectivist culture with them to their workplace, one would expect to observe a high degree of collectivism and group-orientation among them, and, consequently, greater commitment to their company as part of a collectivity. The results of the survey showed that there was in fact no significant difference between the two groups of employees in this respect. Indian employees did not seem to be any less individualistic and more committed to their work organisations than were their English counterparts.

The concepts of 'ingroup' and 'outgroup' may be of relevance here. The scope of ingroup and domain of outgroup denote the extent to which an individual is prepared to have 'close' or 'distant' relationships with others, and the extent to which others will be the object of his or her loyalty (Triandis, 1981). In some cultures the ingroup consists of only family members (e.g. Iran, especially in large cities); in some it encompasses close relations and friends too (e.g. India); and in some societies it includes also one's work organisation (e.g. Japan). Clearly, Indian employees' ingroup does not include their work organisation.

Non-cultural factors, such as organisational climate, may well have had moderating effects here. Indian managers may, for instance, have failed to incorporate their employees' high collectivism into the organisation's own culture and shared value systems. This is an area of management in which Japanese managers appear to be more successful.

Indian employees' low degree of commitment may also have something to do with their hierarchical positions. In a breakdown of the respondents according to their occupations, the author noted that managers in both countries scored much higher on commitment than did other occupational categories. The difference was much more pronounced between senior managers and shopfloor employees. This result, of course, is hardly surprising given the vastly different treatments which the participating organisations accorded to their employees (see Tayeb, 1988, for details).

Also, the class conflict between management and workers, a political economy factor, which is similar in England and India as capitalist countries, may have overridden the cultural differences between the two samples with regard to their commitment. The employees' hierarchical positions 'inside' and 'outside' their organisations appear to have had a combined effect on commitment.

What employees expect from their job and consider as important are assumed to be consistent with their cultural backgrounds. In a predominantly individualistic society such as England employees are likely to consider independence, autonomy and privacy at work to be more important compared with the Indian employees. The latter may attach more importance to 'belongingness'.

The survey showed that Indian employees valued freedom and autonomy, belonging to a group and learning new skills and status as more important than other aspects of a job; whereas to the English employees job security and good pay and fringe benefits were more important.

Here again non-cultural factors might have intervened. At the time the present research was conducted in England, over 3 million people were unemployed and wage increases were severely constrained partly because of government policies, and partly because of the financial hardship that many business organisations experienced. Under these circumstances it was not surprising that the English respondents attached greater importance to job security and good pay.

The Indian employees' preference especially for greater opportunities to learn new skills and to have more freedom and status reflects the shortage and indeed lack of these job features for many employees, particularly those in junior positions.

Given the cultural backgrounds of the respondents, one would expect English employees to express a more egalitarian view regarding management practices and to favour more a participative style, compared to the Indian employees. As Table 4.2 shows, it was the Indian employees who favoured more a participative management style. However, one of the prerequisites of 'participation for all' is the extent to which participants receive information. This in turn depends on how far those who have access to information are willing to share it with others. The table shows quite clearly that it is the English employees who are more in favour of information sharing. Not only is this consistent with the respective cultural backgrounds of the respondents, in terms of the degree of willingness to take other people's opinions into account, but it may also reflect the organisational climate within which the respondents work. The greater preference of the Indian employees for participation may in fact be because of their fewer opportunities to participate in decision-making processes in their workplace.

Organisational structure surveys

This phase of the study was intended to examine whether there was any consistency between English and Indian employees' work-related attitudes and values and their respective organisations' structure and management style.

Seven organisations in each country were selected which were matched in pairs across the two countries with respect to their major contextual variables. The industries in which these organisations engaged were brewery, confectionery, chemicals, pharmaceuticals and electronics. Their technologies varied from simple and stable in the brewery industry to highly complex and changing in the electronics industry. The size of the organisations, in terms of the numbers employed, varied from 133 to 1,670, and the age of the companies from 15 to 144 years. Their ownership and control were determined by the extent to which they were owned and managed by members of a family, shareholders, owner-managers or salaried managers.

Aspects of organisation studied were: degree of centralisation of decision-making power, formalisation (use of written rules and regulations), specialisation of functions, communication and consultation, supervisory spans of control, reward policies, and control strategies.

The Aston Abbreviated Schedule (Inkson, Pugh and Hickson, 1970) was employed in a series of semi-structured interviews in which at least three senior managers from each company participated. The Schedule contained items related to centralisation, formalisation and specialisation. The centralisation scale measured the extent to which decision-making power was concentrated at the top or distributed down the hierarchy. The centralisation items were also used to compute a delegation score for each organisation by counting the number of levels down from the chief executive to the level at which a decision was made. The formalisation scale measured the degree to which written rules, documents, and job descriptions were used in the organisation. The specialisation scale measured the extent to which activities and functions were performed by specialised departments or persons. The Schedule was supplemented by questions about control strategies and reward policies. Also, five scales were included in the work-related attitudes questionnaire, administered among the employees of the same organisations as the second stage of the research, which aimed to measure the degree to which the employees communicated with one another in various directions. Information about control strategies was obtained from the senior managers who participated in the interview programmes. Each organisation's relevent policy manuals were also consulted.

Table 4.3 summarises the findings of this phase of the study.

Table 4.3   Comparison of English and Indian organisations (Mann–Whitney test)

Structural dimensions	English sample (mean) N = 7	Indian sample (mean) N = 7	'U'	Level of confidence p
Centralisation	210	214	19.00	.480
Delegation	167	153	11.00	.080
Joint decisions	19	17	23.00	.840
Formalisation	12	4.71	0.00	.001
Specialisation	10	8.71	21.00	.650
Chief executive's span of control	7	9	18.00	.390
Number of hierarchical levels (height)	6	5.5	18.05	.430
Communication:				
with boss	2.40	2.23	11.50	.090
with subordinates	3.00	2.49	5.50	.010
with colleagues	3.36	2.32	0.00	.001
with people from other areas of work	2.34	2.02	11.50	.090
with people from outside the company	1.96	2.24	11.50	.090

On the basis of the findings of the first two stages of the study, Indian organisations were expected to be more centralised than their English counterparts. The study revealed an interesting pattern in this respect: English organisations were more centralised on strategic and financial decisions but less on operational ones compared to the Indian companies. This seems to have reflected the respective political economic environments of the participating organisations. English firms, as was mentioned earlier, experienced financial hardship and changing economic conditions, reinforced by the open market policies of the Conservative government. Under these conditions, the managers perhaps found it necessary to exert a tighter control over financial and strategic decisions, because of the immense risks involved. In India government political and economic policies are geared towards, among other things, the protection of low-paid manual workers. As a consequence, these employees cannot be fired and their wages cannot be reduced even if they do not perform their jobs properly. Senior managers therefore are frequently personally involved in decisions which concern operatives and their work, in order to avoid unpleasant consequences.

There was more delegation of authority and a smaller supervisory span of control (numbers reporting directly to each manager) in English organisations than in their Indian counterparts. This was consistent with their respective cultural backgrounds.

As the table shows, English employees communicated and consulted with one another to a larger extent than did the Indian employees. The English employees' greater degree of consultation is consistent with their culturally rooted democratic values and their interest in participation, consultation, information sharing, discussion and collective actions. The Indian organisations' lower level of communication reflects Indian people's 'authoritarian' social culture (e.g. Kakar, 1971) where decisions are generally made by seniors (even sometimes on behalf of the juniors, in the case of arranged marriage, for example) with little or no consultation, and submission is expected from the juniors.

The extent of communication and consultation in these organisations also reflects the market conditions they faced. Many of the English organisations in the sample, especially those in the high-technology industries, had smaller market shares and operated in a more competitive environment compared to their Indian counterparts. As a consequence the English employees may have felt it necessary to be in constant touch with their fellow organisational members and to exchange information on a larger scale in order to be able to interact with their environment promptly. On the other hand, the relatively stable environment of the Indian organisations may not have necessitated such extensive communications up and down and across the hierarchy.

Culturalists would argue that the extent to which organisations use functional specialisation and written rules and regulations depends on the extent to which employees can tolerate ambiguity and uncertainty, because rules and regulations and clear-cut definitions of roles and functions provide more security and certainty, which are welcomed by people from an uncertainty-avoiding culture (Hofstede, 1980).

Following this argument, and the Indian employees' relatively lower degree of tolerance for ambiguity, Indian organisations were expected to be more specialised and to use more laid-down rules and job descriptions compared to the English companies. Table 4.3 shows that this was not the case. The Indian organisations were far less formalised and just as specialised as were the English.

The degree of specialisation of the participating organisations appears to have been more influenced by task-related factors than by cultural ones. In a separate analysis of the results of the present surveys reported elsewhere (Tayeb, 1987), the specialisation scores correlated significantly with technology, size, ownership, and control. There was virtually no correlation between specialisation and any of the work attitudes measured.

The results of the study in respect of formalisation and use of rules and regulations are in the opposite direction to that postulated in the culturalists' argument. However, the English organisations' greater use of rules compared to their Indian counterparts indicates a likely connection between organisations and some other cultural traits, namely, attitudes to privacy, independence, and spatiality. The English tend to value their own, and others', privacy, independence and clear-cut spatial territories; the Indians tend to value these less. The English and Indian organisations' degree of formalisation is therefore consistent with their employees' cultural characteristics.

However, the formalisation scale employed in the present study (adapted from Inkson, Pugh and Hickson, 1970) measured the extent to which *written documents* were used in the companies. There might also have been unwritten rules and directives which regulated employees' activities. This might be especially so in the Indian organisations, where most of the shopfloor manual workers were illiterate (a political economy-type factor).

Moreover, formalisation is in effect a means to control employees and to improve their performance (Child, 1984). There are other ways in which control can be exerted. The managers who participated in the interview programmes mentioned a variety of methods that they employed, such as training courses, personal supervision, time-keeping, and verbal contacts. My discussions with these managers suggest that the Indian managers employed direct supervision and personal contacts with shopfloor employees as well as their immediate subordinates to a larger extent than did their English counterparts.

On the whole, in both countries managers and other members of staff were treated differently from the manual workers on the shop floor. There was virtually no external control, such as clocking and close personal supervision for the former, whereas the latter were subject to much tighter measures in this respect. Control over managers and other staff was generally exercised through target setting and progress monitoring; over manual workers through time-keeping and productivity measurements.

In all the organisations in both countries rewards took financial as well as non-financial forms, and the managers said they linked the rewards to the employees' performance. Punishment was less harsh and non-financial for manual workers in the Indian organisations because of the government's regulations, which aim at maintaining employment and a minimum living standard for this group of employees. Also, Indian managers, although they expressed their belief in the effectiveness of financial rewards, for tax purposes rewarded their employees in kind, such as a company house and car, rather than in cash.

It appears that the Indian managers ignored their employees' preferences for the kind of rewards they expected to get from their job, namely, status and prestige, and having an opportunity to learn new things.

Discussion

Culture and work-related attitudes

There are systematic differences between English and Indian employees on some of the work-related attitudes measured in the study. These are attitudes to power and authority, tolerance for ambiguity and uncertainty, expectations from the job and job satisfaction, and attitude to management practices. The direction of the differences is generally consistent with the cultural backgrounds of the respondents. There is a dearth of comparative studies between English and Indian cultures and organisationally relevant attitudes. Some of the previous cross-national studies, such as Haire, Ghiselli and Porter (1966) and Hofstede (1980), included both Britain and India in their samples. The results of the present study are consistent with these researchers' findings for similar attitudes measured.

There is some degree of similarity between the two samples on trust, commitment and individualism. A closer examination of these similarities reveals interesting patterns. The similar scores on trust obtained by the English and Indian employees are consistent with their respective cultural backgrounds, as discussed earlier. The commitment and individualism scores achieved by the English employees are consistent with their cultural backgrounds, but those by the Indian employees are not. The explanation for this discontinuity may lie in non-cultural and situational factors, such as organisational climate, employees' formal position in the organisation, and political economic conditions (e.g. class conflict between management and workers).

It should be noted that the inconsistencies observed between the respondents' cultural backgrounds and some of their work-related attitudes exist virtually only in the Indian sample. This could be because of the influence of the British style of management and workplace relationships on the Indian organisations, which may be a result of the British rule in India over two centuries.

Work-related attitudes and organisational structure

There was some consistency between employees' degree of commitment on the one hand, and the control strategies employed by the management on the other. Also, the employees' attitudes towards management practices matched the extent of communication and consultation in their respective companies. The degree of formalisation in both groups of organisations also appeared to be consistent with the value their respective cultures place on privacy and independence.

There were, however, some inconsistencies between work-related attitudes and the organisational features expected to relate to them. For instance, there was no relationship between the degree of specialisation in the organisations and any of the cultural attitudes held by their members and measured in the study. Also, there were apparent discontinuities between the employees' expectations from their job and the reward policies employed by their managers.

Some of the features of the organisational structures were found to be more closely affected by non-cultural and task-environmental factors than their employees' cultural backgrounds. Specialisation, for example, had a significant correlation with technology and size.

Present study and the multi-perspective model

Weber (1930) pioneered a multi-perspective approach when he developed the thesis that socio-cultural institutions such as religion played an important role in the formation of economic systems and in the degree to which organisations are administered rationally, in addition to materialistic forces of the kind identified by Marx. More recently, Budde *et al.* (1982), comparing a sample of British and West German companies, examined the role of both cultural and contingency factors in explaining the differences and similarities between these companies. Multivariate models have also been suggested by other researchers (see for example Farmer and Richman, 1965; Randolph and Dess, 1984), but they incorporated variables from only one framework.

The multi-perspective thesis proposed here incorporates the variables suggested by contingency, political economy and cultural perspectives in the model presented in Figure 4.1. The model suggests that an understanding of

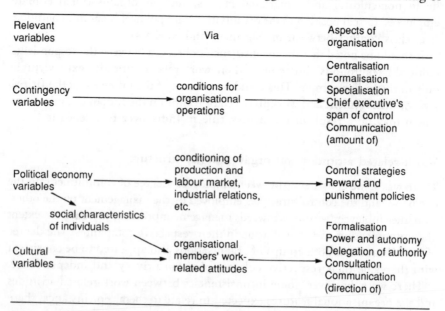

Fig. 4.1 A multi-perspective model for understanding organisational structure and systems
Source: Tayeb (1988), p. 156

organisational structure requires reference both to its formal dimensions, such as centralisation and specialisation, and to the processes which lie behind them, such as consultation and communication.

The contingency factors have implications primarily for formal organisational structure. The relationships between these features of organisation and contextual factors are more or less universal, at least for the samples studied here (see also Hickson *et al.*, 1974). It is indeed common sense to expect, for example, an increase in the number of employees to lead to an increase in the division of labour (specialisation). But the ways in which the degree of specialisation is eventually achieved may vary from culture to culture, or indeed from organisation to organisation.

The processes behind the formal aspects of organisation are performed, managed and implemented by the members of organisations. The members' behaviours and relationships with one another within the workplace are based, to a large extent, on their work-related attitudes, such as attitudes to power and authority, uncertainty and ambiguity, and management philosophy and ideology. These attitudes are strongly associated with the employees' cultural and non-cultural backgrounds, such as their family, religion and social class. These, in turn, have their roots in the cultural and political economic characteristics of the societies within which organisations and their employees live.

Finally, the model suggests that the demarcation lines between contingency, cultural and political economy perspectives are not clear cut. For instance, political economic factors, such as government economic policies, may result in smaller or bigger market shares, and cause, subsequently, higher or lower competition. This in turn constitutes a contingency factor for the affected organisations.

Conclusions

The present study was conducted in three independent stages in England and India in an attempt to examine the role of some cultural, contingency and political economy factors in the structure of organisations and their employees' work-related attitudes.

The study provided some support for the arguments advanced by the proponents of the culturalist approach, who maintain that organisational structure and systems are determined by the socio-cultural characteristics of people inside and outside the organisations. The findings of the three stages of the study show that there is a considerable consistency between English and Indian people's socialisation processes in their homes, schools, religions and societies as a whole, on the one hand, and the degree to which they hold certain attitudes, on the other. There was also some consistency between the employees' cultural backgrounds and their work-related attitudes, and finally, there was some consistency between some of the employees' work-related attitudes and certain aspects of their organisations. The culturalist perspective would provide a rationale for these areas of consistency.

However, the study also indicated that the cultural characteristics of the environments within which Indian and English organisations operated were not the only factors which influenced the way they were managed and structured.

Moreover, employees' work-related attitudes were found to be associated not only with their cultural upbringing, but also with their formal positions in the organisational hierarchy and the standing of their occupational groups in the society as a whole.

The findings of the study suggest that contingency, political economy, and cultural perspectives make valuable contributions to our understanding of organisations, and that the arguments of these perspectives should be integrated and incorporated in a multi-perspective model.

References

Beteille, A. (1969) 'Caste in a South Indian Village', in A. Beteille (Ed.) *Social Inequality*, Penguin, Harmondsworth.

Budde, A., Child, J., Francis, A. and Keiser, A. (1982) 'Corporate Goals, Managerial Objectives, and Organizational Structure in British and West German Companies', *Organization Studies*, Vol. 3, pp. 1–3.

Child, E. (1982) *Individual and Social Factors Associated with the Behaviour of Children in a Play Setting*, unpublished Ph.D. thesis, University of Aston.

Child, J. (1984) *Organization: A Guide to Problems and Practice*, 2nd edition, Harper & Row, London.

Child, J. and Tayeb, M. (1983) 'Theoretical Perspectives in Cross-National Organizational Research', *International Studies of Management and Organization*, Vol. XII, pp. 23–70.

Farmer, R. N. and Richman, B. M. (1965) *Comparative Management and Economic Progress*, Irwin, Homewood.

Haire, M., Ghiselli, E. E. and Porter, L. W. (1966) *Managerial Thinking*, Wiley, New York.

Hickson, D. J., Hinings, C. R., McMillan, C. J. and Schwitter, J. P. (1974) 'The Culture-Free Context of Organization Structure: A Tri-National Comparison', *Sociology*, Vol. 8, pp. 59–80.

Hofstede, G. (1980) *Culture's Consequences*, Sage, California.

Inkson, J. H. K., Pugh, D. S. and Hickson, D. J. (1970) 'Organization Context and Structure: An Abbreviated Replication', *Administrative Science Quarterly*, Vol. 15, pp. 318–29.

Kakar, S. (1971) 'The Theme of Authority in Social Relations in India', *Journal of Social Psychology*, Vol. 84, pp. 93–101.

Koestler, A. (1966) *The Lotus and the Robot*, Danube edition, Hutchinson, London.

Lawrence, P. R. and Lorsch, J. W. (1967) *Organization and Environment*, Harvard Business School, Boston.

Marsh, R. M. and Mannari, H. (1981) 'Technology and Size as Determinants of the Organizational Structure of Japanese Factories', *Administrative Science Quarterly*, Vol. 26, pp. 33–57.

Parekh, B. (1974) 'The Spectre of Self-Consciousness', in B. Parekh (Ed.) *Colour, Culture, and Consciousness*, Allen and Unwin, London.

Randolph, W. A. and Dess, G. G. (1984) 'The Congruence Perspective of Organization Design: A Conceptual Model and Multivariate Research Approach', *Academy of Management Review*, Vol. 9, pp. 114–27.

Segal, R. (1971) *The Crisis of India*, Jaico Publishing House, Bombay.

Tayeb, M. (1981) 'Cultural Influences on Organizational Response to Environmental Demands', University of Aston Management Centre working paper No. 215.

Tayeb, M. (1987) 'Contingency Theory and Culture: A Study of Matched English and Indian Firms', *Organization Studies*, Vol. 8, pp. 241–62.

Tayeb, M. (1988) *Organizations and National Culture: A Comparative Analysis*, Sage, London.

Terry, P. (1979) *An Investigation of Some Cultural Determinants of English Organization Behaviour*, unpublished Ph.D. thesis, University of Bath.

Triandis, H. C. (1981) 'Dimensions of Cultural Variations as Parameters of Organizational Theories', paper presented to the International Symposium on Cross-Cultural Management, Montreal, Canada, October.

Weber, M. (1930) *The Protestant Ethic and the Spirit of Capitalism*, Free Press, Glencoe.

Woodward, J. (1958) *Management and Technology*, HMSO, London.

Part two

Comparisons of human resource practices and strategies

The chapters in this section take broad economic, social and institutional changes and attempt to analyse the consequential strategic human resource policy responses. A feature of all these studies is the relationship between macro-level economic and social trends and the strategies followed at the organisational level.

John Grahl and Paul Teague seek to explain the paradox that while there are diverse industrial relations systems in European countries with different histories, cultures and institutions, common managerial strategies are emerging. They do so by reference to the impact of changes to what they call 'industrial relations trajectories'. These trajectories are guiding principles created by the organisation of work, the institutions and the production system generally in use. Changes to industrial relations trajectories lead to a paradigm shift, with opportunities for new approaches to management according to the fit between the institutional framework in each society and the economic and technical circumstances of production. They proceed to a description of the alternative flexibility strategies available at the level of the firm as a result of the changing trajectory of industrial relations, and the consequences for European institutions and human resource policies of the choices made.

A similar point of departure is taken by Basu Sharma. He applies a 'stage of development' approach to the analysis of industrial relations in Korea and Singapore. According to this theory, different patterns of industrial relations (which are similar to the notion of 'trajectories') are appropriate at different levels of industrialisation. This is because industrial relations policies are brought into line with their general economic policies by the political élites of newly industrialised countries (NICs). Sharma shows how these strategy shifts derived from political changes in Singapore and South Korea when it became necessary to restructure the labour movements according to the economic requirements of industrialisation and competition. Sharma, like Grahl and Teague, therefore reveals how the effective use of human resource management is significant in the process of economic change.

If Grahl and Teague emphasise economic causes, and Sharma political causes of industrial relations change, then the third chapter in this part, by Beverly Springer, looks at the complex social movement towards equal treatment between men and women as one origin of human resource policies. From her comparison of banks in the UK, France and the USA we can see that national value systems are manifested in national legislation concerning women's rights at the workplace. She uses the organisation level of analysis in a case study approach through which she explores the impact of national culture and legislation on equal opportunities.

It is one of the strengths of this chapter that Springer has been able to relate the particular organisation situation to national cultures, legislation, demography and technology. In this way she is able to relate the socially important progress towards women's rights to skill shortages, demographic trends and work systems, and form the link back to the economic and political frameworks discussed in the other two chapters.

5

Industrial relations trajectories and European human resource management

JOHN GRAHL and PAUL TEAGUE

Introduction

The recent decision of the European Community (with the exception of the UK) to introduce a Social Charter to accompany its 1992 programme raises the question of a European system of industrial relations. With the relaunch of the integration process, the notion of a European industrial relations system seems more attractive, but detailed examinations of the issue tend to be cautious. In particular, most studies conclude that because considerable diversity exists among the different national industrial relations systems in Europe any moves toward a single uniform system would involve displacing many existing institutions and practices. Since accepted and finely tuned patterns of industrial relations behaviour would be disrupted in the process, the result could be chaos rather than a new well-functioning pan-European system. In other words, as national industrial relations systems are the product of specific national, historical, cultural and political circumstances, it may be more appropriate for them to remain at the margins of the European integration project (Teague, 1989).

Clearly, this line of argument has substance and unsurprisingly therefore it has become the most accepted view. But an important weakness of the 'institutional diversity' thesis is that it fails to explain why at any given time similar issues and problems tend to determine the industrial relations agenda across Europe despite the differences in national systems. For example, why is it that labour market flexibility is currently a central concern for management, trade unions and governments almost everywhere in Europe? Or why was there a simultaneous upsurge in industrial conflict in many European countries in the late 1960s? Thus, despite institutional diversity similar influences and dynamics are operating on European industrial relations. And it may be that these similar or common factors might provide the foundation of a European system of industrial relations, thereby refuting the 'institutional diversity' thesis that there is no real basis for such an arrangement.

But first it is necessary to examine these similar influences and dynamics and to assess whether they represent the basis for Community-wide industrial relations policies and arrangements. The chapter is organised as follows: first, we describe the extent of intitutional diversity in European industrial relations;

then the common aspects of these different national systems are outlined; in the following section the idea of industrial relations trajectories is developed to explain the apparent paradox of why common or similar developments occur simultaneously in institutionally diverse systems: after that section the rise and demise of the 'Fordist' industrial relations trajectory is described; the fifth section argues that a new 'flexible' industrial relations trajectory may be emerging, but that only some 'production' aspects of the trajectory have appeared; the subsequent section suggests that at present there is a battle between competitive and constructive flexibility models to constitute the 'institutional' parts of the trajectory. The conclusions suggest that the EC Social Charter is an attempt to install constructive flexibility arrangements at Community level.

The extent of diversity in European industrial relations

The degree of divergence among national industrial relations systems in Europe can hardly be doubted. Among the most important differences are the following.

The level of unionisation

Trade union density levels differ significantly across Europe. At one end of the spectrum are countries like France, where trade union membership is low, about 15 per cent of the total workforce. At the other end of the spectrum are the Scandinavian countries, where density rates are high – over 90 per cent of the workforce in Sweden are trade union members. In the middle are a group of countries, like Britain and Germany, in which trade union membership is about 40–50 per cent of those in work.

The degree of centralisation

The level at which most important industrial relations decisions are taken is another difference. Countries like Britain, Italy and Switzerland have relatively decentralised systems, in which most industrial relations matters are resolved at the enterprise level. By contrast, the Scandinavian countries have centralised systems in which round-table discussions between trade unions, employers and government determine rates of pay and other policies relating to working conditions and so on. Countries like Germany and the Benelux states have hybrid systems with elements of both decentralised and centralised arrangements.

The role of law

The extent to which industrial relations policies are embedded in the law is a third source of difference. Employment contracts may be subject to general contract law with some specific legal requirements; or they may be determined by a completely distinct labour code. The highly legalistic industrial relations systems include France and Belgium, where a whole range of employment conditions and rights are underscored by statutory provisions. Countries where the law plays a relatively small role in industrial relations are Britain, Ireland and Denmark. Again, between these two poles there is a group of intermediate cases.

The ideological aspects of the industrial relations system

Although each national industrial relations system has its own ideological dimension, three broad categories can be said to exist across Europe. In countries like Germany, Belgium, the Netherlands, Denmark and perhaps Switzerland the approach is essentially consensual and there is a high level of common values and beliefs among employers, unions and government. In a second group of countries, like Sweden, Norway and Austria, a less consensual ideology exists with the various industrial relations actors regarding themselves as having distinctive and even opposing interests. However, conflict is reduced or averted through the corporatist institutionalisation of the industrial relations system. In other words, political structures are developed to establish a compromise between capital and labour. Britain and Italy represent a third group of countries where the industrial relations system has been essentially adversarial, in which an ideology of 'them' and 'us' prevails.

There are four broad distinctions within European industrial relations. However, there are also many more specific differences. The specific details of the various policies and arrangements differ quite considerably across the Community. For instance, the legal restrictions on working hours differ widely; from the situation where no statutory maximum exists to quite detailed restrictions. Discernible differences can also be seen with regard to employee participation, termination formalities, minimum holiday entitlements and employment contracts. Only with regard to minimum pay and minimum notice to employees is there a degree of conformity. Thus both the broad orientation and the specific details of industrial relations systems vary widely in the Community.

The common features of European industrial relations

Yet despite this diversity a number of common trends and developments in European industrial relations have emerged in recent years. Among the most discernible trends are new forms and new areas of work, decentralisation, the adoption of labour market flexibility strategies and the growth of human resource management. Across Europe there has been a relentless growth of atypical forms of work — part-time and temporary workers, seasonal and short-term contract workers. Moreover, there has been a significant shift in the sectoral composition of full employment, with more service sector workers and fewer manufacturing workers. All these developments must have some bearing on the content and direction of industrial relations across the region.

Another trend is the shift from national or industry-wide collective bargaining to enterprise-level bargaining. This trend is most pronounced in Britain and Italy, but decentralised bargaining is also now much more widespread in countries like Belgium, West Germany, Sweden, the Netherlands, France and Denmark. As a result of these trends, the corporatist arrangements that dominated industrial relations in most of these countries are being weakened, albeit to varying degrees. Furthermore, decentralisation has given rise to a whole new range of enterprise-level employee relations developments such as productivity deals, technology agreements, and innovative consultation and participation arrangements. The issue that has dominated European industrial relations during the last decade is labour market flexibility. In different forms and to a different extent every country in Europe has tackled the qustions, first, of internal flexibility (removal of job demarcations and the development of multi-skilled tasks, increasing the flexibility of working hours and more individualised payment systems), and second, of external flexibility (increasing numerical flexibility, promoting worker mobility and streamlining statutory regulations governing the labour market).

The emergence of decentralisation and flexibility as common themes in industrial relations results from new pressures on enterprises and their adoption of new strategies in response. A closely related development is the growth of human resource management. In essence this means linking employees and employee relations very directly to the commercial needs of the firm. This objective itself requires the removal of non-market institutional constraints on the use of labour. Hence the demand for decentralisation and flexibility.

Industrial relations trajectories

These common trends can be viewed in terms of industrial relations trajectories. The notion of trajectories is predicated on the belief that economic development passes through specific phases within each of which a clearly defined pattern of production becomes the organising principle for most economies. A key feature of such a productive system is that it gives rise to specific forms of social, industrial and work organisation which in turn influence the character and content of industrial relations. In other words, the underlying productive system tends to guide the industrial relations system along a certain path or trajectory. This is for two basic reasons: first, a particular production system tends to give rise to a certain type of labour process; second, the system generates certain 'needs' and tensions which require action within the wider social and political framework: the underlying productive system reaches its optimum only when the labour process and the wider institutional arrangements are adapted to it.

An example might make the argument clearer. During the postwar 'golden age' of economic growth most European economies came to be organised on the basis of mass production and consumption in a way which is often described as Fordism. The emergence of the Fordist system can be seen as being determined by a number of interdependent and mutually reinforcing changes in production processes, in patterns of consumption and in the general institutional framework. Probably the fundamental feature behind the Fordist growth model was its characteristic production process: the mass production of standardised consumer goods, particularly automobiles and other consumer durables. This rested on the introduction of continuous flow techniques such as the conveyor belt and assembly line into much of manufacturing, putting an end to many highly fragmented production methods. High-volume production was the result based on the systematic integration of semi-skilled workers into the production process, displacing a division of labour more centred on craft production. Of course, to sustain high production volumes changes in consumption were necessary. For the first time high and stable levels of working-class consumption became essential to the health of capitalist economies. This was the era when cars and durable consumer goods were first purchased on a mass scale (Aglietta, 1979; Boyer, 1988).

For the purposes of the analysis here it is necessary to highlight two points. First, Fordism gave rise to a production process towards which many enterprises tended to approximate. In particular, large enterprises began to proliferate across Europe, housing similar types of production and work organisations. Thus the nature of car production, for instance, was more or less the same in Italy, France, Britain and elsewhere (Coriat, 1988). Within Fordist systems products tended to be made on a mass homogeneous basis to meet standardised and uniform markets. In many ways this production system was highly inefficient. To secure continuity of output, rudimentary strategic planning was used by enterprises but this approach tended to stockpile intermediate parts and even finished products, which was a considerable financial burden. Rudimentary quality control meant that defective goods were detected only at the end of the production run. Very high volumes were made necessary by long set-up times for conveyor-belt proceses. With regard to labour, this production process gives rise to a certain work organisation. Characteristically, jobs were relatively unskilled as a result of a high degree of specialisation. Most workers performed single tasks repetitively. Little on-the-job training was required and virtually no learning experience took place. Work tasks were organised hierarchically, with close supervision of individual employees. Productivity was encouraged through a range of techniques such as time and motion studies and incentive payments. This type of work organisation was a form of Taylorism, so named after the founder of 'scientific management'. Frederick Taylor.

The second important point is that the system required a variety of institutional arrangements which connected the production process with appropriate consumption norms. Specifically, the institutional structure had to ensure that money wages throughout the economy increased at about the same rate as productivity gains plus inflation so that demand for the output of mass consumption industries kept in line with their expanding productive potential. To some extent, Keynesian demand management helped maintain the linkage between price levels and output volumes. But the burden also fell on the industrial relations system. In particular, through the collective bargaining process a basic formula was struck by the large manufacturing employers and the unions which organised their semi-skilled production line workers. This centred on the productivity bargain, enabling employers to cut costs and accelerate output growth in manufacturing. Through pattern bargaining, administrative practice and legislation the bargains struck in the larger corporations frequently became the centre of the entire national wage negotiation process.

Several important implications arose from these demands placed on the collective bargaining system. First, they gave rise to and sustained industrial trade unions, which effectively ensured the social integration of workers into the industrial order. Thus a basic level of industrial citizenship was secured by mass trade unionism. In this context trade union membership increased rapidly in the postwar period and the role they played in society became much more important.

Thus the social foundation of Fordism was a specific contractual relationship between labour and capital in the enterprise and at wider political and social levels: Fordism gave rise to industrial relations systems based on an explicit contractual exchange. The compromise between labour and capital based on pay and productivity was the core of this key contract while in many Western European societies the corporatist arrangements that grew up in the 1950s and 1960s represented this same exchange relationship at the political level.

The Fordist industrial relations trajectory also gave rise to a certain style of personnel management within the large enterprises, normally organised on 'M'-form lines with specialised and normally independent departments, including personnel. The main function of the personnel department was to maintain industrial peace and ensure that the labour process operated effectively. At the higher levels, this involved personnel managers in rounds of negotiations with the trade unions, mostly over pay. Here the remit was fairly straightforward – to ensure that pay increases were accompanied by equivalent productivity concessions. At the lower levels the main tasks of the personnel function were to supervise the vast numbers of workers carrying out relatively unskilled work tasks, to conduct time and motion studies to ensure that productivity was being maintained and examine how the division of labour could be further specialised or deepened. In other words, the tasks were to implement Taylorist management policies. In most cases, personnel departments were removed from the key corporate strategy-making within the business. Personnel managers were given no initiating role; they were regarded as being basically reactive, responding to the demands made by the trade unions.

Another important institutional aspect of the Fordist industrial relations trajectory was the kind of demand it placed on government economic policies. The emergence of mass production, triggering a major shift from agriculture to industry, increased substantially the numbers of the urban working class, which created new tensions and new demands for government social and economic intervention. Unsurprisingly therefore we see rapid expansion of housing and other urban social services at this time together with an enormous increase in government infrastructural programmes, in particular roads. These social provisions were necessary for the functioning of the underlying productive system and became central themes in political debate. Here it is important to note that the form and character of these social provisions were different in Europe and the USA. In Europe, where social democratic or socialist parties were in government in many countries during this period, government provision prevailed, giving rise to a system described variously as welfare capitalism or social democratic capitalism. In the USA more reliance was placed on the market to provide the new services and infrastructures. Thus, we can call the industrial relations trajectory in Europe 'social Fordism', and that in the USA 'market Fordism'.

The argument is that the organisation of work and the institutional demands created by the underlying production system constitute industrial relations trajectories. These trajectories are the source of the common elements in European industrial relations. The political, social and historical traditions of a given country determine how fully they are implemented within different national systems and to what extent they are adapted to specific national circumstances: it would be excessively functionalist to argue that a trajectory is always implemented in full. It is also these autonomous institutional structures and social traditions that determine the diversity of the industrial relations systems: whether collective bargaining is centralised or decentralised, the extent of unionisation, the exact rules and regulations governing working conditions, and so on.

Furthermore, these institutional and regulatory structures can shape and influence the industrial relations trajectories. Thus, for instance, during the heyday of Fordism – when the emphasis was on the use of relatively unskilled labour – in Germany the national training system created strong institutional pressures on employers to train more workers and afford them broader skills than required by immediate economic circumstances. As a result, employers were induced to pursue commercial strategies which relied more on innovative techniques and highly skilled labour. Similarly, in Sweden a solidaristic wage determination system keeps wages higher than they would be under market conditions, thereby encouraging enterprises to obtain better performance through product diversification, the introduction of new technologies and investing in training and re-training. Cumulatively, the result of these institutional pressures has been to dilute the Fordist industrial relations trajectory in these countries. It is also possible that the institutional structures may fail to accommodate or implement properly the industrial relations trajectory, with the result that asymmetrical linkages and connections exist between the levels of production and of social organisation. For instance, during the 1920s the actual production capabilities of Fordism existed, but it failed to emerge on a wide basis because the institutional part of the industrial relations trajectory was not present. Some attribute the Depression to this disjunction. More recently, it has been argued that the reason Britain experienced slower growth than other European countries during the 1950s and 1960s was because the institutional arrangements and the underlying economic structure were not in harmony (Teague, 1990).

Thus, the implementation of industrial relations trajectories should not be interpreted as a mechanical process in which the underlying productive system determines the industrial superstructure. Industrial relations trajectories are not iron laws but guiding principles and arrangements towards which economies approximate. The influence of trajectories is probably greatest at the early stages of a new productive system and gradually decline as the system progresses through its life-cycle. Trajectories do not collapse or become obsolete simultaneously across countries or even across sectors. This is essentially because enterprises and economies react at different times and with varying speeds to the end of a productive system. Some countries may respond to the demise of a productive system, by reorganising the trajectory in order to revive flagging economic performance through intensification: hence neo-Fordism. Although such actions can bring short-term gains, they tend to be once and for all benefits, and as a result are not the basis of a sustainable long-term solution. Take, for instance, the decline of the European steel industry between 1973 and 1984. Although the actual rates of job loss varied considerably between individual countries on a yearly basis, over the entire period the scale of the rationalisation was basically similar across Europe (Wright and Menz, 1987).

The demise of the Fordist industrial relations trajectory

Considerable upheavals have occurred in European industrial relations during the past decade. From the argument developed in this chapter, these changes can be interpreted as the demise of one industrial relations trajectory followed by the emergence of another. The Fordist industrial relations trajectory, which had existed in Europe from the end of the Second World War, began to decline in the early 1970s as a result of a crisis in the underlying productive system. Both cyclical and structural factors caused this crisis. Probably the most important of the cyclical factors were the oil price shocks and the other massive increases in commodity prices. But the structural factors which arose from contradictions within the mass production system itself played the central role in the system's collapse (De Vroey, 1984).

Essentially, the demise of Fordism was the result of increasing difficulties in maintaining productivity growth via economies of scale. At the core of the Fordist system was the widespread emergence of large-scale production processes. Initially the enterprises concerned were organised on a national basis − with considerable market power. At the start this situation did not cause problems since domestic demand was sufficient to meet the output of these enterprises. But after a while the continuous large-scale investments that occurred produced massive manufacturing units which required world rather than national markets to remain competitive. This process forced large national enterprises into competitive struggles at the international level.

Of course, heightened international competition obliged large firms to control costs and increase productivity. But maintaining high annual productivity increases was becoming more difficult as enterprises started to exhaust methods of expanding production by subdividing labour within the production process. As a result, considerable pressure was put on the capital/labour compromise that had emerged, in which high wages were paid for high productivity. In fact wages levels started to outstrip productivity levels, thereby increasing costs just at a time when many enterprises wanted to reduce them to meet new competitive pressures. The outcome was a massive profit squeeze within industry during the late 1960s and early 1970s: it was not uncommon for large firms to experience substantial losses at this time (Glynn, 1989).

In an effort to raise profit levels many enterprises attempted to diversify their product ranges, but this had the effect of fragmenting world markets, particularly in consumer goods. Firms became reluctant to make long-term investments in product-specific machinery since the product market could well disappear before the machinery's costs were recovered. As a result, a major disjunction opened up between the standardised system of production and the new, fragmented consumption patterns. Thus the combination of reduced profit levels, increased international competition and fragmented consumption patterns produced a major obstacle to the Fordist mass production system, bringing to an end the sustained growth levels of the postwar period. The emergence of 'stagflation' − the simultaneous existence of high inflation and high unemployment − across Europe for the first time testified to this decline. The economic crisis triggered a wave of restructuring in European industry. Plant closures, rationalisations and massive redundancies occurred in every European country as large firms cut back in the face of stagnant world markets. From the mid-1970s until the mid-1980s, the 'shake out' approach dominated industry's response to the crisis. However, since then companies have been following new experimental industrial relations strategies in an effort to find new ways to meet more effectively the challenges of the new economic environment.

A certain economic stabilisation, albeit an unsatisfactory one with very high levels of unemployment, facilitated this type of activity. It is argued below that as a result of both the spontaneous working of markets and of these deliberate efforts on the part of industry to restore profitability through structural and organisational change, there has emerged a new flexible industrial relations trajectory, albeit in a rudimentary or partial form.

The flexible industrial relations trajectory

The aspect of the new industrial relations trajectory, most advanced and thus most transparent, is a new flexible system of production, replacing the old mass production arrangements under Fordism. Termed 'post-Fordism' or 'flexible specialisation', this new production system has begun to emerge as a result of the economic pressures which caused the decline of Fordist mass production. Three factors in particular stand out. One is the internationalisation of economic life. Economic and industrial structures have become truly international in character. Trade flows in the world economy continue to intensify as does international direct investment. Thus outward investment from the top five OECD economies has risen from an average value of $244.6 billion in the 1970s to $419.3 billion in 1988. Their inward investment has increased from $79.9 billion to $107.5 billion. In addition to international direct investment, a myriad of joint ventures, international consortia, marketing and licensing agreements have facilitated the globalisation of industry. With increased internationalisation, competition within world markets has become intense, obliging ambitious enterprises to adopt a highly flexible organisation.

The second pressure is the fragmentation and differentiation of consumption. Not only do consumers now want customised instead of homogeneous products, but the actual period for which each product is in fashion is extremely volatile. As a result, the life-cycle of some products has shortened considerably and the number of distinct products on the market at any one time has risen. Proving that product life-cycles have shortened on a systematic basis is a hazardous task, partly because it is difficult to define a new product as distinct from a refinement of an existing product and partly due to shortcomings in industrial product figures. But isolated evidence does exist in support of the shortened product life-cycle thesis. For instance, Loveman (1989) shows that the life-cycles of IBM and DEC computer products have declined substantially in the past

20 years. He also demonstrates a similar trend in the world car industry: the actual number of different products in any given car range has increased dramatically in the past 20 years or so.

To remain competitive in this new environment of increased market fragmentation and heightened international competition, enterprises have to move away from Fordist production principles. Instead they require the ability to make products in smaller batches and the capacity to move from one product niche to another with relative ease. This flexible and smaller-scale production of a variety of product types is a key aspect of the new system. The third factor, technological innovations, has created the technical possibility of such a production process. As a result a number of industrial sectors have been reorganised so that production is more adaptable. Take, for instance, changes in the car industry. Under Fordism, to survive it was essential that a car manufacturer captured a sufficient share of the market to allow for long production runs of highly standardised products. However, the large-scale diffusion of new technology within the industry has revolutionised the production and design of cars. In particular, the new technology has introduced a level of flexibility which allows for the production of many different types of car in smaller quantities of each and the continuous updating of models. These changes have encouraged European car producers to pursue commercial strategies based on a wider range of products (Altshulter *et al.*, 1984).

Under Fordism the central dynamic driving industry was the creation of economies of scale. Flexible production replaces that dynamic with a new one, economies of scope, with important implications for the organisation of enterprises. Economies of scope can often be realised in smaller units of production with smaller workforces. There is little need for the large-scale plant which dominated the Fordist era. A recent study of smaller units of employment across industrialised market economies argues that its most robust conclusion was that a sharp decentralisation of production to small units has taken place since the 1970s at the expense of larger units (Loveman and Sergenberger, 1988). Thus it seems fair to suggest that the new flexible production system is triggering a shift to smaller production units.

This shift has induced innovations in the internal labour process. In particular, the long assembly lines characteristic of the Fordist factory are giving way to sub-assembly units. The significance of this shift is that it marks the end of a division of production organised into sequential steps in which workers are allocated highly specific and specialised tasks. With sub-assembly arrangements, production tends to be organised on a parallel basis in which teams of workers are responsible for the making of functional and testable parts. A final assembly point exists to combine the different parts to create the final product. Sub-assembly units yield a number of benefits, particularly with regard to improving efficiency and quality. Normally, quality control processes are built into sub-assembly units, giving individual employees or small groups responsibility for inspecting and repairing their own work, which leads to the immediate detection of defective parts. Other innovations have been introduced to improve efficiency and cut costs. For instance, 'just-in-time' systems are now being used more widely. These keep stocks and inventories to a minimum, thereby removing the high sunk costs which were typical in this area during the Fordist era. The significance of just-in-time organisation goes beyond this, however: it reflects a productive structure where products are 'pulled' through the plant by the demand for output, rather than pushed through in response to a production objective set in relative isolation from immediate demand conditions. Thus there is a much closer integration of the productive and commercial functions of the enterprise.

These core features of a flexible production system undermine the Fordist arrangements in which jobs were organised into narrow repetitive tasks. Flexible production heightens the skill levels of manufacturing workers by requiring them to be polyvalent and have the competence to undertake a range of functions. Because of drawbacks in the statistics on occupational skill levels and the problems in monitoring how the skill base of occupations changes over time, it is difficult to be precise about the extent of a shift to skilled workers. But convincing evidence exists supporting the thesis that the demand for skilled workers has increased considerably during the past decade or so. Loveman (1989) shows that since the mid-1970s the percentage of skilled workers in manufacturing has continually increased, breaking with the trend for the rest of the century. And a recent survey of enterprise employment strategies inside the Community concluded that the vast majority of industrial firms in the North European member states are planning to increase the number of skilled workers and reduce the levels of unskilled workers even though two-thirds of those employed in industry are already engaged in skilled work. Table 5.1 outlines these future employment patterns.

Table 5.1 Future probable variation in numbers employed in industry (balances) shown in percentages

Country	Full-time employment		Part-time employment		Total employment	
	skilled	unskilled	skilled	unskilled	skilled	unskilled
B	+ 43	− 13	− 4	+ 10	+ 41	− 14
D	+ 14	− 17	+ 15	− 2	+ 15	− 16
GR	+ 20	+ 8	+ 1	+ 3	+ 11	+ 7
E	+ 28	− 14	0	− 2	+ 22	− 12
F	+ 20	− 40	+ 3	− 14	+ 20	− 37
IRL	+ 25	+ 8	− 1	0	+ 30	+ 17
I	+ 45	− 24	0	− 3	+ 44	− 23
NL	+ 53	− 7	+ 14	− 8	+ 53	− 7
P	+ 39	+ 22	+ 9	+ 5	+ 36	+ 22
UK	+ 33	− 3	+ 4	− 4	+ 26	− 4
EUR	+ 28	− 17	+ 6	− 5	+ 26	− 16

Source: Special EC labour market survey

This new work organisation based on the use of polyvalent employees is a far cry from the old Fordist system. Job demarcations are eliminated to allow workers to perform multiple tasks. Training is sharply increased and is provided on a continuing basis. As a result of these changes, a new agenda has emerged on the arrangements that should govern the relationship between workers, their jobs and their employers. For instance, there has been a proliferation of consultation arrangements, reflecting the autonomy and discretion that many skilled workers now enjoy. Considerable changes have taken place in payment systems, which have led to the growth of personal performance-related pay arrangements, specific firm bonus and incentive schemes, profit sharing and similar measures. More transparent and tightly structured career paths are being organised within firms in an effort to increase job satisfaction and retain skilled workers. All in all, individual workers are now more influential in the shaping of their firm's destiny.

These and similar developments are challenging the institutional aspects of Fordist industrial relations. For instance, the growth of enterprise-related and even individual worker-related payment systems undermines the Fordist tendency towards centralised collective bargaining which establishes a national wage norm for a specific job. And the growth of autonomous forms of work organisation is in direct opposition to the Taylorist assumptions of the need for close supervision of individual workers. Very often new forms of work organisation make this type of monitoring impractical. It follows that it is unlikely that Fordist industrial relations institutions can properly house the underlying flexible productive system. Although elements of a new institutional structure are emerging, it does not yet exist in any full sense. Flexible production has still to be embedded within strong supporting social arrangements.

Thus the current period is analogous to the inter-war years when the productive aspects of the Fordist industrial trajectory existed but the complementary institutional arrangements were missing. Systemic institutional reconstruction has to take place to maximise the economy-wide benefits of flexible production. Of course, it is possible that such a reconstruction may not occur, leading to the persistence of a deformed and incomplete type of flexibility. But from the fragmentary and piecemeal developments so far it appears plausible to suggest that, just as two options emerged from the institutional incorporation of mass production – social Fordism and market Fordism – so two alternative models are appearing for the new flexibility system, which may be termed 'competitive flexibility' and 'constructive flexibility'.

Competitive flexibility

Underlying competitive flexibility strategies is the belief that uncertainty, volatility and market fragmentation are permanent features of advanced economies and that enterprises must adapt their structures and operations to this fact. In other words, strategies in this mould are a reaction, *a competitive response,* to new economic circumstances. Since competitive flexibility initiatives do not represent a neat, distinguishable category, it is hard to give an absolutely clear-cut definition. But it appears to encompass three developments: attempts at removing or minimising the role of external non-market institutions in industrial relations; the emergence of competitive strategies which emphasise cost more than quality; and the growth of strategies aimed at reducing if not eliminating the role of trade unions in industrial relations. Probably the single most important factor here is the upsurge in human resource management. To highlight the content and dynamics of competitive flexibility these developments are examined further below.

If there is any theoretical dimension to competitive flexibility it is the notion that European economies have been suffering from 'Eurosclerosis'. From this point of view, rigid markets and sluggish adjustment processes have been the source of Europe's relatively poor economic performance. Government regulations and extensive trade union power are regarded as the two main causes of market inflexibilities and rigidity. Consequently, if economic and employment growth is to resume governments need to curtail their involvement in the labour market and limit the power of trade unions so as to give enterprises more freedom of action. This view has been highly influential in Europe throughout the 1980s and has given rise to pressures for the streamlining and relaxing of many regulations governing the labour market. Most European governments have introduced some type of change in this direction during the past decade or so. Probably the most common change has been to reduce the indexation links that existed between wage increases and inflation rates. Moreover, statutory provisions with regard to minimum wages have also been streamlined. A further area where some deregulation has occurred is in the recruitment and dismissal of workers – hiring and firing rules. The overall impact of these changes has been to weaken the institutional pressures in Western European industrial relations. From the competitive flexibility point of view, however, many countries have not gone far enough in this direction and regulations are still perceived as causing rigidities and inflexibilities (Grahl and Teague, 1989).

Another facet of competitive flexibility is the preoccupation of some enterprises with cost structures in the face of intensified international competition. In the early years of the economic crisis cost-cutting exercises were pretty crude – mass redundancies and closures. But since then more sophisticated strategies have been pursued. One approach has been to abandon some product lines and through an injection of capital in new technologies focus on being competitive in a narrower range of activities. Although an enterprise's output falls as a result of these rationalisation investments, labour costs are also reduced since less manpower is now needed. In addition, the company is now using less capital and thus able to restore profitability (Boyer,

1989). This type of strategy – the emphasis on investments to improve production processes rather than to develop new products – has been common in British manufacturing during the 1980s: although output has fallen, profits have been at record levels.

Another way of cutting costs has been to reorganise internal labour and production processes. With regard to labour, there has been a drive to obtain greater functional flexibility by removing job demarcations and rewriting job discriptions. Numerical flexibility strategies, particularly by increasing the numbers of part-time and temporary workers, have also been popular since they allow enterprises to adapt labour inputs more easily to changes in demand. In terms of the production process, subcontracting certain tasks has increasingly been seen as a further way of reducing costs without jeopardising the overall efficiency of the business. The 'flexible firm' model developed by Atkinson (1984) embodies many of these strategies. It would be misleading, however, to suggest that they are being implemented by firms in a systematic way. Probably a more accurate view would be that they are being introduced in an *ad hoc* and piecemeal manner.

A third component of competitive flexibility is the growth of human resource management strategies across industries (Storey, 1988). Definitions of human resource management vary considerably, but two factors appear to be at play: first, the thorough application of managerial principles to employee relations; and, second, the creation of structures within firms to increase individual workers' commitment to and identification with the enterprise. Previously, enterprise-level employee relations were separated from general corporate and strategic planning; now the trend is to integrate as far as possible these two functions. On occasions this integration has amounted to employee relations becoming the basis of a company's commercial strategy. As a result of this change, the popular new view is to regard labour as simply another resource which must be fully utilised in the interests of the company. The recent attempt by British Coal to introduce a six-day working week into certain pits so as to maximise capital investments is very much an initiative in this mould.

Of course no manager seriously believes that such a hard-headed and uncompromising approach could be introduced in a naked form. The possibility of generating conflict would be too great, with the effect of undermining the core objective of using labour as a resource to increase competitiveness. Consequently, a range of 'soft' policies and arrangements is seen as simultaneously necessary to counterbalance and facilitate the more hard-headed measures. Obviously, the nature and content of these soft processes vary across firms, but they tend to cover a number of key areas. In the first place, generous rates of pay, increasingly applied on an individual basis, are given to workers regarded as essential to the firm's operations.

Furthermore, consultation packages are being introduced in order to increase employee involvement in the production process. These packages are seldom, if ever, based on the traditional industrial democracy principles and arrangements that were popular in the 1960s and early 1970s. Rather, they focus on creating information flows up, down and sideways within a company through a variety of communication techniques. In many cases this means divisions have to be dismantled through harmonisation. Active consultation is promoted, but mainly with regard to matters dealing with 'real things' (i.e. how an employee thinks the production process could be improved) rather than the broad issues of enterprise strategy. Financial participation through profit-sharing schemes or whatever is a further arrangement used to encourage involvement. Another innovation is that policies governing working conditions tend to be as good if not better than those obtained by unions in national negotiations. Thus health and safety measures, equal opportunity policies, sickness benefits and so on are relatively advanced in firms using modern human resource management techniques. Employment security is sometimes guaranteed by these firms. Elaborate training systems are also developed to give workers firm-specific skills, with the effect of widening internal labour markets as against occupational labour markets. Fringe benefits are another area where fairly favourable provisions exist for employees.

Thus modern human resource management is not about 'Rambo' management techniques. Rather, it concerns establishing a delicate *quid pro quo* in which progressive workplace policies and conditions are introduced as a trade-off and as a facilitator for the unrestrained use of employees for the enterprise's commercial objectives. To some extent this new practice represents the rudiments of a new compromise. For either by default or design, this approach is threatening to replace the contractual orientations of Fordist industrial relations with a more organic, communitarian relationship beween the employee and the enterprise.

In this context the distinction developed by Tonnies between *Gesellschaft* and *Gemeinshaft* is often used – with the enterprise becoming an example of *Gemeinschaft*, that is, a group based on kinship and harmony, in the practice of recent human resource management. The building of green-field sites, moves away from collective bargaining, the reduction of hierarchies within the firm are all signs of the desire to depart from structured exchange relationships. At the same time, the development of comprehensive policies on working conditions, the devising of sophisticated internal training provisions, the offering, in some instances, of lifetime employment are all directed at developing a consensual environment within the firm so that individuals (hopefully) become strongly committed and loyal to the business. With this kind of strategy the enterprise itself becomes the central core of the industrial relations system.

Some commentators think that such decentralised enterprise-level arrangements could constitute the social foundations of the new production system. But it is doubtful whether such an arrangement based on the competitive flexibility strategies of deregulation, cost-reduction policies and the new human resource management techniques could be successful. For one thing, under the competitive flexibility model, the offer of relatively generous working conditions and policies is a heavy financial burden which sooner or later may come into conflict with the firm's cost-reducing strategies and/or impinge on the ability to compete. The recent examples of IBM having to reduce its workforce by 40,000 in spite of having a job-for-life policy is an example of how certain competitive flexibility strategies can sit uneasily together. To circumvent this problem many companies seem to have developed a trade-off through which costs are kept in check by extending soft human resource management policies to only a select group of employees. As a result, groups of insiders and outsiders are created within the companies. Accentuating this tendency are the cost-reducing strategies themselves. For a key aspect of these strategies is to separate out the key productive tasks from the non-essential and low-skill functions and make maximum savings in the latter category. In practice these strategies have contributed to the emergence of core and periphery forms of work, much discussed in the industrial relations literature.

Another problem with competitive flexibility is that while it may be successfully employed by individual enterprises, it may not have the same beneficial impact on the national economy. Take wage formation, for instance. Under competitive flexibility, wage rates are determined by individual enterprises, taking account of local circumstances. In orthodox theory this multitude of separate and unco-ordinated bargaining acts should aggregate into an efficient national wage structure since enterprises are assumed to provide wages which are in line with their productivity levels and their general competitive standing. But seldom does this occur, and economies with decentralised bargaining arrangements tend to display a number of distorted features, for example to exhibit high wage dispersion rates – one indicator of the presence of high income inequality. Furthermore, in periods of recession there is a tenuous relationship between wage and employment levels. And there is a tendency for the aggregate wage level to outstrip aggregate productivity levels, thereby fuelling inflation. This is precisely what happened in Britain during the 1980s. During earlier parts of the decade, wage rates for many groups of workers were persistently above the inflation rates even though unemployment was around the 3 million mark. More recently, wages have started to outstrip productivity levels, which may undermine competitiveness and stoke inflation. In practice, isolated enterprises may not have sufficient information to set wages in full conformity with market conditions. Thus they fall back on a 'going rate' well above that required for macroeconomic stability. Thus the evidence suggests that micro-level wage flexibility is not conducive to efficient national labour market performance.

In a similar vein, whereas an individual company or even a group of companies may benefit from cost-reducing measures, it is doubtful whether the same applies for the whole economy. If the majority of enterprises follow such strategies the competitive dynamic or norm within the economy would be centred on price. The danger of this situation is that companies become entangled in self-defeating price wars, as each strives to obtain lower production costs than the others. As a result, managers are diverted from developing new products and so on as they become exclusively concerned with making rationalisations and savings. Almost certainly, such intensified efforts to reduce costs would result in a widening of the gap beween core and periphery workers. This might be an extreme case, but it serves to highlight the point that the aggregate outcome of cost-reducing competitive strategies is to increase the polarisation tendencies in society.

Thus, if competitive flexibility becomes embedded as the institutional dimension to the new industrial relations trajectory, powerful pressures towards inequality may be unleashed. Since the aim of competitive flexibility is to streamline, if not remove, institutional social protection arrangements, then inequality would probably result. Societies move towards the two-thirds/one-third model, where the majority of the population enjoy a relatively good standard of living at the expense of a large underclass. Although life in the top two-thirds is much better than the bottom one-third, it is not without its problems. In particular, as a result of the promotion of *Gemeinschaft*, large groups of employees become tied to the same firm, with other forms of association marginalised. Their social existence is defined and shaped by the enterprise.

Constructive flexibility

Two key differences separate constructive flexibility from the competitive approach. One is that although the case for greater adaptability across the economy is accepted, constructive flexibility aims to achieve this goal in a manner that does not increase social divisions. The objective is to 'mesh' economic flexibility and adaptability with social protection. The other distinction is that constructive flexibility emphasises output-expanding activities on the part of enterprises, even though they face tough international competition and fragmented markets. Thus product innovation and product development competitive strategies are encouraged rather than the range of activities reduced. These two differences mean that through constructive flexibility initiatives a rather different model is developed for the institutional aspects of the new industrial relations trajectory.

In the first phase, rather than removing institutional influence over labour markets as is the case with competitive flexibility, institutional constraints are modified, updated and even replaced to ensure that they correspond more fully to the new flexible production arrangements. In the social welfare field this involves redrawing the boundaries of the safety net first developed under social Fordism. A range of new proposals, some more developed than others, have been put forward. Among the most topical, but at the same time not particularly advanced in terms of precise detail, is the notion of a basic income guarantee. This proposal has been made in a number of different forms, but the essence is to provide through the social security system a universal standard of income support independent of employment. The aim is to check the growth of the 'poverty trap', which it appears can all too easily get out of control under flexible production. In terms of legal provisions, the popular suggestion is for a body of employment rights, particularly for those workers that make up the new 'atypical' workforce. Protective legislation for part-time and temporary workers and statutes laying down standard maternity and paternity leave systems are probably the most often cited examples of these new employment rights.

Some institutional changes are aimed more directly at improving economic performance. Training systems stand out as the obvious example. It was suggested earlier that under flexible production the level and scope of training would have to increase since the demand is greater for workers with higher and more broadly based skills. In the competitive flexibility approach, the tendency is to internalise training or establish wider training arrangements which are employer- or market-led to cope with this problem. Advocates of more 'constructive' arrangements criticise this approach on a number of grounds. Working from the theory of public good, for example, it is argued that firms will freeride and invest less in training than their own interests demand (Streeck, 1988). Furthermore, developing more or less internal training arrangements undermines occupation-wide training standards, which limits transferability of workers from one enterprise to another since employers cannot be sure of the precise skill levels of a prospective employee. Finally, it is claimed that market-based or enterprise-level training systems will produce a 'lower skills equilibrium' because they fail to recognise that economies which produce a 'high skills' equilibrium do so as a result of a dense network of intitutions committed to that task (Soskice, 1988).

Thus, under constructive flexibility training is provided by a range of external non-market institutions which set down common and high standards so a degree of uniformity is obtained within the system. At the same time, the training provided is closely connected with the production needs of companies. The German model is consistently evoked as the archetypical 'constructive' training system. Here national arrangements bring together the government, employers and unions in a social partnership to define the training needs and undertake the lion's share of the training. The recent overhaul of the entire system so that multi-skilled and not mono-skilled apprentices are produced is an indication that the training institutions have an inbuilt sensitivity to the needs of enterprises, particularly with regard to their meeting the demand of the new technologies. Although the German system is based on national institutions, it is possible that localised institutions could perform this task with equal efficiency. Piore and Sabel (1984) describe how in the 'Third Italy' local institutions produce highly skilled labour for local companies.

Conventionally, it is argued that active labour market policies along the above lines as well as social provisions create pressures on enterprises to follow product innovation strategies since they tend to cut off the cost-reducing route. But this cannot be the full story: otherwise it would simply be a matter of putting in place 'constructive' institutional arrangements. Enterprises have a wide degree of autonomy in choosing the type of production, employment and commercial strategies they follow. Williams *et al.* (1983) describe these decisions by firms as 'enterprise calculations'.

Examples of a 'constructive' enterprise calculation would be making long-term investment decisions and increasing research and development expenditure rather than pursuing strategies aimed at securing profits in the short run. How this type of constructive enterprise calculation emerges is open to debate. Some put it down to the quality of management training. Silvestre, Maurice and Sellier (1986) in a powerful analysis, attribute it to the social and organisational networks that emerge within firms. Stable macroeconomic conditions may be important in lengthening the planning horizons of enterprises. The point we are attempting to convey is that without a 'constructive' enterprise calculation, institutional pressures of a constructive type will not be particularly effective. Conversely, if constructive policies are simultaneously pursued at these two levels, a powerful competitive dynamic is the result.

Thus a recent study suggested that 'an effective product strategy is the key to a more competitive use of microelectronics in manufacturing. Getting the right product to market must come first and to do so you need appropriately skilled and trained personnel' (Warner, 1990). This argument effectively encapsulates the relationship between institutional provisions and enterprise calculation under constructive flexibility. The skilled workforce is provided by the training system while the positive enterprise calculation ensures that the right types of strategy are being employed by the firm. As a result, developments at the two levels reinforce each other, bringing economy-wide benefits. One of the key reasons for the continuing success story of the West German or Swedish economy is precisely because such a symbiotic relationship exists between institutional arrangements and the enterprises. Thus, under constructive flexibility, developing strong linkages and connections between institutions and the market is regarded as indispensable to the smooth running of the economy. This is a far cry from the competitive flexibility approach, which sees institutions as causing rigidities and thereby undermining competitiveness.

With the exception of Britain, and possibly Switzerland, industrial relations in most European countries were organised on a corporatist basis for most of the postwar period. A huge political science literature has grown on the theory of corporatism. Here the term is simply taken to mean centralised institutions which bring together government, employers and trade unions to influence wage formation and other industrial relations decisions. Recently there is a growing tendency across Europe towards greater decentralisation in employee relations. Partly this is the result of some enterprises wanting to implement human resource management policies at the local level and to break loose of the constraints of centralised arrangements. But the pressures towards decentralisation appear to be systematic in character, being the product of the workings of the underlying productive system. For even in economies where constructive flexibility policies predominate there are strong moves towards enterprise-level employee relations. Thus even under constructive flexibility a new relationship between the central and local levels will be required so that enterprises have more scope to pursue their own independent policies.

Soskice (1988) argues the basis of a new balance could be that firms are given more or less complete freedom of action provided that central institutions retain some influence over wage formation so as to connect this process with wide economic policy objectives, and that these institutions should have the capacity to ensure that the workforce is not divided between those with permanent jobs and those without. To some extent, these conditions would constrain the type of policies that enterprises pursue. But even allowing for these constraints, in theory enterprises could introduce human resource management policies more in tune with the competitive approach and thus work against the wider objectives of constructive flexibility. However, the evidence suggests that while some overlap exists between the management of work in competitive and constructive economies, there are also important differences. The policies included in Table 5.2, originally drafted by a Swedish industrial relations organisation, are a good example of the type of enterprise employee relations pursued under constructive flexibility.

Two main differences exist between the policies presented in Table 5.2 and the policies pursued under the banner of human resource management. In the first place, they are more integrative in character since they deliberately attempt to check moves towards the emergence of core and periphery workforces in the enterprise. Furthermore, rather than shifting the enterprise to a *Gemeinschaft*-type organisation, the emphasis of these policies is to reconstruct the basis of the declining Fordist *Gesellschaft* relationship. In other words, the relationship between capital and labour is still regarded as one of exchange. Because pressures to meet the challenge of international competition and fragmented markets apply with equal force to economies adopting constructive flexibility as to those pursuing the competitive approach, the new exchange relationship has focused on ways a new compromise can be established which improves the enterprise's productivity performance. Streeck (1988) argues that these new decentralised forms of compromise represent micro-corporatism, while Windolf (1989) regards them as productivity coalitions. The nature of the compromise is that labour co-operates with capital's efforts to restore or maintain accumulation, and capital pursues accumulation strategies which increase and deepen skill-

Table 5.2 Components of enterprise employee relations under constructive flexibility

1. *Employment security*   This is a precondition for flexibility and a positive attitude to change. Greater employment security leads to a greater willingness to participate in development work.
2. *A fair share of the fruits of production*   An unfair division of the fruits of high-quality performance leads to conflict and erodes the bases for strong industrial development.
3. *Co-determination*   The absence of democracy in society's most important sector – production – means that creativity and initiative perish. Co-determination implies equality between labour and capital. It not only corresponds with demands for improved productivity – it is one of the bases for such improvements.
4. *Work organisation for co-operation*   Work must be organised in groups which foster a sense of community and self-identity. Thus, collective knowledge is enhanced and the threat of worker polarisation is avoided.
5. *Skill enhancement*   Every job – at every level in the firm – must be 'holistic', i.e. have a broad content.
6. *Education in work*   Labour markets and production change. Continuous education allows workers to maintain their value on the labour market. Education and learning must be integrated into every job.
7. *Working hours based on social demands*   As capital costs rise employees are required to work unsociable hours. New ways of manning workplaces must be found. If working hours deteriorate, individual freedom of choice must improve.
8. *Sexual equality in the workplace*   The development of technology and new demands for efficiency threaten to exacerbate sexual inequality in and beyond the workplace. Positive discrimination must be exercised in areas such as education to strengthen women's position at work.
9. *A working environment without health risks and accidents*   Enlightened employers value healthy employees. Workers should not have to face the risk of accident and illness in the workplace.

Source: Elam and Börjeson (1988)

based employment and avoid social inequalities.

Whether or not productivity coalitions become a pervasive arrangement much depends on the presence and outlook of trade unions. In countries previously dominated by corporatist structures and where there are high trade union density levels, the available evidence suggests that labour is disposed towards these coalitions, thus guaranteeing them some type of future. But it is a moot point whether they will emerge on a widespread basis in Britain. Clearly the deregulationary economic approach of the Thatcher government constitutes a major obstacle to their introduction. But even if this barrier were removed, productivity coalitions would face a further hurdle in the form of Britain's adversarial industrial relations tradition. For just as British adversarialism prevented the establishment of a sustainable and effective centralised institutional compromise under Fordism so the same forces could block such an agreement emerging at the enterprise level. Thus, with regard to Britain at any rate, constructive flexibility, or at least certain key elements of it, will not come about by simply defeating or undermining the political forces encouraging a more competitive approach. It will also require the laying of new social foundations for this arrangement.

Overall, then, constructive flexibility offers a rather different scenario for the institutional dimension of the new industrial relations trajectory than the competitive approach. Like the institutions of social Fordism, it attempts to introduce policies which will allow the underlying productive system to reach its maximum feasible potential without accentuating social divisions or creating social anomie. In many ways it constitutes the institutional basis for a modern-day European New Deal. Politically, the form of this new deal will differ from the previous compromise. In particular, because constructive flexibility involves a wider span of support structures and arrangements at various levels to regulate and hold together the underlying productive systems, the new compromise cannot be centred solely on trade unions and managements. A wider range of groups and associations must be incorporated to sustain these arrangements. Hirst (1988) and Thompson (1989) suggest that the old corporatist systems with their heavy orientation towards statism will have to give way to a more associational form of democracy. To a large extent constructive flexibility is predicated on this notion of associational democracy.

Conclusions

As pointed out earlier, neither the competitive nor constructive flexibility models have been introduced on a Europe-wide basis. West Germany and Sweden are probably the economies that approximate most closely to the constructive flexibility model, whereas Britain is the economy in which competitive flexibility is most pronounced. The majority of European countries lie somewhere between these two extremes, introducing aspects of both competitive and constructive flexibility in an *ad hoc* and hybrid manner. In most of these countries, economic policy as well as wider political thinking have been heavily influenced by the neo-liberal ideas which underpin the competitive flexibility approach, but the institutions and structures of welfare capitalism and widespread social and political opposition have limited the extent to which these ideas have been put into effect. It is possible that these tensions will remain for some time, and that most European economies will fail to move to either constructive or competitive flexibility models.

The incomplete nature of the new industrial relations trajectory throws light on the current debates around European social policy. The Social Charter can be seen as an attempt to give institutional endorsement at the Community level to the constructive flexibility approach. Most commentators have seen it otherwise: as yet another scheme by the Commission to obtain monolithic harmonisation in the labour market field. Actually, as a constructive flexibility instrument the Social Charter entails relatively little harmonisation. Just as the social Fordism model was introduced in quite different institutional contexts, so the Social Charter sets out to commit the member states to the principles and objectives of a new social compromise while allowing complete freedom to implement the various measures in line with their own national situations.

Thus the Social Charter is a diffusionist model for the European labour market.

This interpretation tends to weaken the institutional diversity thesis that no concrete basis exists for European social policy, since it sees the member states working towards common goals in the context of existing divergences. Of course this diffusionist model cannot be fully effective without full political support from the member states. When the Social Charter was discussed by the European Council in December 1989 this level of support was not forthcoming and the content of the initiative was watered down. This was not surprising, for it is unrealistic to think that the member states would have given complete endorsement to a constructive flexibility initiative at Community level when they have failed to implement such an arrangement at the national level. The fact that a modified and diluted Social Charter was adopted, however, does not mean it is insignificant. Rather, its adoption has given important additional support to the constructive flexibility model as against the competitive flexibility approach. Through incremental change Europe may yet see the widespread installation of constructive flexibility so that the new flexible productive system develops social and institutional foundations in accordance with European traditions.

References

Altshulter, A., Anderson, M., Jones, D., Ross, W. and Womack, J. (1984) *The Future of the Automobile,* Allen and Unwin, London.

Aglietta, M. (1979) *A Theory of Capitalist Regulation: The US Experience,* New Left Books, London.

Atkinson, J. (1984) *Flexibility, Uncertainty and Manpower Management,* Institute of Manpower Studies, Brighton.

Boyer, R. (1988) *In Search of Labour Market Flexibility: European Economies in Transition,* Clarendon Press, Oxford.

Boyer, R. (1989) 'Le Bout de Tunnel? Stratégies Conservatrices et Nouveau Régime d'Accumulation', mimeo, CEPREMAP, Paris.

Coriat, B. (1988) 'La Théorie du Fordism: Bilan et Perspectives', paper presented to the International Conference on Regulation Theory, Barcelona.

De Vroey, M. (1984) 'A Regulation Approach to the Contemporary Crisis', *Capital and Class,* No. 23, Summer, pp. 45–67.

Elam, M. and Börjeson, M. (1989) 'Languages of workplace reform and the socialisation of flexible production: observations on the identity of Swedish Post-Fordism'. Paper presented to the *European Association for Evolutionary Political Economy,* Keswick, UK.

Glynn, A. (1989) 'Fordism and the Productivity Slowdown', *International Review of Applied Economics,* Vol. 4, No. 2, pp. 173–91.

Grahl, J. and Teague, P. (1989) 'Labour Market Flexibility in West Germany, Britain and France', *West European Politics,* Spring, pp. 83–102.

Hirst, P. (1988) 'Associational Socialism in a Plural State', *Journal of Law and Society,* Vol. 15, No. 1, pp. 139–50.

Loveman, G. (1989) *Structural Change and the Composition of Manufacturing Employment,* mimeo, Department of Economics, MIT, Mass.

Loveman, G. and Sergenberger, W. (1988) *Small Units of Production: A Comparative Survey*, International Institute of Labour Studies, Geneva.

Piore, M. and Sabel, C. (1984) *The Second Industrial Divide*, Basic Books, New York.

Silvestre, J. J., Maurice, M. and Sellier, F. (1986) *The Social Foundations of Industrial Power*, MIT Press, Massachusetts.

Soskice, D. (1988) 'Industrial Relations and Unemployment: The Case for Flexible Corporatism', in J. A. Knegel *et al.* (Eds) *Barrier to Full Employment*, St Martin's Press, New York.

Storey, J. (1988) 'What is Human Resource Management?', Warwick Papers in Industrial Relations, University of Warwick.

Streeck, W. (1984) 'Neo Corporatist Industrial Relations and the Economic Cases in West Germany', in John. H. Goldthorpe (Ed.) *Order and Conflict in Contemporary Capitalism*, Clarendon Press, Oxford.

Streeck, W. (1988) 'Comment on Ronald Dore, "Rigidities in the Labour Market" ', *Government and Opposition*, Vol. 22, No. 4, pp. 413–24.

Teague, P. (1989) 'European Community Labour Market Harmonisation', *Journal of Public Policy*, No. 1, pp. 3–34.

Teague, P. (1990) 'The Political Economy of the French Regulation School and the Flexible Specialisation Scenario', *Journal of Economic Studies*, forthcoming.

Thompson, G. (1989) 'Flexible Specialisation, Industrial Districts, Regional Development: Strategies for Socialists', *Economy and Society*, Vol. 18, No. 3, pp. 527–45.

Warner, M. (1990) 'Flexible Production Systems', *Financial Times*, 23 January.

Williams, K., Williams, J., Haslam, C. and Cutler, T. (1983) *Why Are the British Bad at Manufacturing*, Routledge, London.

Windolf, P. (1989) 'Productivity Coalitions and the Future of Corporatism', *Industrial Relations*, No. 1, Winter, pp. 1–21.

Wright, V. and Menz, Y. (1987) *The Politics of Steel: Western Europe and the Steel Industry in the Crisis Years (1974–1984)*, W. de Gruyter, Berlin.

6

Industrialisation and strategy shifts in industrial relations

A comparative study of South Korea and Singapore

BASU SHARMA

Introduction

South Korea and Singapore are two of the four Asian newly industrialised countries (NICs). They are also called the members of the gang of four, the four little dragons, or the new Japans (Caporaso, 1981; Kraar, 1981; Veit, 1987). The average annual growth rate of gross domestic product from 1963 to 1985 in Singapore was 9.7 per cent. The corresponding rate for South Korea for the same period was 8.7 per cent. The share of manufactures in exports increased from 61 per cent in 1965 to 92 per cent in 1984 in South Korea, and from 31 per cent in 1965 to 53 per cent in 1984 in Singapore. Also, both countries have recently enjoyed a healthy trade surplus as well as a current account surplus (Koh, 1987). Real wages have continuously increased throughout the last two decades. The incomes distribution situation has tremendously improved in both countries. Measured by any traditional standards, theirs is a success story, and this success has commanded much admiration and academic analyses in recent years.

Various factors have been identified to explain the success of the NICs. Trade and structural change (Balassa, 1985; Bradford, 1987), foreign direct investment (Chia, 1985; Koo, 1985), the role of the state (Koo, 1987), weaker distributional coalitions (Chan, 1987), culture and Confucianism (Kahn, 1979; Hicks and Redding, 1983), and wage-setting processes (Fields, 1985) are some of these factors. Of these factors, policies pertaining to foreign direct investment and foreign trade have received a great deal of attention. However, analysis of industrial relations policies is lacking in the literature even though such policies might have played a crucial role in the graduation of these countries from a semi-industrialised to a newly industrialised stage.

In this chapter we analyse industrial relations strategies of the governments in South Korea and Singapore, better to understand their implications for the rapid industrialisation of these countries. First, a conceptual framework is proposed; country case studies are then presented with a view to identifying specific industrial relations strategies adopted at various points in time in these two countries. Explanations for such strategic action and strategy shifts are then offered. A summary of findings together with a discussion of their implications for further research conclude the chapter.

Conceptual framework

Industrial relations strategies comprise a set of policies and techniques used by a given player in the system to deal with the goals and objectives of the other actors (Goodman and Sandberg, 1981). The major players in any industrial relations system are workers, unions, management and the government (Dunlop, 1958). While industrial relations strategies are of central importance to workers and unions, they are only one of several functional strategies for management and government. Hence these two actors formulate and implement industrial relations strategies in association with other strategies pertaining to their overall objectives. Moreover, the government has become the dominant third industrial relations actor in most of the developing countries including the NICs. Given this role for the 'third actor' in these countries, it seems only appropriate to examine the question of strategy formulation, implementation, and industrial relations strategy shifts in NICs within the framework of state autonomy and the dominant objectives of the governing élites.

Recognising the centrality of state autonomy, Sharma (1985) has proposed a three-stage model of the evolution of industrial relations patterns in developing countries. It proposes a logic for a relationship between the requirements for capital accumulation as created by the dictates of industrialisation at various levels of structural transformation moulding the perceptions of governmental élites and the evolution of certain patterns of industrial relations. In this model the stage of industrialisation of a country is the central explanatory variable. A brief recapitulation of the central arguments of the model is in order.

At an earlier stage of economic development, workers' economic concerns do not figure as the dominant objective of the labour movement due to the lack of an antagonistic capitalistic sector and the lack of growth of national incomes. Moreover, in the case of former colonial countries, the alliance formed between the labour movement and the dominant nationalist party during the period of the independence movement remains in force for some time even after independence. Hence political considerations dominate the concerns of both the government and the trade unions as long as a country is in a least-industrialised stage.

As the preoccupation of government shifts to industrialisation, and a country graduates from the least-industrialised stage, structural conditions for both government and unions change, and thereby their objectives as well. With a degree of growing prosperity, the labour movement sees an opportunity to make its claim for higher wages and better benefits. Hence it becomes more concerned with bread-and-butter issues and begins to ask for a larger share of the prosperity brought about by industrialisation. However, savings requirements for sustaining the speed of industrialisation can be adversely affected by realising the trade unions' high wage objective. Aware of this, government tries to persuade unions to abstain from demanding higher wages. Consequently, a rift between government and unions develops. Governments often respond to this situation by introducing restrictive labour legislation so as to weaken the strength of the labour movement. However, when a country continues in its industrialisation programmes and achieves a high level of success over a period of time, it also creates favourable conditions for inflows of foreign capital. Multinational corporations eagerly embrace such growing locations, and international creditors willingly grant credits to such countries. Thus the requirement of a high level of savings for sustaining economic growth can be met partly from foreign capital resources. In addition, savings may be higher at higher income levels. As a result, government can tolerate the high wage objective of trade unions, provided it controls the labour movement. Thus there is a possibility for guided collective bargaining along a corporatist line. Since the economies of the NICs tend to be vulnerable to external shocks, the fear of systems instability is always there. Hence the government's preoccupation with an efficient management of labour relations is further intensified.

The various components of the framework and the interrelationships among and between them are depicted in Fig. 6.1. One of the desirable properties of the framework proposed here is that it also allows for reverse transformations. Nations rise and fall (Olson, 1982). A least-industrialised or a semi-industrialised country can make a structural transformation and move to a higher stage of industrialisation. On the contrary, old-industrialised or even newly industrialised countries may not be able to sustain a required level of economic growth, and be forced to join the league of lesser industrialised countries (Maddison, 1970). The latter process is called the process of reverse transformation – a phenomenon related to the deindustrialisation process of a country. Obviously, the dominant strategies of the actors in industrial relations will change in response to changes in the overall socio-economic environment. Once the dominant strategies change, the dominant patterns will also change. The arrows with broken lines in Fig. 6.1 indicate these reverse paths.

Thus the main hypothesis that follows from the stages of development approach to industrial relations is that different patterns of industrial relations emerge at different levels of industrialisation. The patterns identified are political, repressive, and co-operative. This happens because industrialising élites want to bring industrial relations into line with the global policies pursued for rapid industrialisation of their respective countries. We next test this hypothesis in the context of strategy shifts in industrial relations in Singapore and South Korea.

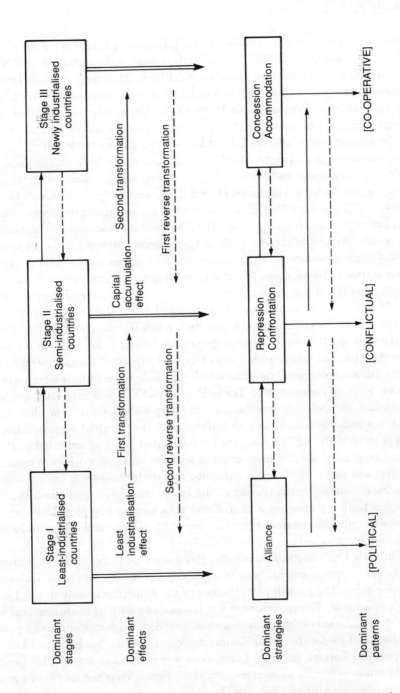

Fig. 6.1 Extent of industrialisation and patterns of industrial relations: an augmented framework

South Korea

Trade unions existed in South Korea in a very limited form during the period of Japanese rule (Shin, 1974). Immediately following the Second World War, labour unions were formed along political lines. However, the government outlawed communist-controlled unions in 1948. A non-communist federation, the Federation of Korean Trade Unions (FKTU), was formed in 1948. The co-operation of business and the government was pivotal in its formation.

The Labour Union Law, the Labour Disputes Adjustment Law and the Labour Committee Act were passed in 1953. These Laws stipulated mechanisms for collective bargaining and resolution of disputes, and emphasised tripartism. However, the leadership of the FKTU was dominated by Syngman Rhee's Liberal Party throughout the 1950s. Trade unions had no autonomy; there was actually very little free collective bargaining. The government's domination of the labour movement eventually created rank and file resentment toward the leadership as well as the government. The political alliance between labour and the Liberal Party started to break down. Workers participated in demonstrations, leading to the downfall of the Rhee government, in the hope that a new government would grant union 'autonomy' (Bognano and Kim, 1981).

The labour movement took a new turn following the coup of May 1961. There were then about 1,200 enterprise-level labour unions. General Chung Hee Park banned labour union activities, and suggested a total restructuring of the labour movement. Seventeen industry-wide trade unions were formed. A new Korean Federation of Trade Unions (KFTU) was established, which controlled the industry unions, and industry-wide unions controlled their branches and chapters. Thus a virtual monopoly to represent organised labour was granted to the KFTU. Also, the Labour Union Law was amended in 1963. This Law granted the constitutional and statutory rights of workers to organise, bargain and strike. However, it stipulated that trade unions stay out of political activities. Thus the restructuring of the labour movement embodied the first strategy shift: by creating a centralised structure and by depoliticising the movement, the government attempted to establish firm control over industrial relations matters.

The early 1960s marked the beginning of a drive for planned economic growth in Korea. Foreign capital was strategically invited to stimulate industrial development. The growth performance of the Korean economy in the 1960s was remarkable. The government was convinced that part of this success was due to the infusion of foreign capital resources. As a reinforcement to this policy, the Special Law for the Trade Union Activities and the Mediation of Labour Disputes in Foreign Invested Enterprises was enacted in 1970. This limited trade union activities in foreign-dominated firms. Thus the extent of control was further intensified (Tak, 1975).

In 1973 the Labour Union Law was again amended. It prohibited trade unions from engaging in political activities and from contributing funds to a political party or a candidate for political office. The Labour Disputes Adjustment Law was also amended, and strikes were banned. For the purpose of promoting labour–management co-operation and maintaining industrial peace, the establishment of labour–management councils within enterprises was encouraged. Thus the objective of this second strategy shift was to depoliticise trade unions and to create a strike-free environment. The overriding concern of the government has been to foster a climate conducive to a higher rate of economic growth to enable the country to make a more rapid transition from its then semi-industrialised stage to a highly industrialised one.

After the assassination of Park in November 1979, Choi Kyu-ha assumed power. However, he was also overthrown in a *coup d'état* in May 1980, and Chun Doo-hwan became President. He quickly realised the strategic role of the labour sector and introduced a series of labour laws. The Labour–Management Council Law was enacted in December 1980. It required the establishment of labour–management councils in enterprises with more than 100 employees. Such councils were to be made up of equal numbers, and they could confer on all industrial relations matters including wages (Chapon, 1984). This measure greatly weakened the effectiveness of collective bargaining. The Labour Union Act was also amended. Strikes were made legal. However, workers could strike only after taking their case to a labour tribunal for arbitration. Thus legal strikes were again effectively ruled out. In addition, the Law gave government the right to decertify a union or to remove a union leader if the union or the leadership were deemed likely to harm 'public benefits' (Launius, 1984). The objective of the legislation was to supplant or weaken trade unions. The Office of Labour Affairs was upgraded and the Ministry of Labour was established in 1981. This was done to oversee the activities of trade unions more closely. As Park (1987, p. 916) has stated, 'The main purpose of government intervention in working class organisations is to control demand articulation, even on the economic level. The popular sector is controlled most systematically by employing legal leverage.' In addition, the structure of the labour movement was once again changed from industrial unionism to a system of company unionism. All these developments mark the third strategy shift in industrial relations, the major objective of which was to fragment the labour movement so that it could no longer function as a pressure group.

The consequencies of the new strategies were quite significant. Trade union membership decreased considerably. The KFTU lost about half its 1.5 million membership. The collective bargaining institutions became ineffective because of the overuse of labour–management councils. The labour movement once more began to look for a political role as there were very few industrial relations functions left for it to perform. Eventually, workers and students began to form alliances to fight for democracy and for workers' rights. Once they heard then presidential candidate Roh Tae-woo's 29 June 1987 democratisation announcement, the suppressed anger of the workers was openly expressed. Mark Clifford (1987, p. 53) has colourfully depicted the mood of the time: 'From burly longshoremen in the port of Ulsan to teenage girls at the huge Kukje-ICC shoe factory across the city, from bus drivers in Seoul to taxi drivers in the southern city of Pohang, labour is using South Korea's summer of democracy to its advantage.' In fact, about 3,000 strikes were fought in the summer of 1987 alone.

Singapore

The Singapore Trades Union Congress (STUC) was formed in 1951. It was supported by the colonial government as a counter-measure to avoid communist-influenced unions. However, the STUC was politically orientated from the very beginning. It supported the Labour Front, which won the election in 1955. Nonetheless, the hard-won labour support appeared too difficult for the Labour Front to maintain as unions demanded higher wages and took militant action, sometimes to back up political demands. The Labour Front government soon found itself in a defensive role and tried to curb the industrial activities of militant unions. In the meantime, the struggle for political power between the Labour Front and the People's Action Party (PAP) was going on. Several unions shifted their alliance to the PAP, a consequence of which was the defeat of the Labour Front in the 1959 election.

Voluntarism dominated industrial relations in Singapore before self-government was granted in 1959. However, in 1960 the PAP government passed the Industrial Relations Ordinance to introduce a system of compulsory arbitration. The Industrial Arbitrtion Court was established under the Ordinance. The major functions of the court have been to register and certify collective agreements, to interpret disputed provisions in those agreements, and to refer disputes to referees. Once the Court takes cognizance of a dispute, strikes cannot be fought over it, and the Court's award is not subject to review or appeal.

Although the PAP thwarted the growth of economic unionism by mobilising unions for political objectives before it became the government, it found itself in difficulty in encouraging that trend after it came to power. Its major objective in passing the Industrial Relations Ordinance and establishing the Industrial Arbitration Court was to promote industrial peace. However, an intense rivalry between left-wing and government-backed moderate unions led to a very high level of industrial conflict. Associated with this rivalry was the split of the Singapore Trades Union Congress into the Singapore Association of Trade Unions (SATU) and the National Trades Union Congress (NTUC). The government cancelled registration of several leading left-wing unions affiliated to SATU in 1963, alleging they were involved in communist activities. The

NTUC, supported by the People's Action Party of Lee Kuan Yew, was then successfully able to consolidate its power base.

Even though Singapore joined Malaysia to form the Malaysian Federation in September 1963, it was expelled from the Federation in August 1965. The expulsion meant immediate hardship for Singapore. The PAP government therefore decided to embark immediately on a programme of rapid industrialisation. Part of this programme was to create a strike-free environment by curtailing the rights of trade unions. In 1966 the Trade Union Amendment Ordinance was passed. It required a two-thirds majority vote for strikes, and made registration of union officials compulsory. It also prohibited strikes in essential services. In 1967 a new Bill was passed which made sympathy strikes illegal; in 1968 the Employment Act and the Industrial Relations Amendment Act were passed. The former standardised employment conditions and imposed a ceiling on fringe benefits, while the latter removed such matters as promotion, transfer, retirement and dismissal from the scope of collective bargaining. This was one of the major strategy shifts in industrial relations.

The legislative changes of 1968 forced the union leadership to seek to justify the relevance of the labour movement to workers. To examine this issue and to chart a new direction, a historic labour modernisation seminar was held in 1969. The union leaders agreed to co-operate with the government by supporting tripartism and by becoming involved in a campaign for higher national productivity. Since then, labour unions have played an active role in setting up productivity committees and works' councils. It is also worth mentioning that the NTUC has been active in establishing transport, insurance and consumer co-operatives.

Another major strategy shift in industrial relations took place with the establishment of the National Wage Council (NWC) in 1972. The underlying logic behind its establishment was to make wage policy a part of overall industrialisation strategy. The NWC is a tripartite institution, and it has set annual wage guidelines for the economy, often linking them to productivity growth. Unions and management are expected to follow these guidelines in their wage negotiations. In most cases they have done so. Consequently, a system of guided collective bargaining has emerged in Singapore.

The comparative advantage of Singapore with respect to low-wage manufactured exports was gradually being eroded due to the new competition created by the low-wage second-tier South East Asian NICs: Thailand, Malaysia and the Philippines. The government was thus forced to restructure its industrialisation policy. It wanted to phase out labour-intensive manufacturing industries and to promote capital-intensive ones. It did so by implementing a new high wage policy through the NWC in 1979.

Despite the existence of a co-opted NTUC, the government perceived the general unions as still powerful enough to block some of its actions, and therefore decided to restructure the labour movement. The two general unions, the

Singapore Industrial Labour Organisation and the Pioneer Industries Employees Union, were divided into nine industry unions. Furthermore, the government wanted unions to be organised along company lines. As *The Economist* (1983, p. 73) reported on this development, 'Some unions were vexed about this intervention. The 3,000-strong United Workers of the Petroleum Industry voted to stop its members forming company unions. In October it recanted under pressure from the National Trade Union Congress.' The Trade Unions Act was amended in December 1982. Various other legislative amendments to existing labour legislation were proposed, with a view to providing greater flexibility to employers in labour matters. By restructuring the labour movement the government was interested in emulating the Japanese enterprise unionism model in the hope of promoting labour – management co-operation and joint consultation (Lim and Pang, 1984).

The corrective high wage policy remained in practice until 1984. However, signs of trouble in the economy were apparent by then. Indeed, in 1985 the economy had a negative growth rate for the first time in more than two decades. An economic committee was formed to look into ways to get out of trouble. The policy recommendations of the committee included a reduction in the rate of employers' contributions to the Central Provident Fund (CPF) by 15 per cent for two years, wage restraint for 1986 and 1987, changes in the wage system with use of wage levels reflecting job worth and employee productivity, and changes in the structure of collective bargaining with wage negotiations taking place annually. The first two recommendations were supposed to be short term, and the remainder the long-term measures to correct the wage system. The recommendations were subsequently implemented. The CPF contribution was first reduced to 35 per cent, 10 per cent being contributed by employers and 25 per cent by employees. In July 1987 the Minister of Labour announced a long-run CPF policy. In July 1988 the employers' contribution was increased, and the employees' contribution decreased, to 20 per cent.

Explaining the strategy shifts

The two preceding sections have examined the evolution of industrial relations systems in South Korea and Singapore to identify major strategy shifts in industrial relations in these two countries. Table 6.1 summarises these shifts.

The import-substitution-type industrialisation policy South Korea pursued during the 1950s led to a chronic balance of payments deficit. By 1961 South Korea's exports were less than a quarter of its imports. In response the Park government adopted an export-orientated industrialisation policy, emphasising the expansion of labour-intensive manufactured exports. This policy measure produced good results. As Kuznets (1985, p. 56) has noted. 'Export receipts

Table 6.1   Major industrial relations strategy shifts in Singapore and South Korea

Singapore			South Korea		
Tentative date	Strategic action/s	Objective of strategy shift	Tentative date	Strategic action/s	Objective of strategy shift
1950s	Seeking support of the STUC	To win the general election	1948	Formation of the FKTU	To form alliance between unions and political parties
1963	Banning of the left-wing unions	To depoliticise the labour movement	1963	Restructuring of the labour movement	To create a centralised structure
1966–8	Introduction of a series of restrictive laws	To curtail strike power and to limit the scope of bargaining	1973	Banning strikes and prohibiting unions from political activities	To depoliticise unions and to create a strike-free climate
1972	Establishment of the National Wage Council	To introduce a system of guided collective bargaining	1980	Introduction of labour–management councils and company unionism	To fragment the labour movement so that it cannot function as a pressure group
1985–6	Introduction of a new wage policy	To resume competitiveness of Singapore economy	1987	Lessening of government intervention	Yet to emerge at time of writing

quadrupled from 1965 to 1970, tripled from 1970 to 1973, quadrupled again from 1973 to 1978, and doubled from 1978 to 1983.'

The supply of labour was almost unlimited in South Korea in the 1960s. Export success has been attributed largely to this cheap and abundant labour. However, real wages began to increase in the late 1960s, probably indicating a beginning of the Lewis-type (Lewis, 1954) turning point. In addition, beginning in the late 1960s, countries like Malaysia, the Philippines, Thailand and Indonesia began to emerge as the second-tier NICs. This posed a serious threat to South Korea's relative wage advantage and the resulting success in export-orientated industrialisation. The government responded to these changes in a number of ways. First, the government shifted its emphasis from labour-intensive to capital-intensive manufactured exports. It then introduced a Heavy Industry and Chemicals Plan in 1973. Second, the government provided subsidies by means of rationed, low-interest loans to preferred firms in preferred sectors. Third, it introduced wage–price control by a decree issued on 3 August 1972. (The control was lifted in 1974.) Fourth, there was a shift in industrial relations strategy in the early 1970s, with strikes being banned and trade unions being prohibited from political activities. Real wages increased only moderately from 1971 to 1975.

Wages were increasing faster than productivity. The world economy was in recession and the harvest was not good. Suddenly the long-sustained political stability disappeared with the assassination of President Park in 1979. The poor harvests of 1978 and 1980 together with the political turmoil of 1979 played havoc with the economy: real GDP fell in 1980. Expectations of political freedom loomed large following the assassination of Park. However, President Chun decided to establish the legitimacy of his regime on the basis of economic performance rather than an abrupt political liberalisation. He therefore introduced a host of policies to reverse this trend. These included selectivity and restructuring of heavy industries, changes in interest rate and credit policies, and a shift in industrial relations strategy. The traditional rate of economic growth was soon restored.

In the mid-1980s the political climate began to change gradually. Opposition parties were permitted to contest elections in 1985. The 1988 Olympics, the presidential election, and a general call for restoration of democracy preoccupied the Koreans for a while. This new mood in the country led to another strategy shift in industrial relations: the lessening of government intervention. Labour has still been exploiting 'South Korea's summer of democracy'. However, its full course is not known yet.

Singapore is a city-state. Hence its economy is far more manageable than that of South Korea. Even then, the success of Singapore would not have been achieved without appropriate industrialisation policies.

Singapore started with the import-substitution type of industrialisation. This policy was based on the assumption that the Malaysian Federation would provide a larger domestic market. However, Singapore's separation from the Federation in August 1965 ran contrary to this assumption. Moreover, as Wong (1985, p. 381) has pointed out, 'achievements during 1960–65 were modest because of political uncertainty and labour unrest'. The government therefore restructured its industrialisation policy. The unemployment rate was quite high in the early 1960s. The impending withdrawal of the British military base and an annual entry of some 20,000 school-leavers into the labour market sent a warning alarm to the government. It therefore decided to move to an export-orientated industrialisation policy by encouraging foreign direct investment to produce labour-intensive manufactured goods for export. Consequently, a host of legislation and policy measures pertaining to trade, investment and industrial relations were introduced during 1966–8. These policy measures produced the desired results.

The success of a labour-intensive export-orientated industrialisation strategy made Singapore a labour-short economy by early 1970s. However, this posed a danger to the industrialisation objective as a tight labour market could lead to high wage increases and easily wipe out the advantages Singapore had in the world market. The government produced two major policies to avoid this: first, the NWC was established to allow orderly wage increases; second, immigration laws were relaxed so that firms unable to hire workers in the local labour market could bring in foreign workers.

Although wage restraint and foreign workers helped Singapore to maintain its economic performance in the short term, these measures also appeared to impede the restructuring of the economy. The reasons are obvious: imports of foreign workers would depress wage increases; this would in turn discourage employers and firms from upgrading their technology. The policy of restrained wage increases would lead to the same result as there would be no incentive for firms to abandon labour-intensive production methods and switch to capital-intensive ones. However, it was unlikely that Singapore would be able to compete with other NICs and the second-tier NICs without restructuring the economy. Hence the government proposed a wage correction policy. The NWC therefore recommended wage increases of 14–20 per cent a year for the period from 1979 to 1982.

The growth of labour costs exceeded productivity growth during 1979–85. Unit labour costs increased by 40 per cent in manufacturing compared with 11 per cent in Taiwan, 1 per cent in South Korea – and a decrease of 22 per cent in Hong Kong. The real GDP of Singapore had a negative growth rate in 1985 (for the first time in more than 20 years). Although external factors might have played some role in this, the high wage policy was assumed to have backfired and contributed greatly to this reversal. The economic committee formed in April 1985 (and mentioned in an earlier section) examined various factors that might have affected Singapore's economic growth. Wage policy was one such factor identified; consequently, a new wage policy figures prominently in the committee's report. Wage restraint for the years 1986 and 1987 and changes in the CPF contribution rates were the measures taken by the government following this report. The economy of Singapore has come back on track. This may be seen from the data contained in Table 6.2.

Park Chung-hee, Chun Doo-hwan and Lee Kuan Yew sought legitimacy of their regimes by means of a high-growth economic policy. Since there was no old agrarian upper class or *bourgeoisie,* the class structure was fluid in both countries. The emerging *petite bourgeoisie* class was quite different from an established capitalist class. In the words of Koo (1987, p. 171), 'The grip of tradition and status concerns had by and large disappeared, and society was full of small entrepreneurs who were continuously searching for new sources of incomes.' Hence resistance to new policies from this class was negligible. The labour movement has been co-opted in both countries. In addition, the government of South Korea has reminded Koreans frequently of the fear of invasion by the communist regime and the government of Singapore has reminded Singaporeans of the danger of resurgent militarism in Vietnam. Thus a supportive general public sentiment was created by invoking the so-called 'imminence of destruction' thesis (Chan, 1987). And in both countries internal insulation from domestic pressure groups would be complete once a full control

Table 6.2 Growth rates of GDP, real wages and number of industrial disputes in South Korea and Singapore, 1960–87

| | South Korea | | | Singapore | |
| | Growth of: | | Industrial | Growth of | Industrial |
Year	GDP	Real wages	disputes	GDP	disputes
1960	0.9	n.a.	256	n.a.	45
1961	6.2	1.5	122	8.5	116
1962	1.7	−1.5	n.a.	7.1	88
1963	9.1	−8.4	70	10.5	47
1964	9.9	−6.8	7	−4.3	39
1965	5.3	2.3	12	6.6	31
1966	12.1	5.8	12	10.6	14
1967	5.2	11.4	18	13.0	11
1968	10.7	12.5	16	14.3	4
1969	13.6	3.9	7	13.4	n.a.
1970	7.9	6.3	4	13.4	5
1971	8.8	2.4	10	12.5	2
1972	5.7	2.0	n.a.	13.3	10
1973	14.4	8.0	n.a.	11.3	7
1974	7.5	8.8	58	6.8	4
1975	7.8	1.4	52	4.0	7
1976	12.4	16.8	49	7.2	4
1977	10.1	21.5	58	7.8	1
1978	11.3	17.4	102	8.6	–
1979	7.1	8.4	105	9.3	–
1980	−3.0	−4.1	206	10.2	–
1981	7.1	−2.6	186	9.9	–
1982	6.0	n.a.	88	6.3	–
1983	7.5	n.a.	98	7.9	–
1984	9.7	n.a.	114	8.2	–
1985	5.1	n.a.	n.a.	−1.7	–
1986	12.5	n.a.	n.a.	1.9	–
1987	12.2	n.a.	n.a.	8.6	n.a.

Source: For GDP growth rates, United Nations (various years); for number of labour disputes, International Labour Office (various years); for real wage growth rates in South Korea, from 1961 to 1970, Ogle (1978), Table 4; from 1971 to 1981, Launius (1984), Table 3.

over labour is established. Furthermore, an export-orientated industrialisation strategy was based on keeping the wage pressure down. However, this could not be done without firm control over the labour movement. In addition, state élites wanted as long a tenure as possible and as much political independence as feasible. Any organised interest group could eventually become a threat to these objectives. Thus strategy shifts in industrial relations were motivated by these economic considerations and political interests of the state élites in both countries.

Economic nationalism has thus remained the dominant ideological force behind authoritarian government actions in both Singapore and South Korea throughout the post-independence period. Rapid industrialisation has been the goal, and export-orientation the means (Foster-Carter, 1987). The governing élites have pursued this goal even though often at variance with other social groups, including labour. Since both countries have a legacy of the Confucian tradition, this has further enhanced the political independence of state élites, which have consequently been able to bring about strategy shifts in industrial relations in response to the constraints, created internally as well as externally, on industrialisation.

To summarise, industrial relations strategies evolved largely in line with the exigencies of broader macroeconomic policies in both countries. In the 1950s there was lesser concern with investment incentives to enhance capital accumulation and to promote exports. Establishing an alliance with the labour movement for political gain was the government industrial relations strategy. As a result, the dominant pattern of industrial relations was political. However, in the 1960s and the 1970s the economies of both the countries were in the semi-industrialised stage. The governments' industrial relations strategies shifted to a more repressive cast. This resulted in a more conflictual pattern of industrial relations. In the 1980s Singapore and South Korea joined the rank of NICs. The dominant government strategies were to make some concession to trade unions and to seek ways to accommodate the interests of the unions and the employers. The Singapore government was quite successful in doing so. Hence a co-operative pattern of industrial relations has emerged there. However, the story has been quite different in the case of South Korea. With some reversal in the economic growth in the early 1980s, the trade union movement has remained still highly confrontative even though the government has shown some willingness to reduce its intervention in industrial relations. This evidence generally supports the predictions of the model presented earlier.

It is also evident from the discussion presented above that there have been some differences in the modes of strategy shifts in industrial relations between these two countries. These are the results of the variations in internal and external conditions and constraints faced by these countries. Major features of some of these variations are summarised in Table 6.3.

Table 6.3   Major differences between the two countries

	Singapore	South Korea
Major policy variable/s	Wages	Wages and credits
Target firms for policy implement- ation	Subsidiaries of multinational corporations	Domestic firms (big conglomerates)
Demand Structure	66 per cent of the total demand – external	Only 26 per cent of the total demand – external
Dominant form of foreign capital	Foreign direct investment by multinational corporations	Foreign aid and foreign debts

Foreign capital has played an important role in the industrialisation of both countries. However, Singapore has relied more heavily on foreign direct investment (FDI) by multinational corporations. The government was able to attract multinational corporations by creating a favourable investment climate through fiscal incentives, orderly wage increases, and industrial peace. Strategy shifts in industrial relations were largely instrumental in establishing such an investment climate.

FDI has played some part in the industrialisation of South Korea but to a far less extent than in Singapore. South Korea has relied more heavily on foreign borrowings. For example, the share of FDI in gross domestic capital formation has been close to 25 per cent in Singapore, whereas it has never been above 3 per cent in South Korea (Haggard and Cheng, 1987). However, South Korea is one of the major debtor nations, with foreign debt of more than US$50 billion. Debt servicing requires good export performance; and industrial order remains at the centre of good export performance. Strategy shifts were effected at various points in time to establish such an order.

These two countries also differ in terms of size, endowments, and historical legacy. Singapore is a city-state whose domestic market is quite small. On the contrary, South Korea has a fairly large domestic market. External demand accounts for about two-thirds of the total in Singapore, but for only a quarter in South Korea. Furthermore, subsidiaries of multinational corporations account for much of the exports of Singapore; in South Korea it is the domestic conglomerate firms. Since Singapore is very much dependent on FDI, the industrial relations strategies of the government are more focused toward labour cost. On the other hand, South Korea is more dependent on foreign borrowings. Export success depends partly on labour cost and partly on credit facilities to exporting firms. Hence the government strategies focus on both wage and credit policies.

Regardless of these variations, the governmental élites in both countries have set the same basic objective: to transform the economies of their respective countries. Trade, credit, investment and industrial relations policies were all designed to serve this basic objective. Most important of all, trade, credit and investment policies would not have produced the desired results in the absence of appropriate industrial relations policies. Hence industrial relations strategies played a central role in the transformation of these economies and in their emergence as the prominent Asian NICs.

Conclusions

This chapter has identified major strategy shifts in industrial relations in South Korea and Singapore in the past four decades. It has then applied the 'stages of growth' approach to industrial relations to analyse these shifts. This approach examines industrial relations in terms of macroeconomic strategies of development pursued by the governing élites, and explains strategy shifts in industrial relations principally in terms of stages of development.

The analysis presented suggests that the governments in both Singapore and South Korea first experimented with a political unionism-orientated industrial relations system, and then gradually moved toward a restrictive legislation-based system. The logic underlying such a shift was largely economic. Since the capital accumulation process required rapid industrialisation, this created a need for an industrial relations climate conducive to export-orientated economic growth, so the governments consciously made industrial relations strategies part of their macroeconomic policies. This result is consistent with the predictions of the conceptual framework presented in the second section of the chapter.

Much of the existing literature pertaining to industrial relations in NICs is guided by Dunlopian-type thinking. In this tradition, industrial relations are simply outcomes of the tripartite interactions among labour, management and government agencies. This literature often underplays the role of an effective use of human resource management in the process of industrialisation. However, as experiences of the Asian NICs show, human resource management policies can become strategic inputs to macroeconomic strategies for rapid industrialisation. It is therefore important to look at industrial relations strategies in a global perspective to appreciate fully their importance. More research is needed along this line.

References

Balassa, B. (1985) 'The Role of Foreign Trade in the Economic Development of Korea', in Walter Galenson (Ed.) *op. cit.,* pp. 141–75.

Bognano, M. F. and Sookon K. (1981) 'Collective Bargaining in Korea', *Proceedings of the 34th Annual Meeting of the Industrial Relations Research Association,* Industrial Relations Research Association, Madison, pp. 193–201.

Bradford, C. I. (1987) 'Trade and Structural Change: NICs and Next-Tier NICs as Transitional Economies', *World Development,* Vol. 15, No. 3, pp. 299–316.

Caporaso, J. A. (1981) 'Industrialization in the Periphery: The Evolving Global Division of Labour', *International Studies Quarterly,* Vol. 25, No. 3, pp. 347–84.

Chan, S. (1987) 'Growth with Equity: A Test of Olson's Theory for the Asian Pacific-Rim Countries', *Journal of Peace Research,* Vol. 24, No. 2, pp. 136–49.

Chapon, Marie-Claude (1984) 'Labour Conditions in South Korea: New Needs, New Direction', *Euro-Asia Business Review,* Vol. 3, No. 2, pp. 37–40.

Chia Siow Yue (1985) 'The Role of Foreign Trade and Investment in the Development of Singapore', in W. Galenson (Ed.) *op. cit.,* pp. 259–97.

Clifford, M. (1987) 'Price of Democracy', *Far Eastern Economic Review,* 20 August, pp. 53–5.

Dunlop, J. (1958) *Industrial Relations Systems,* Henry Hold and Co., New York.

Economist (1983) 'South-east Asian Unions: Bossed About', *The Economist,* 10 December, p. 73.

Fields, G. S. (1985) 'Industrialization and Employment in Hong Kong, Korea, Singapore, and Taiwan', in W. Galenson (Ed.) *op. cit.*, pp. 333–75.

Foster-Carter, A. (1987) 'Korea: From Dependency to Democracy?', *Capital and Class*, No. 33, Winter, pp. 7–19.

Galenson, W. (Ed.) (1985) *Foreign Trade and Investment: Economic Development in the Newly Industrializing Asian Countries*, University of Wisconsin Press, Madison.

Goodman, J. P. and Sandberg, W. R. (1981) 'A Contingency Approach to Labour Relations Strategies', *Academy of Management Review*, Vol. 6, No. 1, pp. 145–54.

Haggard, S. and Cheng, T. (1987) 'State and Foreign Capital in the East Asian NICs', in F. C. Deyo (Ed.) *The Political Economy of the New Asian Industrialism*, Cornell University Press, Ithaca, pp. 84–135.

Hicks, G. L. and Redding, S. G. (1983) 'The Story of the East Asian Miracle', *Euro-Asia Business Review*, Vol. 2, No. 4, pp. 18–22.

International Labour Office (various years) *Yearbook of Labour Statistics*, ILO, Geneva.

Kahn, H. (1979) *World Economic Development: 1979 and beyond*, Croom Helm, London.

Koh, T. (1987) 'Tigers with Different Stripes', *The Straits Times* (Singapore), 31 August, p. 20.

Koo, B. Y. (1985) 'The Role of Direct Investment in Korea's Recent Economic Growth', in W. Galenson (Ed.) *op. cit.*, pp. 176–216.

Koo, H. (1987) 'The Interplay of State, Social Class, and World System in East Asian Development: The Cases of South Korea and Taiwan', in F. C. Deyo (Ed.) *The Political Economy of the New Asian Industrialism*, Cornell University Press, Ithaca, pp. 165–81.

Kraar, L. (1981) 'Make Way for the New Japans', *Fortune*, August, pp. 76–84.

Kuznets, P. W. (1985) 'Government and Economic Strategy in Contemporary South Korea', *Pacific Affairs*, Vol. 58, No. 1, pp. 44–67.

Launius, M. A. (1984) 'The State and Industrial Labour in South Korea', *Bulletin of Concerned Asian Scholars*, Vol. 16, No. 4, pp. 2–10.

Lewis, W. A. (1954) 'Economic Development with Unlimited Supplies of Labour', *The Manchester School of Economic and Social Studies*, Vol. XXII, No. 2, pp. 139–91.

Lim, L. and Pang E. F. (1984) 'Labour Strategies and the High-Tech Challenge: The Case of Singapore', *Euro-Asia Business Review*, Vol. 3, No. 2, pp. 27–31.

Maddison, A. (1970) *Economic Progress and Policy in Developing Countries*, W. W. Norton, New York.

Ogle, G. (1978) 'Changing Character of Labour–Government–Management Relations in the Republic of Korea', in E. M. Kassalow and U. G. Damachi (Eds) *The Role of Trade Unions in Developing Societies*, International Institute for Labour Studies, Geneva, pp. 141–60.

Olson, M. (1982) *The Rise and Decline of Nations*, Yale University Press, New Haven.

Park, M. K. (1987) 'Interest Representation in South Korea: The Limits of Corporatist Control', *Asian Survey*, Vol. XXVII, No. 8, pp. 903–17.

Sharma, B. (1985) *Aspects of Industrial Relations in ASEAN*, Institute of Southeast Asian Studies, Singapore.

Shin, H. (1974) 'Industrial Relations System in Korea – What Should be Done?', *Asian Economies*, No. 8, March, pp. 5–26.

Tak, H. J. (1975) 'Foreign Investment and Industrial Relations in Korea', in *Foreign Investment and Labour in Asian Countries*, Japan Institute of Labour, Tokyo, pp. 43–52.

United Nations (various years) *Yearbook of National Accounts Statistics*, UN, New York.

Veit, L. A. (1987) 'Time of the New Asian Tigers', *Challenge*, Vol. 30, (July-August

1987), pp. 49–55.

Wong, C. M. (1985) 'Trends and Patterns of Singapore's Trade in Manufacturing', in W. Galenson (Ed.) *Foreign Trade and Investment: Economic Development in the Newly Industrializing Asian Countries* (Madison, Wisconsin: University of Wisconsin Press, 1985) pp. 379–432.

7

Changing patterns of employment for women in banks
Case studies in the UK, France and the USA

BEVERLY SPRINGER

The personnel needs of banks from the 1950s until very recently were quite simple. Banks hired a steadily increasing number of young, relatively unskilled and inexperienced persons. The job structure of banks was a steep pyramid in which the persons at the top of the pyramid usually arrived there through internal promotion. The harmony in the pyramid was maintained because most of those in its base did not seek to climb higher or even to remain in the pyramid for a full career.

Today that harmonious pyramid is disrupted by a three-pronged attack. Authorities agree that the changes in personnel needs in banks are little less than revolutionary. A volatile and competitive market is forcing banks to be more concerned about the cost and effectiveness of their workforce. New technologies are disturbing job categories inside the pyramid and bringing new training needs. The changing expectations and career patterns of women make up the third prong and provide the primary focus of this chapter. Traditionally, women provided the passive and flexible base of the pyramid; they still provide the majority of persons found at the base of the pyramid but, for a variety of reasons, their role in banks is changing.

The purpose of this chapter is to compare the employment pattern for women in three banks, each of which operates in a different country. The three countries are the UK, France and the USA. Each of these countries has a dynamic banking sector. Each also has public policies to promote the employment of women. The banking structure differs in the three countries so that the banks are not exactly comparable but each bank is considered 'typical' in its own country. In each case information will be presented concerning changing personnel needs in the bank and personnel policies the bank has regarding women. Information will also be noted regarding the competitive climate in which the bank operates and the new technologies adopted by the bank and the impact of the two on the employment of women.

A large amount of research has already been done concerning employment patterns for women in banks. For a number of years experts have been concerned to learn about the impact of technology on the employment of women. Experts have also studied banks to ascertain if women are benefiting from equal opportunity policies. The Commission of the European Community, in particular, has targeted banks for studies regarding the employment of women. The findings of these studies generally support the conclusion that jobs for women in banks are at high risk and that bank employment will decrease significantly. The experts who study equal opportunity also generally agree that banks have been more receptive to equal opportunity for women than many sectors of the economy. However, they have found little statistical evidence that women are, indeed, experiencing equal opportunity in banks. I want to ascertain the extent to which both the generalisation regarding job loss and the generalisation regarding equal opportunity are supported at the present time in the three banks to be studied. The world of banking is in rapid change. Generalisations need to be tested frequently. Also, national differences may result in significant variations despite the commonality of the changes.

The United Kingdom

British clearing banks have had to adapt to a major change in recent years. The traditional structure of finance that defined the sphere of operation of clearing banks has been replaced by a competitive environment with many new participants. The banks, in turn, have had to seek new forms of business. They have had to reorganise and modernise their operations while containing costs in order to remain competitive. The banks have met the challenge with a highly successful surge in activity and in profits. However, they cannot afford to slow their pace of change because the post-Big Bang environment in Britain and the anticipated European internal market of 1992 keep the environment highly volatile.

The personnel needs of British banks generally matched the pyramid structure previously mentioned. Each year the banks hired thousands of school leavers. A large proportion left after a few years, but a few were groomed for upward mobility. Banks were able to make necessary personnel changes in response to the challenge of recent decades with relative tranquillity. This tranquillity is quite surprising when compared to the turmoil taking place in manufacturing industries in the throes of competitive change in the same period, and can probably be accounted for by several differences from the manufacturing sector. Banks did not have to implement involuntary redundancies. Jobs in London clearing banks actually increased throughout the period. Moreover, the high rate of voluntary attrition among low-level employees decreased the pressure for the new, more highly skilled positions. Other possible reasons include the low membership rate in trade unions, internal competition among the unions that organise bank employees, and the traditional passivity of both white-collar and female employees (Morris, 1986).

During the same period that the number of bank jobs in Britain were doubling, the proportion of the jobs held by women increased steadily, reaching 57 per cent by 1982 (Povall, 1986). Banks are now one of the most important employers of women in a country which has a higher than average participation rate for women compared to other countries in the OECD. (The labour force participation rate for British women was 60.1 per cent in 1985, which is 4 per cent above the OECD average (OECD, 1987).) Most of the women who work in banks work full time. Part-time work is increasing in British banking but it is not as common in banking as it is in many other sectors. The typical female bank employee is hired at the age of 16, just after she has completed her basic education. She then works in a highly feminised workplace and is unlikely to rise more than a few steps in the job hierarchy.

Employment practices for women in banking came under scrutiny in the 1970s in Britain as they did in many countries. Britain enacted laws establishing the principles of equal pay and equal treatment at work. Banks responded by appointing equal opportunity managers and initiating policies directed to the interests of their female employees (Hackett, 1988). The major criticism of banks in regard to their employment of women was and is their failure to promote women beyond the lower levels of job categories. Banks have answered this charge by asserting that women working in banks have not sought careers as bankers and have not taken the necessary steps to prepare for promotion.

National Westminster Bank

National Westminster Bank (NatWest) is one of the major British clearing banks. The domestic banking division is divided into eight regions, 51 areas and 3,200 branches, with a total of 70,500 employees. The bank rationalised its operations in the 1970s and closed a number of branches without a decrease in personnel. In the future it plans further rationalisation which will entail the replacement of existing regional and area operations by 22 regional offices.

Since the 1970s the work in the bank has been transformed by new technology. Microprocessors, automatic teller machines, a computer-based transmission system and a clearing house automated payment system have been introduced, entailing major changes in skill requirements. The only change which led to a significant labour dispute was the introduction of the clearing house automated payment system because it resulted in redundancies. The bank has made a major financial commitment to further innovations in technology so that the personnel needs and training needs of the bank will be in a state of flux for the foreseeable future.

NatWest uses a standard job classification scheme. The three main categories are clerical grades (G1 to G4), appointed staff (A1 to A4) and management (M1 to M5). Newly hired personnel are placed in clerical grades G1 to G3 depending on their level of education and their initial evaluation. (A few university graduates start at A1.) New entrants are divided into three groups.

The smallest group is composed of persons who are regarded as having good managerial potential. They are put on a fast track for training and promotion. A second group is given an opportunity to move into the fast track after initial training, upon evidence of a potential for managerial success. The third and largest group is composed of individuals who are informed that they should expect to rise to the level of senior clerk or junior manager if they remain with the bank. This information is found in the employee handbooks.

Training is available at all levels but it varies greatly and ranges from on-the-job training to special seminars held at the bank's training centre in London and its staff college at Heythrop Park in Oxfordshire. Training is obviously extremely important for success in British banks since they have not had specific educational requirements for new employees. Individuals are expected to take the initiative to participate in training opportunities. Promising entrants at NatWest are also urged to prepare for the Associateship of the Chartered Institute of Bankers, which is a generally recognised qualification in British banking.

The three major fctors that determine a successful career at NatWest are:

(*a*) the initial assessment of the entrant, which is based on the educational level of the entrant and the assessment made by the person responsible for the hiring;

(*b*) in-service training;

(*c*) periodic assessment of the person by his or her superior.

It is obvious that a successful personnel policy depends on the ability to screen large numbers of entrants in order to find the few who are to be groomed for upward mobility. It is equally obvious that the process cannot be completely foolproof or even completely objective given the limited range of instruments available for such selections.

It is against this background that the subject of women employees at NatWest needs to be considered. The bank is widely recognised in the UK for its commitment to equal opportunity. Since the 1970s the bank has had an active programme to bring women into management and to remove vestiges of sexism from its operations. In 1980 the bank created the position of equal opportunity manager. The position appears to have more status than an affirmative action director in an American firm and to be a legitimate career step (Hackett, 1988). The bank has held seminars for personnel managers to make them aware of the commitment for equal opportunity. The firm complies with legislation for maternity leave and equal pay and it lists itself as an equal opportunity employer on all relevant materials. In addition, NatWest is famous for its 're-entry' or 'career break' scheme which entitles men or women who are considered to have senior management potential to up to five years' leave to raise their children. The bank guarantees to re-employ the person at the same grade and to retrain him or her. During the leave the person is expected to work at least two weeks a year and to attend an annual one-day seminar. This very interesting scheme is still too new to evaluate but 135 women are currently taking the leave. Many of the women who have participated in the scheme have not taken the full five years and have worked more time than the required two weeks a year.

A consideration of employment trends for full-time employees from 1977 to 1987 shows small but interesting developments in the different levels. The total number of employees in the two lowest levels (G1 and G2) remained relatively stable, indicating a counterbalancing impact from the expanding bank business and the introduction of new technology. The proportion of the staff that was female also remained steady (65 and 75 per cent). In contrast the total workforce at the G3 and G4 levels increased dramatically and women increased their participation rates as well. (Women increased from 48.4 to 67.1 per cent of the G3 staff between 1977 and 1987. They made dramatic gains at the G4 level, increasing from 16 per cent in 1977 to 41.5 per cent in 1987. These figures are based on information supplied by both NatWest and the Banking, Insurance and Finance Union. The two sets of figures are very close.) These are positive signs but they do not constitute proof that women are now on the ladder to the top. These two levels include both people who are passing through to the top and those who have reached their top career level.

The evidence found for the next level − the lowest level of the appointed grades (A1) − suggests that many of the women in G4 will rise no higher. In 1987, 3,240 women worked at the G4 level and only 747 worked at the A1 level. Since women formed 41.5 per cent of the lower level and only 21.7 per cent of the higher level, the divide between the two obviously represents an important career cut-off point. The proportion of women at the next three appointed grades declines steadily to a low of 4 per cent by A4.

A breakdown by grade was not available for women in management but the average for the four grades indicates that women have increased from about 1 per cent of bank management to about 2 per cent. This increase represents a doubling of the number of women in management since there was a large increase in personnel in this category between 1977 and 1988.

In regard to the future, the developments discussed below are anticipated.

Employment levels
Since bank business is not expected to grow as it has recently and the introduction of new technology is expected to continue, the demand for personnel at G1 and G2 levels will decline. This decline is expected to be handled without redundancies, according to people interviewed in the bank. They assume that slower hiring rates plus the usual relatively high attrition rates at these levels will solve the problem. From a personnel point of view, the developments do not represent a problem. In the past, many of the people who took these jobs were content with limited opportunities and worked only a few years.

The Banking, Insurance and Finance Union (BIFU), which represents bank employees, is less sanguine about the future. The researchers for the union note a worrying trend toward the use of part-time employees. (Britain has a much larger part-time workforce than do other European countries. While part-time work can be a benefit for working mothers, it is not advocated by unions concerned about promotion opportunities for their members.) The proportion of part-time employees in banks is lower than the national average but it has increased recently. NatWest has the smallest percentage of its workforce in part-time work of any of the major British clearing banks. Part-time employees comprised 7.3 per cent of the workforce in 1986 (BIFU figures).

Union researchers are also sceptical about the opportunities for people to be promoted out of these levels. They note that in 1984 over 1,000 employees had been in the G1 level for at least five years and all but 29 of this group were female. Moreover, they assert that training for this group is almost nonexistent (BIFU). They fear that the introduction of new technology will lead to redundancies for people in the lower grades, and plan a large campaign to alert employees to the consequences of new technology on jobs. They believe that the negative consequences will particularly affect women not only because they are a large proportion of employees at the low levels but also because women have a lower education level when they are hired than do men.

There is no consensus in Britain about how sharp will be the job loss at the bottom of the employment pyramid as a result of new technology. General literature on the subject is more complacent than is comparable literature in France. However, it is difficult to see how the changes can be implemented without redundancies. It seems that NatWest should, perhaps, be addressing the subject with more caution. It could find itself with a large pool of surplus labour that is neither promotable nor as passive as it was in the past.

Skill shortage

A skill shortage is the most obvious problem on the horizon for the bank. The bank anticipates a decline of 25 per cent in the number of school-leavers between 1981 and 1991. The total working age population is expected to decline by 0.2 per cent and participation rates are expected to decline as well (OECD, 1987). Add to this the shocking facts that 40 per cent of British school-leavers have no formal qualifications and only 14 per cent go on to universities (Economist, 1987). The current personnel policy of the bank is designed around this projected skill shortage. The bank must attract and retain employees who will absorb increasing amounts of capital in training costs at a time when the pool of talent is shrinking.

The future for female employees

What does this mean for the future of women as employees at NatWest? It would seem that female employees cannot be considered as a single group. The future will be very different for educated women who enter the bank with an awareness of career opportunities and for those who enter with minimal education and no view of the future. The latter will provide the bulk of the disposable workforce.

Educated women will benefit from the fact that the traditional pool of bank talent – young educated men – is diminishing. This is the single most important fact for their future opportunities. Neither British law nor banking personnel practices provide the grounds to anticipate a surge of women into managerial ranks at the bank. British law does not require affirmative action. Promotion practices in the bank allow for the continuation of subtle discrimination if those in authority so desire. Individuals are expected to make career decisions early and to be assertive in seeking training opportunities. Encouragement from supervisors can be crucial at this point. In the past supervisors looked to men to encourage, but now bank policy encourages them to consider women as well. However, bank policy still leaves in place two other practices that can work against women. One is the requirement that all new employees who want to be considered for management must agree that they will accept positions anywhere in the country. Another is the promotion policy of the bank for higher positions. Potential candidates are not notified when such openings exist. Women have no way of knowing if they are being considered for a position or if they have been passed over in favour of a less qualified male candidate.

It appears that women will continue to penetrate the ranks of management in the bank. They are perceived as having the human skills that modern banking requires and the ability to learn the technological skills as well. However, the absolute growth in their numbers (in contrast to the proportion) will not be large. The demand for bank management has probably peaked, so future promotions will result largely from attrition. Women managers will slowly replace the vanishing male manager. Only a change in government policy could force a more dramatic increase and that is not under consideration in present-day Britain.

France

Prior to 1982 the banking structure in France was more diversified than in the UK. Between 1967 and 1981 many new branches were opened and the country was transformed from being considered underbanked to overbanked (Leveque, 1983). Banking practices were greatly modernised in the same period. Since 1982 new laws have changed the operation of French financial services and banks have been under pressure to improve the quality of their services in order to attract and retain customers. The nationalisation and privatisation that have taken place in this decade have also affected the organisation of the banking sector so that data before 1982 is not always comparable with data after that year. Information about the French financial sector usually distinguishes among the 37 principal banks which belong to the Association of French Banks (AFB), special banks such as Crédit Agricole and 900 small financial societies.

Employment growth in French banks started to decline in 1979, recovered slightly in 1982 and 1983, and has continued its downward trend since then. Total employment was only 2.3 per cent higher in 1986 than it was in 1979 (AFB, 1986/87). Indeed, the big three deposit banks in Paris actually reduced their employees by 4.6 per cent. The French Banking Association (AFB) anticipates that current trends will continue. The Association also notes that banks are using more part-time employees. (The percentage was 7.8 in 1987 compared to about 10.3 for the major British clearing banks.)

Jobs are classified into three categories in France as they are in the UK. Between 1977 and 1987 the proportion in the top two classifications increased relative to that in the lowest category. The practice of internal promotion is not as binding in France as it is in the UK. Entry-level personnel may be hired on fixed-term contracts. More senior posts may be filled by external hiring. As a result, it will be interesting to examine how a specific bank adjusted its workforce in response to the redistribution of banking personnel into higher job classifications.

Women comprised 52 per cent of the workforce in French banks in 1987. The most unusual feature of the employment profile of women in French banks is their relatively strong participation rates in higher-level positions. Moreover, this is not a recent phenomenon: in the 1970s France was noted for the number of women it had in various management levels compared to other countries in the European Community. Table 7.1 gives the percentages of women and men working in the three categories in 1979 and 1987.

Table 7.1 Employment in French banks by category

	Women (%)		Men (%)	
	1979	1987	1979	1987
Clerical	51.4	36.2	34.0	20.0
Appointed	44.4	57.7	43.4	53.0
Management	4.2	6.1	22.6	27.0

Source: AFB (1986/87), p. 22

French law requires that women employees be treated equally with male employees as does the law in other European Community countries. However, new legislation passed in 1983 appears stronger than British legislation. It requires that employers prepare an annual report regarding their personnel policies for women. It provides clear sanctions for transgressions as well as protections for an employee making charges against an employer. It also moved in the direction of affirmative action and comparable worth at a time when these concepts were not a part of government policy in the UK and were losing favour in the USA, for example the French Law 83-635 of 13 July 1983.

French firms are required by law to spend a portion of their revenue on training. The firms may not discriminate in their selection of personnel for training. The banking industry spends 4 per cent of turnover on training (European Communities, 1985).

French social policy is very beneficial for working women. In addition to maternity leave and child allowances, public authorities also provide day-care services that range from child minders for infants to after-school programmes for older children. These services were increased in the 1970s due to public pressure. Today French working women find it much easier than either British or American working women to obtain qualified and inexpensive care for their children.

F Bank

The French bank which was studied for this research did not wish to be identified so it will be referred to as F Bank. Its structure was changed in 1982 so that only data after that date will be used and refers only to the Paris region. The bank has 110 branches and a total of 5,100 personnel. It is part of a larger financial group and is an AFB bank.

The personnel needs of the bank are in line with general trends in the banking world today. It has a surplus of clerical staff, an increasing need for appointed staff and a stable demand for management personnel. In addition, the skills of its current workforce do not match the skills required for many of the tasks necessary for modern banking. This problem is compounded by the fact that the bank has an ageing workforce. Two-thirds of the employees have been with the bank for 11 years or longer.

Recently the bank has sought to assure more flexibility in its workforce through the use of fixed-term contracts. The majority of new clerical staff are employed on these terms. In 1987 the number who left the bank due to the expiration of their contract exceeded the number hired on fixed-term contracts. The bank also obtains flexibility through the use of part-time employees (7 per cent). The bank is also much more likely than the British bank to hire new personnel with appropriate skills as the need arises rather than to re-train existing employees. The bank has the usual educational opportunities for personnel but no major programme to re-train personnel for the new positions in banking.

Women comprise 60 per cent of the total workforce, which is above the national average for bank employees (52 per cent). They comprise 74 per cent of the clerical staff, 67 per cent of the appointed staff and a surprising 30 per cent of the management. (This information is largely drawn from the 1988 report of the bank on professional equality.) An interesting feature is the fact that the largest proportion of women are in the bottom level of the appointed staff and the total of women at the appointed level is greater than at the clerical level. This is accounted for partly by the fact that the bank personnel structure no longer resembles the classical pyramid and partly by the fact that women outnumber men at this level as well as at the clerical level.

Women in the management level increased by 24 per cent in five years while the total number of men in that category decreased. Fifteen years ago the bank had no female directors of its branches; now it has 15. No special reason is given for the change except that the women had the necessary skills. The positions were not advertised and decisions were made at the discretion of the bank managers.

While the bank has no policy of affirmative action, it does have social policies that assist working mothers. It gives a monthly supplement for child care based on the number of children and a sum to help with the expenses entailed at the start of each school year depending on the number of children and their ages. The workers' council has a budget for vacations for the children as well. In addition, the bank provides for a paid maternity leave for six and a half months with a possible unpaid leave until the child is three years old. The mother is entitled to a minimum of six days' leave a year to take care of sick children. She also gets special assistance in order to participate in bank training courses.

In regard to the future, it appears that the largest problem the bank faces is what to do with the large number of employees who are aged from 30 to 45 and who are staying for longer periods in the same grade level. Longevity pushes up their pay scale, but not necessarily their value to the bank. The majority of those in this category are female. The bank has an earlier retirement age for females than males, but that still does not solve the problem. Large-scale redundancies would not be socially acceptable especially since few alternative jobs are available. No doubt members of the bank are watching with interest an ambitious re-training programme which the government is conducting with two regional banks. Employees are given some release time for the programme but they must also attend after working hours. It is a major test to determine if midlife employees can be re-trained from routine administrative jobs to the more dynamic and marketing positions which banks need today.

The United States

The banking sector in the USA is even more volatile and complicated than it is in the UK and France. This is due to the federal system which subjects banks to both national and state policies and results in deregulation policies that are moving at different rates of speed in different states. Banks that were long accustomed to operating within the stable confines of a single state find themselves in competition with large national banks that are now free to enter the state. They also find other firms encroaching on financial opportunities that were formerly reserved for banks. The competition is intense. Small banks are being absorbed by larger ones and bank failures are at a postwar high.

The USA's record in job creation is well known. The average annual rate of growth in employment between 1979 and 1985 was 1.4 per cent. The rate for the finance sector was 4.4 per cent – which was higher than any other sector except business services and real estate (OECD, 1987). Projections for the future of employment in banking are more difficult to make in the USA than in France and the UK due to the important restructuring that is taking place since the legalisation of inter-state banking, in addition to the impact of new technology and increased competition. However, the US Department of Labor forecasts that employment in finance will continue to grow but that growth for bank teller jobs will be slower than the average for all jobs (US Department of Labor, 1988).

American women are more likely to participate in the workforce than are either British or French women. In 1980, 60 per cent of women between the ages of 16 and 64 were in paid employment. The majority of American mothers work. In the 1970s three out of every five persons entering the workforce were female. Moreover, these women remained in the workforce – unlike women in the previous decade, who left during their child-bearing years (US Congress, 1982). A recent study concluded that most American women now in the labour market are full time and career-orientated. This generalisation applies regardless of age, race and marital status. The study also discerned convergence in male and female labour force patterns over the life-cycle and predicted that the convergence would continue (Shank, 1988).

The finance sector is the single largest provider of jobs for women. Women comprise an amazing 70 per cent of bank employees (Miller, 1985). Opportunities for women in banking expanded rapidly in the 1950s and 1960s when banks responded to the needs of a newly affluent public. The demand for bank tellers, in particular, escalated and the occupation changed from a male to a female one. Before the Second World War, a female teller was a rarity. By 1980, 91 per cent of tellers were female (Strober and Arnold, 1987).

The laws that apply to women in the workforce are an important variable that must be considered in any comparison of employment of women in the USA with the employment of women in Europe. American law does not provide the social protections of maternity leave and public day-care centres that French law does. However, American law does require employers to be very conscious about the ways that they utilise their female employees and does provide for legal redress when employers do discriminate. The three most important laws are the Equal Pay Act of 1963, Title VII of the Civil Rights Act of 1964 and the Equal Employment Opportunity Act of 1972. The Equal Opportunity Commission exists to oversee compliance.

Another important variable that has distinguished employment practices in the USA from those in Europe concerns redundancies. The employment at will doctrine is quite deeply embedded in the USA. Employers are deemed to have quite broad powers to hire and fire employees. The social and legal concerns that constrain NatWest and F Bank play a much smaller role for an American bank.

US Bank

The American bank studied in this chapter also did not want to be identified. It is located in the state of Arizona, where the banking laws were changed in 1987 to permit banks from other states to enter. The bank, which will be referred to as US Bank, is the last major Arizona bank to maintain its independence. Other large banks in the state have been taken over by the big national banks such as Citibank. US Bank was the largest bank in the state and was proud of its pioneer roots. Now, however, it has lost market share to its new competitors and is struggling to adapt to the new competitive environment.

The bank continued to grow until 1987, adding personnel, opening new branches and undertaking new activities. Now the bank is trying to streamline its operation and cut costs. It plans to close branches that are not profitable and has already made staff cuts. The bank is utilising new technologies to expand its activities while at the same time operating with a smaller staff. The crucial variable will be the quality and training of the remaining staff.

Each year the bank makes a report on its personnel that conforms to national guidelines set by the Equal Opportunity Commission. The report utilises nine categories for different types of jobs. (These categories are not easily matched with the categories noted in Europe.) The three largest are (1) office and clerical, (2) professional and (3) officials and managers. The first is composed mainly of tellers. In 1987 women comprised 86.4 per cent of this group. The professional group has a large proportion of college graduates who are specialists such as accountants. Women make up 48.3 per cent of the category. Women comprise 50.1 per cent of the third category compared to 24 per cent ten years ago. (In 1984 women made up 42 per cent of officials and managers in the entire country (Quinn, 1987).)

Care should be taken not to misinterpret the strong showing that women have in the officials and management category. It is a broad category which is about one-third the size of the office and clerical category. It lists positions that would be included in the appointed ranks in the French system. The bank subdivides the category into three levels: line manager, middle managers and executives. Women comprise 60, 38 and 12 per cent respectively of the three levels.

A distinctive feature of the personnel department in the US Bank is the sophisticated analysis which is made of the bank employees in relation to the population at large. This practice was developed in response to national policies against racial and sex discrimination. The bank uses an eight-factor availability analysis to measure its utilisation of females and minorities. For example, the bank compares the percentage of women it has at a particular job level against percentages of women in the labour force, of women among employees qualified for the position, etc. Each of the eight factors is weighted according to its importance. The bank can then determine whether it is utilising its female employees in a non-discriminatory manner. The bank has used this form of analysis for more than a decade.

The personnel director of the bank believes that women will continue to move into the ranks of top management. He believes that education and skills are the crucial attributes today, not sex. However, women are not yet in positions of real power in the bank. Also, they are in the positions most at risk in the competitive labour market in Arizona banking – tellers and middle level managers. The personnel director stated that the bank could not afford to wait for attrition or education to adapt its existing personnel to the needs of tomorrow's banking. Staff will be cut. People who have worked their way up the ladder but who do not have the requisite skills will be given severance pay and assistance in finding other jobs. It is fair to assume that a significant proportion of the people selected will be women. However, the bank will be careful to ensure that it does not leave itself vulnerable to a lawsuit by selecting the persons to be made redundant in a discriminatory manner. These policies go beyond the requirements of US law and are enlightened by US standards.

Conclusions

Generalisations regarding the findings for the three banks should be regarded with caution due to the fact that they are not the 'matched pair' foreseen in the research design. However, the historical differences that distinguished banks in the three countries have diminished. A recent comparative study of bank policy and structure concluded that there is 'an increasing degree of similarity in commercial-banking operations' (Wilson, 1986, p. 424). The interrelated factors of competition, technology and deregulation are forcing the pace of change and placing heavy demands on the personnel function.

The findings support the conclusion that banks will no longer be 'the leading job creator' in the service sector (Pastre, 1985). Banks will also no longer be the provider of jobs for vast numbers of young, unskilled women who want to spend a few years in the workforce. On the other hand, the banks have not yet given evidence to support the more pessimistic predictions concerning job losses (Cheve, 1986). The trend seems to be toward a slow contraction at the base, with the result that the traditional pyramid is gradually becoming a diamond. The crucial problem today is not yet redundancies but re-training in regard to the two European banks. On the other hand, the US Bank, which faces similar personnel needs, accepts the need for redundancies in a very matter-of-fact manner.

The personnel directors of all three banks are struggling with similar problems. However, they are operating within different parameters. The British bank follows the British tradition of hiring young and grooming the best for the top. Those not destined for the top are still urged to anticipate a lifetime of work in the bank with modest promotion possibilities. The French bank, in contrast, appears to be freer to renew its workforce through the use of fixed-term contracts and external hiring. However, the French personnel director also accepts the cost of an ageing workforce and the need to consider how employees selected in a different era can be moulded for the new banking culture. These concerns are quite foreign to the American personnel director, who did not believe that such a transformation is possible.

In regard to women, all the banks employ more women than men and are constrained by laws that prohibit discrimination. The banks have taken steps to eliminate vestiges of discrimination. However, important and surprising differences do exist in regard to policies and the distribution of women in the workforce. The British bank's primary policy for women is directed toward women who are targeted for top positions and is designed to retain them in the workforce during their child-bearing years. It is a policy that clearly responds to British conditions (internal promotion, anticipated skill shortages, the feminisation of the job pool and lowered participation rates for women aged 25 to 35). The French bank has no special policies for a select group of women. Rather, its policies supplement state social policies which reflect traditional French concern with the family.

Women form a larger percentage of the workforce in each of the three categories in the French bank than in the British, as Table 7.2 shows.

Table 7.2 Women as percentage of the workforce in British and French banks

	French bank	British bank
Clerical	74%	64%
Appointed	67%	12%
Management	30%	2%

The differences are significant and cannot be fully explained by differences in the two banks. The percentages accord with national averages except that the percentage of women in management in the French bank is higher than the national average, which is 16 per cent. A large part of the explanation has to be general differences in Britain and France, since the banks are not atypical for their countries. One possible explanation may be the differences in participation rates, which have been apparent since about 1973. Figure 7.1 shows the lifetime work participation rate for British women forms an 'M' with peak participation rates at about the ages of 21 and 45 and a sharp drop in between. In contrast, the curve for France resembles an inverted 'U'. French women stay in the workforce during those critical years when careers develop. Evidence indicates that French social policy is a major factor in explaining the difference. The pattern for French women changed in the early 1970s and coincided with the period of expansion of programmes for children (OECD, 1985).

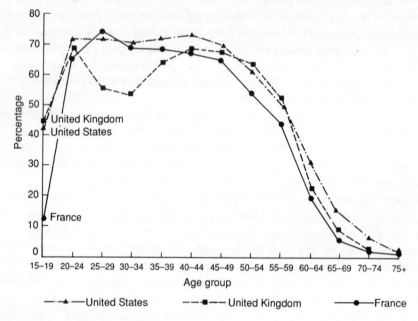

Fig. 7.1 Labour force – women by age group
Source: Based on figures in the Yearbook of Labor Statistics (International Labour Organization, 1987) pp. 27, 40, 44

A possible explanation for the fact that French women have had a relatively high participation rate in the management of banks since the early 1970s may be simply that French banks had a less plentiful supply of qualified men. During the period of the French economic miracle, banks had to compete with industry for a smaller supply of educated young men. Britain did not experience comparable growth rates, and banks were a more attractive option than industry. Such an explanation is difficult to prove but it is supported by the fact that in 1973 Britain had over twice as many unemployed men as France had (OECD, 1987).

The rapid increase in female managers noted in F Bank since 1982 has at least two possible explanations. The increase coincides with a period when the government had special concern for the conditions for women and came close to an affirmative action policy. Only one person interviewed on the topic was willing to state categorically that government policy explains the increase. Others were more cautious. The other possible explanation is that qualified women were already in the job stream and so the increase is normal when sex discrimination no longer takes place.

The impact of technology has changed the content and demand for work in both banks. The impact on the number of jobs has been limited by increased banking activities but both banks anticipate that they are reaching a plateau in growth and forecast a slow-down in employment. Neither bank will hold an open door for young, unskilled persons nor will it be as easy for the newly hired to climb up the promotion ladder. The two-tier employment situation that has always been implicit in banking (but was not noticed since the bottom tier had a 'natural' rotation) is now more noticeable and troublesome. There is an ageing of the workforce in the bottom tier with a resulting increase in costs. Both banks have cut recruitment, increased part-time work and, at least in the French case, resorted to fixed-term contracts. That is the bad news for women. The good news is that educated women have better prospects in the higher tier since both banks – for different reasons – will be likely to continue to increase the proportion of their managers who are female.

In conclusion, the findings show that both banks are reacting to new developments with cautious and moderate policies. Both deny that major redundancies are planned. Neither has a comprehensive policy to transform its existing workforce into the bankers of tomorrow. Both state that qualified women will have a good future with them. Neither has much to say about the future of unqualified women. In both cases it seems that the changes experienced by women in the banks as well as the differences noted between the two banks are more a result of broader national trends than they are of initiatives taken by the banks.

When the US Bank is brought into the comparison, the topic becomes more complicated. In many respects, the comparison is closer between the US Bank and F Bank. Both have a relatively large proportion of women in management. Both have been subject to more active government policy regarding the employment of women. Moreover, the labour force participation rate for American women is closer to the French than to the British so that neither bank appears greatly concerned over the loss of their female employees during their child-bearing years. However, explanations concerning why the two banks have more women in management and why women in the two countries remain in the workforce are more elusive. The possibility was raised above that French women remain in the workforce because they have public day-care centres. This is not the case in the USA. Indeed, a recent book on women states 'the United States does less than any other advanced country to make like easier for working mothers' (Hewlett, 1986, p. 174). However, a study comparing British and American women (Dex and Shaw, 1986) argues that the reason that American women are more likely to remain at work than British women is due to favourable tax provisions for child-care. (The study also speculates that the need for health insurance, which is available only with a full-time job, may account for the fact that American women are less likely than British women to work part time.) Obviously, the topic of national participation rates requires more study than it has had in the past.

It does appear clear from the research in this chapter that legislation is an important factor in moving women into the ranks of management. Legislation against sex discrimination is necessary as a starting point but the more vigorous French and American affirmative action policies appear to be one of the reasons that women in those two countries are in a stronger position in banks than are women in Britain. A study on employment protection in the USA asserts, 'over a 20 year period, federal equal employment legislation has slowly but significantly altered the personnel policies of employers' (Levitan, Carlson and Shapiro, 1986, p. 76). The detailed reports which the personnel director of US Bank regularly compiles keep him constantly aware of the need to be able to justify his personnel decisions in terms of sexual equality.

The final point to be made concerns the impact of competition and technology on the employment of women in US Bank in comparison to the British and French banks. Forces of competition appear to be much greater on US Bank and the labour force is already being reduced. The changes will be quicker and deeper than in Europe. However, the resulting workforce is not likely to have a significantly different gender composition than it has had in the past. Women who do not have the necessary skills will lose their jobs, but women who have the skills will be hired to replace them. The task of the American personnel director is easier than that of the French or the British in adapting to the new competitive environment as long as he does not overtly make personnel changes in ways that are discriminatory.

References

AFB (1986/87) *Rapport sur l'Evolution de l'Emploi dans les Banques AFB*, AFB, Paris.
BIFU (undated) *Jobs for the Girls*, monograph, BIFU, London.
Cheve, H. (1986) 'Menaces sur l'Emploi dans les Banques', *Économie et Politique*, February, pp. 40–1.
Dex, S. and Shaw, L. (1986) *British and American Women at Work*, St Martin's Press, New York.
Economist (1987) 'Britain: Survey', *Economist*, 21 February, p. 10.
European Communities (1985) *The Social Implications of Introducing New Technology in the Banking Sector* (V/641/85-EN), EC, Brussels.
Hackett, G. (1988) 'Who'd Be an Equal Opportunity Manager?', *Personnel Management*, April, pp. 48–55.
Hewlett, S. (1986) *A Lesser Life*, William Morrow, New York.
Leveque, J. M. (1983) 'European Comparisons', in *The Banks and Personal Customers*, Institute of Bankers, London, pp. 39–43.

Levitan, S., Carlson, P. and Shapiro, I. (1986) *Protecting American Workers,* Bureau of National Affairs Inc, Washington DC.

Miller, R. (1985) 'New Directions for the NABW', *Bankers Monthly,* September, p. 24.

Morris, T. (1986) *Innovation in Banking,* Croom Helm, London.

OECD (1985) *The Integration of Women into the Economy,* OECD, Paris.

OECD (1987) *Employment Outlook,* September.

Pastre, O. (1985) 'Employment', in *The Social Implication of Introducing New Technologies in the Banking Sector* (European Communities, V/641/85-EN), p. 39.

Povall, M. (1986) 'Equal Opportunities for Women in British Banking', *Equal Opportunities International,* p. 27.

Quinn, L. (1987) 'Bank Women on the Fast Track', *Bankers Monthly,* September, pp. 41–4.

Shank, S. (1988) 'Women and the Labor Market: the Link Grows Stronger', *Monthly Labor Review* (Bureau of Labor Statistics), March, pp. 5 and 8.

Strober, M. and Arnold, C. (1987) 'The Dynamics of Occupational Segregation among Bank Tellers', in C. Brown and J. Pechman (Eds) *Gender in the Workplace,* Brookings Institution, Washington DC, p. 121.

US Congress (1982) *Economic Status of Women,* Hearing before the Joint Economic Committee Congress of the United States, Ninety-Seventh Congress, 3 February.

US Department of Labor (1988) *Occupational Outlook Handbook,* 1988–9 edition, pp. 9 and 229, Washington DC.

Wilson, J. S. G. (1986) *Banking Policy and Structure,* New York University Press.

Part three

Comparisons of human resource roles and structures

The three chapters following focus on the specialist personnel or human resources (HR) department as their subject. This is the specialist function of management which is at the nexus of competing values, and frequently takes the cultural strain when new industrial relations trajectories and strategies are brought into being.

Peter Lawrence compares the personnel specialist role between Germany and the UK. His description bears out the popular impression that German management is required to be more formal and legalistic than its British counterpart. He shows how the laws and institutions in Germany produce formal processes of consultation, rule observance, and an emphasis on training and technical competence. This contrasts with the British 'ad hocracy' and informality. However, the British HR specialist's involvement with industrial relations negotiations, with the management of change and with planning and management development can bring him or her more into the arena of top management decision-making than is typical in Germany.

As Lawrence points out, his findings are based on certain assumptions about British HR specialists – about whom it is difficult to generalise because in the UK there is no formal legal structure governing the detail of employee relations, and there is great variability between organisations.

The chapter by Nancy Papalexandris shows that while organisations may exist in the same geographical areas, their ownership, management philosophy and techniques can vary greatly. Her chapter demonstrates both the distinctions between the formal, systematic policies of the multinational corporations (MNCs) and the informal relationship-based policies of local and often family-owned firms in Greece.

This chapter brings out two important points. First, that there are legitimate differences in the way HRM is performed in organisations – there is no one correct way – and, second, that the application of advanced systems and procedures by MNCs, while seen as developmental for locals working in their HR departments, also serves to spread common approaches and techniques in solving HR problems around the world.

The struggle for a version of professionalism in personnel management, which is compatible with the social and economic needs of three nations in Africa, is the subject of D. M. Akinnusi's chapter. He examines the personnel function within the context of renewed economic, social and political development in Ghana, Kenya and Nigeria. By tracing the growth and development of the personnel function in both private and public sectors he identifies many of the cultural and social influences which create the agenda for African personnel managers today.

The meaning of professionalism in HR management is explored in these chapters, therefore. They set out the related dilemmas of formal versus informal policies, the issue of the appropriateness of the model of HR management to business and social needs, and they raise the question whether there is now forming a universally relevant body of knowledge on which an international claim to professional status can be made.

8

The personnel function

An Anglo–German comparison

PETER LAWRENCE

Introduction

The traditional view has been that management and for that matter industrial organisation are much the same around the world, or at least among the conspectus of advanced industrial countries. On the one hand, management is constrained by its social environment and the available production technology; on the other, drives for efficiency and profitability are forces leading to a presumptive homogeneity.

This traditional view has been dismantled only relatively recently. In Britain in particular the idea that there might indeed be patterned and interacting differences from country to country emerged in the course of the 1970s debate over Britain's relative economic underperformance. If many other industrial countries were measurably wealthier than Britain, it appeared desirable to probe for internal features which might help to explain overall differences in national wealth. This is the period that gave us comparative surveys of the qualifications of managers (Glover, 1978), of wage differentials (Sylvestre, 1974), of company structures (Brossard and Maurice, 1974), of the growth of the divisionalised company (Dyas and Thanheiser, 1976), of productivity (Panic, 1976), of the effectiveness of first-line supervisors (Fores, Lawrence and Sorge, 1978), of engineering education systems (Chisholm, 1975), as well as occasional monographs seeking to characterise management in another country (Lawrence, 1980). Significantly, all these comparative studies involve West Germany, usually in comparison with Britain, France, or both.

The study of comparative management has received a further thrust in the 1980s due to the universal interest in Japan, a desire to know how the Japanese do it, and whether constructive emulation is possible. The discipline is now proceeding at two levels, the broad characterisation of management in more distant (or inscrutable) countries, side by side with more particularistic comparisons: this chapter belongs to the second strand of the subject's development.

It is a relevant consideration in comparative management to know, in the American phrase, where the researcher is coming from. In this instance the author is British, with research and other experience in West Germany. The tendency is to look at Germany, or elsewhere, as an outsider, and to ask what is different and interesting about the subject under examination from a British point of view. In this chapter we will tend to assume an approximate familiarity with Britain, but provide a more detailed account of the German side of the equation. Furthermore, it maybe helpful at this point to offer some basic, background information on German trade unions, and the nature of wage negotiations in West Germany and on the co-determination system.

Trade unions and pay bargaining

The German equivalent of the TUC is the *Deutscher Gewerkschaftsbund* (DGB), with its headquarters in Düsseldorf. There are 17 unions affiliated to it, and these are industrial unions. That is to say, membership of any given industrial union is open to *all* employees in that industry, whatever their rank, skill level or particular trade. This system of industrial unions keeps the number of unions very low by British standards; it is also generally held to eliminate the possibility of demarcation disputes. Employers are similarly organised in *Arbeitgeberverbände* (employers' associations), by industry and region, and there is an umbrella organisation, the *Bundesvereinigung deutscher Arbeitgeberverbände* (BDA), with its headquarters in Cologne. It is located next door to, and works closely with, the *Bundersverband der deutschen Industrie* (BDI), an organisation roughly comparable with the CBI in Britain.

The structure of wage negotiations in West Germany is rather simple. They are typically bipartite, where one union negotiates with one employer federation on a *Land* basis. The differences between the *Länder* have some importance in this matter. The richest *Land* is Baden-Württemberg in the south, and it also has the lowest unemployment rate. When negotiated wage rates are compared nationally Baden-Württemberg will tend to come out best; the poorer states are Saarland, Rheinland-Pfalz, Niedersachsen, and Schleswig-Holstein. Not all companies are members of the relevant employers' federation (the expression is being *'verbandspflichtig'*) but most are. The result is that the typical company is not directly involved in wage negotiations, and neither is the typical personnel manager, no matter how senior.

German trade unions are wealthy and well staffed by British standards. In the works they are represented by *Vertrauensleute,* union members who seek to propagate the name of the union and recruit new members. Thus they might be said to have the same formal *raison d'être* as shop stewards in Britain, but their role in practice is much more limited, and they do not have the power and importance which shop stewards in Britain usually have. The shopfloor representative in a German factory is in fact the works' council member, which brings us to the co-determination system.

Industrial democracy in West Germany

The co-determination system is rather complicated, and only an outline account is offered here. It is probably easiest to start at the top. The German public company, the type with AG after its name, is a two-tier board system. At the top, there is the *Aufsichtsrat*, a supervisory board of non-executive directors having the power of veto. Traditionally the *Aufsichtsrat* is composed of shareholders' representatives, but the various co-determination laws from 1951 to 1976 provided for employee representatives on the *Aufsichtsrat* too. Depending on the type and size of firm, the employee representatives will make up a third or half of the membership. The *Aufsichtsrat* in turn has the power to appoint the *Vorstand,* or executive committee, comprising full-time senior managers of the firm.

It is the *Vorstand* which initiates policy and actually runs a public company. Since 1950 the *Vorstand* of companies in what Germans call the *Montanindustrie* (iron, steel, and coal) has included an *Arbeitsdirektor* (labour director). The *Vorstand* members are elected by the *Aufsichtsrat* anyway (as mentioned above) but in addition the *Arbeitsdirektor* has to be chosen by the majority of the *employee* representatives on the *Aufsichtsrat*. That is to say, the *Arbeitsdirektor* is a genuine representative of worker interests, in terms of the mechanism of his election.

The last co-determination law, that dating from 1976, extended the institution of the *Arbeitsdirektor,* though in a modified form. It requires the appointment of an *Arbeitsdirektor* in all large public (AG-type) companies, though in these cases the *Arbeitsdirektor* does not have to be elected by the employee representatives on the *Aufsichtsrat*. In other words, the new-style *Arbeitsdirektor,* outside the *Montanindustrie* is not (usually) a workers' representative, but a career manager with special responsibility for industrial relations and personnel questions. So the 1976 law represents a gain for the co-determination protagoniest in the sense of official recognition of the importance of industrial relations, and a (potential) strengthening of the personnel function. At the same time it can hardly be represented as a radical gain.

The works council

Then at a more humble level, that of the works, there is the *Betriebsrat* or works council. These exist in all places of employment, not just manufacturing industry, and date from 1950; that is to say, they are very well established and German managers can hardly imagine any more the world without the elected works council.

The law setting up the works councils dates from 1950, but subsequent legislation has strengthened these councils and added to their powers. These may be divided under three headings:

(*a*) *Mitbestimmungsrecht* (co-determination right) or the right to give its consent to certain things: appointment of workers to new positions, internal transfers, transfers between wage groups, dismissals, setting the start and end of the working day, introducing shift-working or overtime, and canteen prices.

(*b*) *Mitwirkungsrecht* (right to be consulted): this refers particularly to planning questions, such as decisions to close plants, open new plants, investment decisions and business policy issues.

(*c*) *Informationsrecht* (or the right to be given information): in practice information about the firm's economic performance and prospects.

This in brief is the co-determination system. The works councils are an important reference point for the German personnel manager and much of his time is spent in negotiation or discussion with the council.

The German personnel function compared

A broad and pervasive difference between personnel management in Great Britain and West Germany is that in the latter it is marked by a higher degree of both legalism and formalism, with laws, documents and written agreements being more salient.

Legalism

The German system is legalistic, first, in the literal sense that much that exists and occurs does so because laws have been passed. As was made clear in a previous section, the entire co-determination system is based on federal legislation, as was the establishment of the works councils, and so is their complex of rights and duties. Similarly, there is a system of labour courts to which employees may resort, and while involvement in such courts is hardly a daily event for German personnel officers, the existence of the courts is always a significant consideration. In doing their job (applying the law!) German personnel managers will implicitly ask themselves how their actions would look if they ever came to be reviewed in a labour court. The instance which most often figures in accounts given by personnel managers concerns the implications of instant dismissal, where an employee would be caught out in some grave offence and the enraged superior would demand instant dismissal and the offender's immediate removal from the plant. On such occasions the personnel manager would temporise, calm down indignant superiors, and above all lay the case before the works council. If a dismissed employee appealed to the labour court, and it emerged that 'the works council had not been heard', the company would be in a very vulnerable position.

Formalism

This leads to the next consideration: the German system might be described as formalistic, or legalistic in a metaphorical sense, in that forms, procedures and rules are important, and are treated as though they are laws, whether or not they are in the strict sense. This applies at the top, and at the bottom; to big things and small things. An example at the top of the scale which has already been outlined is wage bargaining. This does not 'just happen' because employees suddenly feel like a rise. It occurs in a formal, procedural, and scheduled way between recognised bargaining partners. To take a smaller example, a firm with a rush of orders to be completed does not just offer or institute overtime working in the way that an English company often does. It must approach the works council with a request to institute overtime, and secure the council's agreement. Incidentally, while in Britain overtime is generally welcomed as an addition to the employee's income, and such a state of affairs is by no means unknown in Germany, we have actually seen several instances in German companies where overtime was resisted by workers, and management had to fight hard to get them to do it. Furthermore, a company in Germany cannot institute unlimited overtime working, even with the consent of the works council; above a certain amount the company is legally obliged to inform and obtain the consent of the federal labour office (though violations of this requirement are not unknown). Right at the bottom of the scale quite small issues between management and workforce can be said to be 'settled' only when they have been formally agreed with the works council and the decision written down in a formal way.

This leads to a third general consideration: the German *modus operandi* might be said to be legalistic in the sense that it is embedded in a written culture. Things do not get done by nods and winks, hints or nudges, by diplomatic fudging or impression management; issues are resolved by formal processes whose outcomes are recorded in writing.

There is a fourth general consideration. Quite simply, it is that there seems to be much less of an informal system in German companies than in British. 'Informal system' is the term used by sociologists to refer to the totality of actual practices – authority relations, communication channels, job standards and working methods, employee performance and behaviour, and so on – in so far as these depart from what is formally prescribed by the company, contained in its rules or job specifications, its agreements and codes, its handbook and organisation chart. These departures appear to us to be less common and less important in German companies.

A cautionary word should be added to the effect that it is obviously difficult for a foreign researcher to identify or uncover such informal practices, much more difficult than it is to collect information of a more formal type. Even with this proviso there are two considerations which tend to support our contention that the informal system is less developed in German companies.

The first is that to postulate an attenuated informal system in German companies is entirely compatible with other characteristics, discussed in the last few pages. Germany is a society where the formal dominates the informal, or put more modestly, one where the rigour and comprehensiveness of what is formally ordained do not require informal buttressing or elaboration, and leave less room for such practices than in Britain or the USA.

The second is that if interviews with managers, which have formed part of our research, do not offer an opportunity to observe such informal practices it is still possible to probe for them with 'What happens if . . .?' type questions. This works in Britain where one gets answers of the, 'Well, what they really do is . . .' or 'The way they do it in practice is . . .' or 'You ought not to take the organisation chart too seriously . . .' kind. In the German context answers were more of the 'It would not happen' or 'That would be referred to the *Tarifkommission*' or 'We have a committee to deal with this' or 'I would need to check the Works Council Act on that one' kind.

Documents, contracts and written agreements

So far German personnel management has been characterised as legalistic, formal and procedural, written-culture-orientated and, in comparison with Britain and the USA, operating in the relative absence of an informal system. It may help to put flesh on these bones if some of the particular documents and agreements which impinge on the life of German personnel managers are described.

First, there is the *Arbeitsordnung* (literally, work order). The English equivalent would be the company rule book, but the *Arbeitsordnung* is typically more extensive and more omnipresent. Every German company has an *Arbeitsordnung* and they are quite lengthy documents by British standards. Sometimes they begin with a statement of general values along the lines of: we are engaged in profit-making activity, but it is important to maintain constantly democratic behaviour, and to have respect for human dignity. A grandiloquent plea for top-quality products is common. These documents will tend to cover things such as the rights and treatment of handicapped employees, improvements and suggestions schemes, the right of employees to inspect their personal files, reminders about the powers and responsibilities of the works council, and so on – in short, the *Arbeitsordnung* ranges more widely than a list of dos and don'ts typically associated with the English company rule book. Some of the items are also details; specifying, for instance, what kinds of jewellery are considered a danger in the workplace, detailing the parking arrangements for handicapped employees, or explaining which collections (in the sense of collections for charity) may with legal propriety be made on company premises. A final, and very characteristic, point concerning the *Arbeitsordnung* – it is the joint work of management and the works council and comes into force only when signed by representatives of both.

When it comes to negotiations between the employers' federation and the trade union, detailed earlier, two documents arise, but at different time intervals. First, there is the *Manteltarifvertrag* (something like overall wage contract), which specifies everything except the actual pay rates. The sort of issues dealt with in this document will include the duration of the working week, shift work and overtime rates (as percentage additions to basic rates), arrangements for the remuneration of part-time employees, what happens if the company has to introduce short-time working, paid breaks, special payments, holiday entitlements, bonuses and extras of various kinds again expressed in percentage terms, sickness provisions, the circumstances in which a worker is entitled to time off, probationary periods for new employees, termination of the work contract and pension arrangements. In other words, this is not a brief document either, but one requiring close reading by those with personnel responsibilities. The *Manteltarifvertrag* will last for about four or five years and then be renegotiated.

Second, there is the annual wage contract variously known as the *Lohnvertrag, Lohntarifvertrag* or *Gehaltstarifvertrag*. This document contains information of two kinds. There are, of course, the wage rates for various grades of workers. To give an example from one of the wage contracts obtained in the course of the research reported here, this source stipulates monthly base wage rates for 35 categories of employee based on a points system of $0-186$. This is a fairly simple example relating to a low-technology industry where semi-skilled workers predominate. It also leads to the second kind of information contained in the wages contract, that dealing with *Eintarifung*, or fitting people into the categories. For this to happen there has to be some agreed method of classifying the jobs, so that worker X can be said to be occupying, for example, a senior experienced semi-skilled job Y carrying a group 5A salary, or whatever. Sometimes the classification of the job is straightforward commonsense stuff, which can easily be agreed to; sometimes it is based on an elaborate analytical model where all jobs are graded in terms of several analytical criteria yielding an overall pay grade for each.

In Germany there is relatively little dispute over differentials – the pay gaps corresponding to skill differences. It is the *Eintarifung,* the fitting of people into the system, which tends to be controversial.

Moving to a new body of documentation, we have referred already to the Works Council Act, and to subsequent legislation which tends to strengthen the power of the works councils. The result is a complex web of rights and duties, procedures and obligations. This complexity, and the basic importance of the works council in the working life of the German personnel manager, has given rise to the publication of detailed, interpretative commentaries; the one most frequently used by German personnel managers runs to some 4,000 pages.

This is not to say that the works council legislation covers everything. There are gaps, omissions, and occasions when management and council are exhorted to come to an agreement without the content of the agreement being specified. Such instances may give rise to a *Betriebsvereinbarung* (literally, works agreement) between management and the works council, management being represented by a personnel manager of course. These *Betriebsvereinbarungen* (works agreements) are naturally in written form.

The general point urged is that the *Arbeitsordnung* (sometimes called a *Sozialordnung*), the *Manteltarifvertrag,* the *Tarifvertrag,* the works council legislation, and finally the role of the *Betriebsvereinbarung,* do substantiate quite tangibly the claim that personnel and industrial relations have a legalistic – procedural – documentary character in West Germany.

The personnel manager and the employees' representative committee

Again taking West Germany as the starting point it can be argued that the works council, the employees' representative committee, impinges on the work role of the German personnel manager in several ways.

First, the existence of the works council system and its myriad of supporting legislation conditions in large measure what the German personnel manager needs to know to do the job (cf. the 4,000-page interpretative handbook). Given the legalistic nature of personnel work in Germany in general, and the need for mastery of the works council legislation in particular, it is not surprising that the traditional qualification for the German personnel manager is the Dr.Jur. (first degree and Doctor's degree in law).

Second, the existence and operation of the works council conditions the German personnel manager's job in terms of activity as well as sapientially. Although the German personnel manager does not run or chair the works council, he or she will facilitate its meetings, take cognisance of its agenda, provide information at its request, respond to issues which the council raises, and, of course, negotiate with the council with respect to any *Betriebsvereinbarung* that may be required. With regard to the implementation of wage agreements (*Eintarifung* – described earlier), appointments, transfers, termination of employment, redundancies, and changes in working hours – start and stop times, overtime, shift work, holiday arrangements, and so on – the German personnel manager will again be dealing with the works council.

Third, the works council also conditions the character or ethos of the German personnel manager's job. Compared with his or her British counterpart, the German personnel manager tends to be reactive rather than proactive. Several factors contribute to this greater reactivity, and this issue is explored in more detail in the final section. But clearly the institution of the works council is one of these factors: it structures the German personnel manager's deployment of time and the profile of professionally required knowledge; it requires his or her attention, cognisance and response.

In Britain, of course, there are no co-determination system and works councils of the German kind. The Bullock report of the 1970s recommending a co-determination system for Britain has been politely forgotten, and industrial democracy is not a priority for British trade unions in the 1980s. At the same time, probably most British companies do have some kind of employee representative body, a works committee or whatever, so that the contrast with West Germany is not the black and white one that it is sometimes depicted as being, especially by Continental Europeans who know more about the law than British industrial practice.

These British works committees, of course, are less important in the British scheme of things than is the works council in the German context – but they do commonly exist. The British works committee differs from the German works council by being without legal foundation, variable in form and operation, and in lacking any precise or commonly agreed set of rights or obligations. These British committees exist with the consent of companies rather than the support of law, and it has been argued elsewhere that they are often used by management as downward communication channels (Lawrence, 1984). What is more, British personnel managers are typically less involved in these works committees, which are more often chaired by a senior production manager or general manager.

Production, personnel, and the industrial relations incidents

In both Great Britain and West Germany personnel managers are involved in serious industrial relations issues – strikes, threatened strikes and negotiations on important issues – but there are relatively few of these in either Britain or Germany. An interesting difference in the work of British and German personnel managers, however, emerges at a more humble level, at the level of 'the small change' of industrial relations incidents: complaints and disagreements about, for example, supervision, working conditions, safety, the allocation of overtime, subcontracting, working arrangements, and so on. It is often noted, rightly, that there are fewer such incidents in Germany: in part because of a more disciplined climate, and in part because the works council system in Germany 'takes out' some of these issues as matters of potential conflict (the works council, for example, sets the tea breaks so these cannot be the subject of a dispute with management!). Our purpose here, however, is to note a different contrast. In Britain the first 'port of call' for employees with a grievance is typically someone in the production hierarchy – a foreman, superintendent or production manager. The personnel department is likely to be involved only where such industrial relations issues reach a certain 'critical mass'. In Germany, on the other hand, such issues are more likely to be routed through the works council and on to the personnel department. The fact that there are fewer incidents of this kind in Germany should not disguise the fact that their 'critical path' is different. The greater proactivity of the German production manager is in part purchased at the expense of the greater reactivity of the German personnel manager (Hutton and Lawrence, 1979).

Personnel management and pay bargaining

It is easier to generalise about the German system of pay bargaining and the involvement of the personnel management therein, than about the British system. As we have seen, pay negotiations in West Germany are between trade unions and the employers' federations: the typical German personnel manager plays no role in this. Personnel management in Germany is involved only in the implementation of pay agreements, in the form of *Eintarifungen*. This is often complicated, detailed and demanding work; but it is not proactive, policy-making or status enhancing.

In Britain, on the other hand, pay bargaining arrangements are more variable, but plant-level bargaining is common (and increasing). Where this is the case British personnel managers are involved, often centrally involved, as management's representative. This tends to raise the profile of personnel overall in Britain, and sustain the claim of personnel to be involved in policy and planning and not just execution and implementation.

Personnel management and apprenticeship

It has been argued elsewhere that the institution of apprenticeship has developed differently in West Germany. While in both countries apprenticeship has its origins with the craft guilds of the Middle Ages, in Britain it came to be regarded as restrictive by employers, whereas in Germany apprenticeship has been adapted and developed to take account of new industries, technologies and specialisms (Sorge and Warner, 1978). The net result is that a recognised apprenticeship is available for approximately 500 occupations in Germany (Lawrence, 1980). Or, to put it another way, some 54 per cent of the age group undergoes apprentice training in Germany as opposed to 17 per cent in Britain (Windolf and Wood, 1988).

This contrast has a straightforward implication for the comparison of personnel management work in Britain and Germany. Apprentice recruitment, selection and care are typically a more important part of German personnel management work: there are more apprentices, and German companies invest more resources (and aspiration) in their training.

Personnel and management development

The final difference to which we wish to draw attention is a matter of relative emphasis. Starting with Britain, we would argue that it is common for British personnel management to feel that management itself as well as the workforce is a legitimate object of its attention. This is manifest in two ways. First, there is the characteristic desire of British personnel departments to be involved in management development. In the picking and training of (young) managers – also their career planning and counselling. Second, there is the tendency of British personnel managers to see themselves as specialists in 'the human side of enterprise', as having a superior understanding of the arts of communication and motivation, knowing about relationships and social behaviour and being willing to counsel management colleagues in these matters. In interviews with German personnel managers, questioning them about the nature of their job, there were fewer references to management development work and what involvement there was tended to be more formal (Lawrence, 1982).

Professionalism, proactivity and status

It is easier to write about personnel management in Germany than in Britain. Generalisations can be firmer, advanced with greater confidence; descriptions more precise and formulations of the work role more tangible. The role of personnel managers is less variable in Germany than in Britain, there are more constraints, and more fixed points.

Proactive v. reactive

A leitmotiv of the foregoing characterisation of the work role of the German personnel manager is that it is less proactive than that of his or her British colleague. There are several elements in this lack of proactivity. First, there is the plethora of legal constraints. Second, the importance of the works council in Germany, to which the personnel manager is obliged to react. Third is the fact that via the works council the German personnel manager is cast a little in the role of having to do the production manager's trouble-shooting in minor industrial relations matters. Fourth, the personnel manager in Germany has no initiative, indeed no role, in salary negotiations, while still being charged with the minutiae of implementation. And, lastly in this connection, the German personnel manager suffers from a traditional German tendency to favour those who bear front-line responsibility. To employ for a moment the old fashioned distinction between line and staff, in the German scheme of things status and strength accrue to the line (production and general management) rather than to the staff (advisory and support positions) – and personnel is certainly staff.

Professionalism

There is a further distinction which is certainly consistent with the Anglo – German, proactive – reactive, contrast, without exactly having been caused by it, and this concerns professionalism.

Sometimes the word 'professional' is used as a generalised term of praise, so that to call, for instance, German personnel managers 'professional' would mean they were good. The intention here, however, is to use the word in a more precise and restricted way, and to raise the question of professionalism among German personnel managers in terms of distinctive occupational consciousness and attachment to a body of knowledge and set of techniques. On the basis of this narrower understanding of the term we would argue that the German personnel managers do not exhibit a very marked professionalism. Their understanding of their work appears largely pragmatic; they see themselves as doing a job, concerned particularly with the tangible issues of recruitment and works council liaison. They are not inclined to put the world to rights, or to make major changes in the working life of employees. Their preoccupations are mostly short term and operational.

On the whole, an interviewed sample of German personnel managers (Lawrence, 1982) showed no great enthusiasm for what might be termed the distinctive apparatus of personnel work, that is, for employee appraisal, for job descriptions and job evaluation, for personnel planning, succession planning, and career development. Employee appraisal and job evaluation tend to be viewed positively only when they are necessary adjuncts to the payments system.

In particular it was noticeable, as suggested earlier, that when the managers interviewed described the activities and responsibilities of the personnel function as a whole there was usually little reference to management development, or to an advisory function *vis-à-vis* the management body. But we would hold that both these are common in Britain, where personnel departments would think of management development as their concern, and as being a status-enhancing activity, and would feel it right and proper to advise other managers on personnel questions and the human relations aspect of the job when opportunity arose.

Finally in this connection, there was little interest in Germany in the relevant professional association, the German equivalent of the Institute of Personnel Managers in Britain. Taking the first dozen companies visited in Germany, the personnel chief at one of the 12 reported involvement in the personnel management institute, and one other senior personnel manager referred to it and could quote its address (in Düsseldorf) from memory. But frequently there was no apparent knowledge even of the institute's existence. Paratypical of this phenomenon was the response of two personnel managers to a query as to the existence of such an organisation:

First personnel manager: 'No, no, we don't have anything like that.'
Younger colleague: 'Hold on, maybe there is even if we never heard of it.'

There are two qualifications to the judgement made here on professionalism. The first has been discussed at some length already in a different connection, and refers to the legalist-procedural nature of industrial relations in Germany. From the point of view of the German personnel manager this involves the mastery of a considerable body of legislation and procedures. So, in so far as professionalism is defined in terms of the possession of relevant and specialist information it might be claimed that German personnel managers have it in this form. A possible counter-argument is that this particular knowledge is peculiar to the German system rather than to personnel management practice in general.

The second qualification refers to the importance of training. We would take the view that the organisation of training is a major and classic responsibility of the personnel function. In our study there was considerable evidence of the commitment of personnel managers to training, and Germany compares favourably with Britain in this respect.

The status of personnel

In one of the first in our series of interviews with German personnel managers, it was suggested that personnel is typically a low-status function in German firms as, for instance, design and production have been reckoned to be in Britain. Responding to this impetus we raised the status issue at all the subsequent interviews, and found considerable support for the view that it is indeed a low-status function. At the same time it is fair to say that much of this support was oblique.

It may be helpful to elaborate this last remark. there were two broad responses among the German interviewees to questions about the relative standing of personnel. The minority response was: 'Yes, that's right; personnel lacks standing in the typical German firm.' The majority response was a more cautious, conditional one, taking the form of saying personnel used to lack status, lacks status now in old-fashioned firms, in other firms (but not here of course), in other sectors of the economy, or even if it is not true really one can see why the question has been put. Our view is that such responses do tend to confirm the proposition, albeit with qualifications.

If we accept that there is something in this contention that personnel lacks standing in Germany, and the same view is not generally prevalent in Britain, then it may be of interest to seek causes and explanations.

Two obvious causes have already been canvassed – the lesser proactivity of the personnel function in Germany, and the slighter attachment to canons of professional (personnel) knowledge and practice. A final consideration deserves to be cited.

In consideration of the relative prestige of the various departments or functions – sales, production, personnel, finance, and so on – status is a zero sum game. Not all functions can be high-status; the gain of one is at the expense of the others. Now it has already been suggested that German management is different and un-American in its glorification of the line at the expense of the staff. But perhaps the more important dynamic is the importance attached to the 'technical' in the German industrial culture. The valorisation of *Technik* in German companies is sometimes at the expense of that which merely relates to professional management.

References

Brossard, M. and Maurice, M. (1974) 'Existe-il un Modèle Universel des Structures d'Organisation?', *Sociologie du Travail,* Vol. XVI, No. 4.

Chisholm, A. W. J. (1975) 'First Report on the Education and Training of Engineers on the Continent of Europe, with special reference to courses in total technology', University of Salford, June.

Dyas, G. P. and Thanheiser, H. T. (1976) *The Emerging European Enterprise,* Macmillan, London.

Fores, M., Lawrence, P. and Sorge, A. (1978) 'Germany's Front Line Force', *Management Today,* March.

Glover, I. A. (1978) 'Executive Career Patterns: Britain, France, Germany and Sweden', in M. Fores and I. Glover (Eds) *Manufacturing and Management,* HMSO, London.

Hutton, S. P. and Lawrence, P. A. (1979) 'The Work of Production Managers: Case Studies at Manufacturing Companies in West Germany', Report to the Department of Industry, London.

Lawrence, P. A. (1980) *Managers and Management in West Germany,* Croom Helm, London.

Lawrence, P. A. (1982) 'Personnel Management in West Germany: Portrait of a Function', Report to the International Institute of Management, Berlin.

Lawrence, P. A. (1984) *Management in Action,* Routledge, London.

Panic, M. (1976) *The UK and West German Manufacturing Industry 1954 – 72,* NEDO, London.

Soreg, A. and Warner, M. (1978) 'Manufacturing Organisation and Work Roles in Great Britain and West Germany', discussion paper of the International Institute of Management, Berlin.

Sylvestre, J. J. (1974) 'Industrial Wage Differentials: A Two-Way Comparison', *International Labour Review,* Vol. 110, No. 6 (December).

Windolf, P. and Wood, S. (1988) *Recruitment and Selection in the Labour Market,* Gower, Aldershot.

9

A comparative study of human resource management in selected Greek and foreign-owned subsidiaries in Greece

NANCY PAPALEXANDRIS

Background and objectives of this research

In the early 1960s there was a spectacular improvement in the growth of the Greek economy, due to a large extent to the association agreement of Greece to the European Community (EC) and the foreign capital which was attracted and invested in the country.

Throughout the 1960s and till the end of the 1970s Greece enjoyed an economic boom during which the manufacturing sector showed an average annual growth rate of 9.6 per cent and the country was officially classified by the OECD as a 'newly industrialised country' along with the Pacific Rim countries.

However, after the 1980s, the two oil crises of the previous decade, some long-existing structural imbalances and an increasing current account deficit have resulted in the lower performance of the economy.

Greece became a full member of the EC in 1981 and from 1992 will have to meet the challenge of the European Single Market, which allows for free movement of capital, goods and individuals within the Community.

Research findings based on empirical surveys of Greek industry (Hassid, 1980) point to the fact that the limited use of modern management practices must be seen as a major source of lower effectiveness and that managerial performance could well improve if special attention is given to the management of human resources within Greek firms.

With reference to human resource management (HRM), research evidence of previous years (Greek Management Association, 1972) had shown that the establishment of multinational companies (MNCs) in Greece had provided a challenge to Greek company owners' attitudes to the practice of management and that MNCs were successfully using sophisticated management staffing techniques which their Greek counterparts seemed to ignore at the time. Similar differences were found during a research project among a paired sample of Greek firms and European subsidiaries (Georgoulis, 1978), where the latter were found to operate with greater managerial efficiency than their Greek, almost entirely family-owned, pairs. More recent research among a representative sample of larger Greek manufacturing firms (Papalexandris, 1986) has shown that in the 1980s some Greek firms have started to implement HRM practices quite similar to those applied by MNCs. These firms are led by Greeks who have studied abroad at postgraduate level or are using the guidance of management consultants. Thus, there is a growing awareness among top managers about the importance of systematic recruitment, selection, appraisal and training methods, which are considered by some respondents as issues of equal importance to those of markets or technology.

In view of this increasing role which HRM seems to play among Greek firms, it appeared interesting to make a follow-up study with two main objectives in mind: to compare HRM practices applied by MNCs to those applied by some of the larger Greek companies which, acording to the 1986 research project mentioned above, were found quite progressive in management practices; and to examine the sources of these differences and the major difficulties met by both types of firms in applying HRM practices as a result of the Greek external environment.

With these objectives in mind this research gathered a considerable body of information, part of which will be described and analysed in the following sections of this chapter.

Major research findings

For the purposes of this research five Greek firms were compared to MNCs of similar size (number of persons employed) and activity (manufacturing branches).

All firms employed more than 500 persons, which classifies them as large according to Greek standards. The research was conducted in spring 1988 in the Athens area, where these firms have their headquarters, and executives responsible for the HRM function were interviewed. The information gathered covered HRM practices such as:

(a) policy and planning;
(b) recruitment and selection;
(c) appraisal and promotion; and
(d) management training,

as applied by companies, with a special emphasis on managerial personnel.

Policy and planning

The main points investigated under this were:

(a) the degree to which personnel practices were the responsibility of a certain department or group of people; and

(b) the degree to which staffing practices followed specified policies and planning techniques.

All ten firms examined had personnel departments – which in three cases had recently changed their name to human resources department, thus indicating a change in the philosophy towards the human factor. Personnel departments of MNCs had more subdivisions and more employees compared to Greek firms. While there was no difference in the way personnel managers viewed their role and the importance they attached to the personnel function, there was a difference in the background and qualifications they possessed. In Greek firms personnel managers were older, with qualifications ranging from a degree in law or economics to that of a military academy, and with experience ranging from long service in the various departments of the same company to that of an ex-service army officer. In MNCs personnel managers had received systematic education in personnel management or psychology and were assisted by junior managers who had received relevant education in foreign universities.

Detailed policies related to planning about managerial personnel existed in all foreign firms and in two of the Greek firms. The remaining three Greek manufacturing firms said that, due to the unpredictability of the external environment of firms, they would rather meet needs as they appeared. As reported, whenever they had made such planning attempts, changes in the market situation had completely reversed their plans.

Various planning techniques for meeting needs in managerial personnel were used by foreign firms, such as a management inventory, managerial supply forecasting and management succession schemes. In one US manufacturing firm an analytical annual manpower plan existed and every manager had an appointed successor. Another European subsidiary drew an annual manpower plan which covered the three subsequent years and was checked and adjusted annually.

All Greek firms expressed their intention to implement planning in management staffing in order both to avoid the possibility of simultaneous retirement of a large number of key executives and to have available resources for expansion. They all showed a growing awareness of the increasing importance of the personnel function and of the fact that manpower planning was a key factor to managerial efficiency.

However, as a respondent from a Greek firm stressed, although a detailed policy existed on personnel matters, this was in fact seldom applied but remained among other formal documents that were very rarely referred to, not unlike what tended to happen with organisational charts.

Furthermore, two respondents from Greek firms stressed that management succession schemes could not be easily applied by Greek firms, where few organisational members would be willing to develop their successor for fear of losing control or of being replaced.

Comparing the information described so far, policy and planning of human resources showed a higher degree of efficiency in MNCs in terms of systematisation, use of tools available and in the overall qualifications of organisational members charged with implementation.

Recruitment and selection

The major source of recruitment in our sample of Greek firms was persons belonging to the firms' immediate surroundings, such as family, relatives or acquaintances of owners, or of organisational members. Only in those cases where such persons were not available was recruitment carried out by advertising in newspapers, using personnel consultancy firms or from unsolicited applications.

On the contrary, foreign firms used mainly personnel consultants and advertisements for recruiting applicants. Consulting firms, which are booming in Greece, also undertook the initial selection.

Both Greek and foreign firms expressed the complaint that some of their young recruits who had proved to be very competent were taken away by firms who applied headhunting practices or had left their jobs to join state jobs which offered security and tenure.

In all firms academic qualifications played an important role in selection. However, when considering applications from relatives or friends in Greek firms, lack of these qualifications would not necessarily be an obstacle to selection. Absence of job descriptions in four out of five Greek firms allowed for flexibility in selection criteria while the great availability of university graduates accounted for the emphasis Greek firms placed on the additional criterion of previous experience, which is almost a necessary prerequisite for entry into junior management.

On the other hand, foreign firms would rather select junior staff which met their standards in terms of personality or educational qualifications but did not necessarily possess previous experience. This difference is due to the fact that MNCs have developed their own training function and prefer to train their junior managers systematically, something which Greek firms seem to lack. Also, MNCs have a preference for young recruits possessing an MBA from abroad; they believe the possession of such a degree shows the relative competence of the candidate.

All firms reported the importance of the selection interview among methods for hiring a candidate. Foreign firms would also add personality, intelligence and achievement tests. Depth or stress interviewing was practised by two foreign firms. The interviewing procedure seemed to include two or three sessions in foreign firms, and usually one session in Greek firms. In three Greek firms it was reported that results of the selection interview were often misleading as candidates sometimes managed to display totally different personality charcteristics from those they really possessed. Thus firms would rather rely on personal introduction or references. Furthermore, all Greek firms seemed to express their concern that the university degrees which all managerial candidates seemed to possess were not professional qualifications enabling them to perform effectively: hence the preference for experienced recruits.

On the other hand, MNCs did not seem to bother about the nature of Greek degrees as they relied much more on degrees obtained abroad and on training and developing their young recruits.

Comparing the information described so far, recruitment and selection of human resources, and especially of junior managerial staff, showed a higher degree of efficiency in MNCs. More extensive use of sources available for recruitment, more objective selection criteria, more sophisticated selection techniques, more experienced selection interviewers and a preference for higher degrees from abroad account for their selection of better junior staff.

Frequently Greek firms oppose these techniques, and place reliance on personal acquaintances and on previous experience. Although these may sometimes prove very useful criteria for recruitment and selection, they include a degree of risk and deprive Greek firms of many competent young candidates who do not happen to match them.

Performance appraisal and promotion

Performance appraisal practices were used by all firms but to varying degrees. A complete appraisal system was found to exist in three subsidiaries which were following guidelines suggested by parent companies abroad. Three persons were involved in the appraisal: the immediate supervisor, the personnel manager and the department manager. Appraisal was based on management by objectives (MBO) or target-setting, and managers were informed of the results of the appraisal. The personnel managers interviewed in these three firms placed great value on the discussion of the results between the manager and his superior and thought the interview provided a good opportunity to establish the preferences and expectations of managers, which could be used for future placements. Of the remaining firms, in two foreign and four Greek ones the immediate superior was required to conduct an appraisal annually with the help of standard printed forms. Subordinates were appraised according to some rather general and subjective criteria such as loyalty to the firm, integrity, hardwork, theoretical knowledge and the ability to communicate with subordinates. In the three foreign firms and in one Greek firm some type of objective criteria such as meeting deadlines in preparing financial statements and filling orders were used while target-setting was reported to work only in marketing departments. Thus we can conclude that performance was the major basis for promotion decisions in foreign firms whereas seniority seemed to play a more important role in Greek firms.

In all cases Greek firms favoured promotion from within and would stress its advantages for the firm, which included improved morale in view of opportunities lying ahead and identification with the firm.

In one Greek firm it was said that once a manager joins the firm and spends his first two probational months he very seldom leaves, and in the remaining Greek firms the turnover among managerial staff does not exceed 2 per cent a year. To compensate for their inability to promote all their staff, firms increase managers' salaries or change their job titles. Only in those cases where changes in job requirements meant lack of persons available within the firm, outsiders had to be found for senior managerial positions.

Promotion from within was also found to be a standard policy in all subsidiaries. Most of them had started with foreigners in top management which were later replaced by Greeks who had moved up in the hierarchy. Similar to what was reported in Greek firms, changing job requirements meant that some outsiders had to be hired and this made it necessary to postpone promotion decisions on already existing staff. It was stressed that hiring outsiders created serious resentment among employees; this was a major concern for all firms and they tried to avoid it as much as possible.

Equally difficult appeared to be the situation mentioned by one Greek firm when it came to promote one manager from among colleagues of equal rank. A committee was set up for the purpose of the assessment but members of the committee did not wish to 'commit' themselves. Lack of systematic appraisal information and objective criteria hindered a sound promotion decision. So, it was finally decided to hire an outsider through the assistance of a consultancy firm. The existence of a committee for promotion decision was mentioned by all firms in our sample. However, the final decision always lies with the chief executive in both Greek and foreign firms. The main difference lies in the fact that foreign firms will follow efficiency-based criteria dictated by parent companies to a much larger extent than will Greek firms.

Yet, as was mentioned by all respondents, there is always room for the chief executive – a Greek national in all cases – to exercise arbitrary judgement. As a result of this, seniority is mostly preferred by organisational members, who view it as a safeguard against favouritism, friction and tension. Hence all firms tend to adhere to it especially in middle management jobs, often at the expense of efficiency.

To sum up, as it appeared from our investigation, appraisal and promotion practices are less systematic and subjective among Greek firms while objective criteria are used by foreign firms. However, in both types of firms promotion decisions present difficulties, among which easing the dissatisfaction of unpromotable managers and selecting from among equal-rank employees appear to be the most important.

Management training

As explained to our respondents, by management training we meant all company-sponsored training, whether courses or other methods, theoretical or practical, which were intended to provide additional knowledge and skills to managerial personnel.

One of the common features among respondents was their strong belief in the value of training as a means of improving individual, group or company performance. In all Greek firms training was described as a panacea for improved performance although the favourable opinions expressed were not matched by a corresponding degree of systematisation in training activities. Although all Greek firms in the sample provided some kind of training for their managers, a formal training policy linking training with planning, recruitment, appraisal or promotion practices existed only in foreign subsidiaries. MNCs would consider promotion possibilities when deciding upon a manager's training and would take his or her participation in training courses as a positive element when appraising his or her performance.

In Greek firms training was usually conducted in response to external courses offered by management centres rather than on the basis of systematic identification of training needs. Also, there was no evidence of defined training objectives and training methods were largely confined to lecture-type instruction.

Evaluation of training results consisted of distributing an evaluation form at the end of the course on which participants had to rate the instructors; no attempts to obtain feedback about the effect of training on job performance were reported. Training for managers in Greek firms was based primarily on off-the-job practices, consisting of a limited number of internal courses and rather more external courses.

A more encouraging situation was found in the field of technical or production management, where all Greek manufacturing firms provided training for technical middle managers in subjects such as production control, stock and quality control and accident prevention. As well as acting as trainers, production managers kept in close contact with machinery suppliers abroad. Also, under 'know-how' or consulting agreements, there were exchanges of visits between Greek managers and foreign manufacturers of machinery as well as frequent visits to international technical exhibitions abroad. Still, technical managers were considered to be lacking in managerial skills and financial knowledge and some courses in finance or in management were offered to non-financial managers to meet this need.

On-the-job practices were reported in two Greek firms and consisted of job-rotation practices, while all foreign firms used some form of job rotation especially at entry-level managerial jobs, or occasionally sent their younger managers to work for their parent companies abroad.

Foreign firms were much more active than Greek firms in organising *internal training courses.* Greeks who had replaced foreign nationals in top positions in these firms had continued to follow guidelines provided by parent companies, which invariably gave support to extensive training. Thus managers in foreign firms were sent to attend courses or conferences at the headquarters' training centres abroad, while in-house seminars were organised locally in Greece by the company departments responsible for the co-ordination of training activities. Internal training seemed to have gained popularity also among Greek firms although to a much more limited extent. Two Greek firms were found to organise courses quite frequently, while the remaining three firms would invite foreign experts to give seminars on issues requiring immediate attention.

External courses were used by all firms. For Greek firms they played a major role whereas foreign firms which organised their own training activities were using external seminars whenever the subject offered was of special interest.

The two main management training centres in Greece attracted 90 per cent of participants. A small percentage of courses was offered by private firms such as banking, insurance or computer companies. Few executives had in the past attended courses held at the American Management Association, the Harvard Business School, INSEAD or IMEDE. It was evident that attendance on these courses was considered as an extra fringe benefit rather than as a training event.

Attitudes on the value of training as practised in Greece were not so favourable as attitudes towards training in general described earlier. Comments differed between Greek firms, which used mainly external training activities, and foreign firms, which used mainly internal ones.

Internal courses had been found very useful by foreign firms in introducing new organisational tools and methods, in bridging the gap between different departments, in improving communications between managers and their subordinates and in developing supervisory skills among middle managers.

External courses were viewed with mixed feelings by Greek firms which were using them as their main training option. Respondents felt that the main asset of courses was the fact that they promoted interaction among managers from different firms and that they provided a stimulus to the mind and a break from the monotony of everyday work. Some reservations concerning the instruction methods or the instructors used by training institutions were also expressed but it was appreciated that instructors could not possibly cope with the different backgrounds and learning needs of managers on each course. As a result of this, all the Greek firms were considering the possibility of organising more internal training courses geared to their actual needs but had not yet begun to tackle this possibility in a systematic way.

A comparison of the information on management training among firms in our two samples shows that Greek firms which have no internal training function use external courses while foreign subsidiaries prefer internal courses plus the occasional use of external courses both in Greece and abroad. Reactions to internal courses of both types of firms are more favourable than reactions to external courses, which cannot possibly cover the differing needs of a heterogeneous group of participants. Regardless of the type of courses used, the overall approach to management training appears to be more systematic in foreign firms as it includes identification of training needs, evaluation of training results and co-ordination with other management staffing practices such as recruitment, appraisal and promotion. Lack of such co-ordination among Greek firms indicates that despite the favourable attitudes towards training in general, training is carried out in a much less systematic manner.

Summary of research findings

In order to present an overall picture of the situation prevailing in both the Greek firms and the MNCs, every firm was graded as to the systematic use of the various aspects of human resource practices examined so far. A five-point scale was used for this purpose, and the results are shown in Table 9.1.

Table 9.1 Systematic use of human resource management practices

	Ratings	
	Multinational firms	Greek firms
1. Policy and planning		
(a) Formalisation of policy	4	1
(b) Efficiency of personnel dept.	4	2
(c) Sophistication of planning	3	1
(d) Adequacy of planning	3	1
2. Recruitment and selection		
(a) Adequacy of recruitment sources	4	2
(b) Objectivity of recruitment methods	4	2
(c) Sophistication of selection criteria	4	2
(d) Efficiency of selection methods	4	3
3. Appraisal and promotion		
(a) Formalisation of appraisal procedure	5	2
(b) Objectivity of appraisal results	5	2
(c) Objectivity of promotion policy	4	2
(d) Efficiency of promotion decisions	4	3
4. Internal training activities		
(a) Extent of on-the-job training	3	1
(b) Extent of internal courses	4	2
(c) Efficiency of training resources	4	1
(d) Possibilities for implementation	4	1
5. External training activities		
(a) Extent of external courses	2	4
(b) Relevance of subject matter	3	2
(c) Efficiency of trainers	3	3
(d) Possibilities for implementation	3	2

Key: 1: very low; 2: low; 3: moderate; 4: high; 5: very high.

Every aspect of the practices applied by firms surveyed is given a grade. The numbers represent the rounded mean score for all firms in the sample. The rating of firms is based both on respondents' opinions and on personal estimations made by the researcher according to the information provided during interviews with respondents.

The simplicity of this quantification is due to the qualitative nature of the responses and the exploratory nature of this study, but was used as a means to convey the existing differences.

As can be seen, use of systematic practices is lower for Greek firms; the only exception is in the use of external training practices, which are used more extensively by Greek firms to compensate for the limited use of internal or in-house training applied to MNCs. Still even in the case of external training, the relevance of subject matter and the possibilities for implementation are lower for Greek firms than for MNCs.

Discussion of findings

The introduction of MNCs and of their management practices in Greece has undoubtedly contributed to the improvement of Greek management. Today, no one can question the better managerial performance of foreign subsidiaries operating in Greece, as well as the efforts of Greek firms to follow their example. Still, as described, differences exist even when comparing MNCs to larger and better organised Greek firms.

Given the fact that both types of firms operate within the same external environment and are run by Greeks, it is interesting to comment on the sources of differences and to try to identify the reasons for the less systematic use of HRM practices in Greek firms.

During the research among a representative sample of Greek manufacturing firms (Papalexandris, 1986), respondents had repeatedly stressed the fact that their actions were limited by certain environmental characteristics which interacted with their firms, influenced their managerial decisions and shaped the way they operated. Following up on this information, we asked our respondents to comment on the environmental factors which seemed to influence HRM practices applied by their firms. Answers included factors which can be classified under the economic, legal-administrative, socio-cultural and educational environments of Greece.

Economic environment

The Greek economy is at present in a stage of development lying mid-way between the developing countries and the industrialised countries of the EC. Starting in the 1980s, the economy has suffered from a low rate of growth, and a high inflation rate compared to other EC member countries. The main problems facing Greek manufacturing firms in our sample were:

(*a*) high competition due to import penetration;

(*b*) low labour productivity relative to standards in other EC member countries;

(*c*) limited exploitation of economies of scale in production and in distribution; and

(*d*) a high debt to equity ratio.

All these problems seem to lower the capacity of firms to invest money in better organising the HRM function. On the other hand, MNCs had overcome most of these problems due to appropriate managerial staffing, sound debt to equity ratios, better technical know-how supplied by their parent companies, the services provided by their research and development departments abroad and better access of their products to foreign markets due to organised global networks of distribution.

While some of the advantages enjoyed by MNCs due to their connection with parent companies abroad cannot be secured by Greek firms, the latter could meet unfavourable economic conditions through better managerial performance.

Legal-administrative environment

It is widely recognised that some of the difficulties facing manufacturing firms in Greece are due to the bewildering complexities of the law and the inefficiency of public administration. Both Greek and MNCs characterised the state as unpredictable, inconsistent in its policies and bureaucratic in its procedures. Every change in government, or even change in the head of a ministry, could result in a change in legislation.

All firms reported that they felt insecurity and anxiety about the future, which had an adverse impact on their corporate policy and planning. This did not, however, keep MNCs from planning and adjusting plans continuously on the basis of information which they gathered systematically as well as planning and investing in human resources. On the other hand, Greek firms felt less able to plan in human resources and were reluctant to spend as much on developing their managers as they would like.

Two additional characteristics of the legal-administrative environment mentioned by respondents were:

(*a*) the Greek banking system, which is controlled by the state and which provides funds at a high cost and with strict requirements in collateral; and

(*b*) the serious weaknesses of the capital market, due to which firms have to rely almost entirely on the banking system.

MNCs can obtain funds from foreign banks and equity capital from their shares which are traded on foreign stock exchanges. Thus they are less affected by these characteristics and can utilise their managerial time in exploiting market opportunities instead of dealing with the complexities of the Greek banking system.

Socio-cultural environment

Greece was officially recognised as a free state in 1828, following four centuries of Turkish occupation. Even during those years some remarkable entrepreneurial dynamism was shown in shipping and trading activities outside the country. In the nineteenth century the Greek state lacked any effective development policy and people in search of work in the cities had to rely on political parties in order to secure jobs offered in exchange for political support. Political favouritism and family connections have ever since been major features in staffing decisions in both the private and public sectors. Even today young graduates prefer the security and tenure of state jobs and thus many competent candidates are lost for private industry. Subjective staffing decisions are a culturally rooted characteristic still prevailing today both in Greek firms and in the public sector, which often goes hand in hand with lower productivity.

Staffing decisions in MNCs are geared more to objective criteria due to the fact that top managers in MNCs cannot afford to show low productivity to their parent companies abroad.

The family structure and the lack of separation between ownership and control were found to be responsible for poor management in Greek firms (Alexander, 1968). Owner–managers were afraid of losing control and would prefer excessive borrowing from the banking system to equity capital. This was to some extent due to the origins of Greek industrialists, most of whom had started their careers as craftsmen or merchants.

Craftsmen usually have a low level of education and a negative attitude towards public ownership, while merchants are mostly interested in high per-unit profit rather than in improved effectiveness – high profit being a trade characteristic still prevailing today in Greek manufacturing industry.

Although many years have elapsed since the Greek companies of our sample were established, and top managers were not necessarily family members, management is more centralised in Greek firms than in MNCs. As reported, decision-making in most Greek firms centres around one man or a few men who would refuse to delegate authority from fear of losing control over performance or results. This means that younger managers are not allowed to assume responsibility themselves but are expected only to carry out orders.

However, assuming responsibility is the main device for developing managerial talent. This managerial talent which MNCs seem to be able to detect and develop among their young recruits is often wasted or remains unidentified in Greek firms.

It is believed that the strong individualism found among Greeks stands as a major barrier when it comes to delegating authority and accounts for the readiness of Greeks to engage in entrepreneurial activities. This leads to the creation of numerous small-size firms which often face serious problems of survival.

Again, this results in a loss of more dynamic young candidates for private industry and a waste of valuable human resources.

Educational environment

Greeks attach great value to higher education as a prerequisite to future success, social status and economic prosperity. A study of the Greek sociology of education points out that the Greek educational system is surprisingly open, even compared to those of highly industrialised countries (Dimaki, 1974).

Business education is offered in a number of university schools which have recently modernised their programmes. However, the low ratio of teaching staff to students and the absence of attendance requirements lead to inadequate training for a considerable number of these graduates. To this must be added the emphasis on theory rather than on practice and frequent examples of political conflict, which often mean loss of time and energy for both students and professors. Due to the large supply of business graduates and the prevailing unemployment, the most competent among them follow postgraduate studies abroad and are to a large extent employed upon their return by MNCs.

This means that MNCs have the comparative advantage of recruiting among better-trained personnel. In Greek firms, however, young candidates possessing degrees from abroad are often viewed with suspicion and, as mentioned by one respondent, their knowledge and skills do not fit the reality of Greek firms.

Conclusions

We have seen in the first part of this research some of the complexities associated with the functioning of Greek enterprises and we have compared some aspects of recruitment, selection, appraisal, promotion and training as applied in Greek versus foreign-owned subsidiaries.

Serious efforts to improve HRM in Greek firms are being made, but there is still much thought to be devoted and action taken by those charged with the responsibility of running Greek business firms, to meet the changing realities of organisational life.

The second part of this research has shown that the peculiarities and the various characteristics imposed by the Greek external environment seem to exercise a much more adverse influence on Greek firms than on MNCs. Foreign firms seem to have developed among their members a variety of competencies which managers in Greek firms need and could develop in order to compete effectively within the enlarged European Community market.

The Greek political, social and economic framework can at present be regarded as moving towards a more fluid, complex condition, such as that encountered in other EC countries. Thus, one aspect of management capability which becomes more important is an awareness of such social and political movements.

References

Alexander, A. (1968) *Greek Industrialists,* Research Monograph Series, Centre of Planning and Economic Research, Athens.

Dimaki, J. (1974) *Towards a Greek Sociology of Education,* 2 Vols. (in Greek), National Centre of Social Studies, Athens.

Georgoulis, V. (1978) *A Comparative Management Study of Selected Greek and European Multinational Manufacturing Firms Operating in Greece,* Ph.D. thesis, University of Bath.

Greek Management Association (1972) *The Management of Greek Firms,* GMA, Athens.

Hassid, J. (1980) *Greek Industry and the EEC: A Study of the Impact from Entry,* Vol. 1, Institute of Economics and Industrial Research, Athens.

Papalexandris, N. (1986) *Management Development Practices in Manufacturing Firms in Greece,* Ph.D. thesis, University of Bath.

10

Personnel management in Africa
A comparative analysis of Ghana, Kenya and Nigeria

D. M. AKINNUSI

Introduction

Presently, Africa's economic, social and political outlook is a grim one indeed. Most African nations are under the threat of political instability. Economic performance in most African countries in recent years has been disappointing in spite of the abundant resources that the continent possesses. Characteristic features in their economic situation could be summarised as a slow rate of growth in gross domestic product, near stagnation in per capita income, a high rate of inflation, huge external indebtedness, widespread unfavourable crop conditions and consequent rising bills on food imports, hunger and starvation, high infant mortality, high illiteracy, high unemployment and underemployment. These and many others undoubtedly serve as impelling forces toward political, social and economic restructuring, a concern shared by all African nations since independence but more so in recent times when their dreams of true nationhood are becoming elusive.

Today self-reliance is the watchword for most African nations, as symbolised by Nigeria, the so-called giant of Africa. In 1986 Nigeria, faced with the grim prospect of an economic collapse, had to take the bull by the horns by attempting to restructure its economy to make it more self-reliant and self-sustaining through diversifying its base, developing agriculture, improving the rural areas, developing infrastructural facilities and reducing dependence on foreign imports and technology. In short, the primary objective of the Structural Adjustment Programme is to mobilise local resources to meet the needs of the people. In the arena of politics Nigeria has also drawn up a political programme that will ensure a smoth transition from a military to a civilian government and also create, in the process, a disciplined and patriotic citizenry through programmes of social mobilisation. These fundamental changes are occurring in greater or lesser magnitude in many other African nations today.

However, translating development policies, priorities and strategies into actual development projects, programmes and plans that are consistent with declared goals, and the implementation of those projects, programmes and plans also pose management challenges in terms of decision-making, resource allocation, co-ordination of efforts, monitoring, implementation, identifying and removing bottlenecks and reporting on performance and results. This, essentially, is a managerial problem and one of Africa's greatest weaknesses and a major handicap to its development efforts.

The focus and scope of this chapter

It is in the light of the above and in the context of renewed economic, social and political development taking place across Africa that we intend in this chapter to examine the role of the personnel function as being that aspect of management directly concerned with the management of human resources. Interest in this area has arisen from three factors: first, the African economy is essentially labour-intensive so that the management of human resources takes on additional priority; second, the productivity of African labour is one of the lowest in the world; third, personnel management is an area which has engaged more indigenous managers in sub-Saharan Africa than any other area of management.

The plan of this chapter will be, first, to indicate the role of human resources management in development and to describe the personnel function as that part of management responsible for the human resources management of an organisation. Following this, an attempt will be made to describe the growth, development and character of personnel management in Africa. Third, contemporary issues in personnel management in Africa will be examined and the challenges which personnel management faces in the future development of Africa will be underscored. The implication of this for professionalism in the practice of personnel management in Africa will be discussed. The final section will summarise and draw appropriate conclusions.

While Africa is the purview of this study, special reference will be made to the personnel functions as practised in Ghana, Kenya and Nigeria. These three countries have many things in common and are yet in sharp contrast to one another. They were once colonies of Britain, from which they derived their political, legal and administrative systems, although much has changed since Ghana secured independence in 1957, Nigeria in 1960 and Kenya in 1963. All of them embarked on programmes of political, social and economic development after independence with varying degrees of success. While Kenya has had a relatively stable government, Ghana and Nigeria have experienced a series of political changes and both are now under military regimes.

Socially, the countries are multilingual and multicultural and there are ethnic rivalries which pose serious problems to national unity. Economically, although Nigeria is by far the richest in terms of natural endowments, mismanagement of the economies of these nations has resulted in a poor standard of living in the face of rising populations, high rates of inflation and unemployment and heavy external indebtedness. A common problem facing these nations is how to modernise their agriculture, improve rural life and reduce dependence on foreign technology and imports, and how to shape acceptable political systems especially in Nigeria and Ghana.

Yet these countries differ in some fundamental ways such as in their size, population, social and economic variables.

The role of human resource management

Human resource management is an ever critical factor in the economic development of a nation. After all as Harbison (1973) points out, human beings are the source of all creative energy in organisations, and the capacity to develop this resource is the key to national development.

At the organisational level, the quality of human resources – especially the managerial class – is often the single most important factor that determines the success or otherwise of an organisation.

A model of personnel functions

According to the Institute of Personnel Management, London, personnel management is integral to general management, its distinctive contribution being the concern to assist individuals to make a significant contribution as members of work groups to the effectiveness of the organisation. Thus, personnel management is a basic function of management, permeating all levels and types of management and not necessarily the sole responsibility of the department in charge of that function. This means, in effect, that the personnel function may suffer if managers are ill-equipped to perform the personnel functions associated with their work.

The personnel function's activities are conceived as comprising a set of interrelated and mutually reinforcing sub-functions which cumulatively influence job satisfaction and organisational effectiveness. The effect of personnel functions on workers and how this in turn affects overall organisational effectiveness can be illustrated as in Fig. 10.1.

The growth and development of personnel management in Africa

In traditional African societies, the personnel functions as we now know them did exist in some respects but they were not as formalised or systematised as we now have them. The armies and the administrations of kings, the guild system and other social institutions had their own mode of selecting recruits,

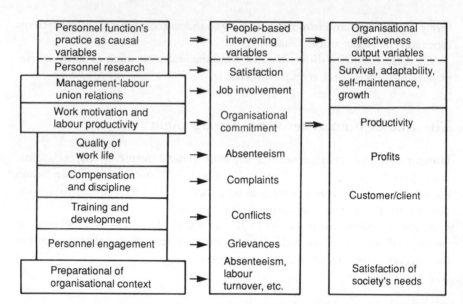

Fig. 10.1 A model of personnel functions, practice and organisational effectiveness
Source: Ekpo-Ufot (1986) p. 295

inducting and training them, maintaining discipline and rewarding employees (Enahoro *et al.*, 1987) but the advent of colonialism saw the importing of modern organisations based on bureaucratic principles.

The personnel function was one of the areas that first engaged the attention of the colonialists, trading companies and European settlers in Africa as local staff were needed to carry out the functions of messengers, clerks, interpreters and labourers. Incidentally, too, the personnel function was the first area of management to be indigenised for reasons of expediency. Initially, African chiefs were relied upon as recruiters of labour and, later, African chief clerks and personal assistants were appointed as labour officers with the primary responsibility of pacifying their fellow Africans when the latter began making vociferous demands and complaints about their conditions of work, especially after the official recognition of trade unions in Nigeria in 1938, in Kenya in 1949 and in Ghana in 1941.

Although indigenised early, the personnel function did not enjoy much prestige as the occupants of the function lacked the academic preparation and the power really to influence decisions which were mostly taken by the expatriate staff. However, with independence and more so with programmes of indigenisation, more responsibilities were entrusted to the indigenous personnel managers.

Several factors have contributed to the growth of personnel management functions in Africa in the last two or three decades. First, all African nations after independence proceeded to replace the foreign staff which had dominated the economies of these nations. This process was known in Ghana, Kenya and

Nigeria as Ghanainisation, Kenyanisation and Nigerianisation respectively. This created the dire need to employ, train and develop indigenous manpower, thereby expanding the scope of personnel functions of public sector organisations. Subsequently, in 1968 and 1974 respectively, Ghana and Nigeria also embarked on indigenising the private sectors of their economies, thereby again expanding the scope of personnel functions, this time in the private sector organisations.

Second, apart from these programmes of indigenisation, the governments of African nations also embarked on programmes of economic development through encouraging local and foreign investment as well as embarking on direct investment or joint ventures. All these activities have necessarily resulted in the rapid growth in the number and sizes of organisations and, correspondingly, the volume and character of personnel functions changed.

Third, parallel to the growth of industrialisation is the increase in trade union activities. For example, in Nigeria in 1981, 131 trade disputes were recorded involving 181,678 employees and 1,040,042 lost man-days. This contrasted sharply with 1978 when 67 trade disputes were recorded involving 29,892 workers and a total loss of 200,515 man-hours. All this meant that organisations had to employ competent personnel and industrial relations managers to deal with increasingly militant trade unions.

Fourth, the scope of personnel functions in Africa also increased tremendously due to government enactments designed to regulate the relationship between employer and employee. The enactment of health and safety laws, labour disputes Acts, minimum wage laws, indigenisation decrees and many others have all directly influenced the scope of the personnel function in Africa.

Thus, the personnel function – which used to be one of the general administrative functions in the early 1950s – has now grown both in scope and function to become a specialist function with several sub-departments. Correspondingly, too, the personnel manager has gained more power and status among other functional heads in most medium to large organisations. However, in the small organisations that predominate in the economies of African nations, the personnel function is still very much underdeveloped, just as are the management systems of these organisations. In these small, non-unionised and under-organised establishments, paternalistic management, about which we shall say more later, is the norm. In the section that follows, an assessment of personnel practices in Africa is undertaken.

Personnel management in the public sector

The public sectors of most African nations are the largest employers of labour. In terms of staff size, in 1988 the Nigeria Federal Civil Service has a staff strength of about 170,000 (excluding the police and armed forces) while the 21 state civil services had about 400,000.

Several factors have contributed to make public sector personnel management a major problem area of management in Africa. The Nigerian case is illustrative of the situation that exists in most African countries. Prior to independence in 1960, the four regional governments together with the federal government had different civil services with different conditions of service. The public sector personnel functions were shared between the ministries of establishments, the public service commissions and the offices of heads of service at both federal and state levels. The ministries of establishments were responsible for job description and specification, implementation of conditions of service, maintenance and review of civil service rules, the determination of staff numerical strength, maintenance of staff records, statistics and gradings. The public service commissions, on the other hand, were responsible for the appointment, promotion and discipline of officers above salary level 07. The offices of the heads of service were responsible for ensuring the efficiency of the machinery of government and the management of personnel functions. There was a lack of co-ordination among these bodies, with the result that the conduct of personnel management practices in the public sector was characterised by delays, red tape and too much buck-passing (Banjoko, 1987).

Another important development that has adversely affected the personnel function in the public sector was the rapid speed with which independent African states embarked on programmes of replacing foreign personnel with local staff in the shortest possible time, calling into question the capability of the new helmsmen to master the controls and guide the system along the chosen direction without crashing. This was the case in Kenya, Ghana and Nigeria.

The Africanisation of the public service also coincided with intense political activities characterised by ethnic chauvinism and sectionalism. The bureaucracy was used as part of the means of achieving partisan objectives or rewarding political loyalists to the detriment of overall public service efficiency and effectiveness.

Besides, the public sector of most African nations also witnessed phenomenal growth and expansion which complicated the personnel problems already evident in the system. For example, in Nigeria in 1966 there were just five civil services – which increased to 13 in 1968, 19 in 1977 and 22 in 1987. There were also parallel developments in the local government system. All this growth meant greater strain on the personnel function.

Moreover, the direct involvement of most African states in economic development through ownership or joint ownership of productive enterprises further expanded the scope of public personnel management. This is true of all three countries under consideration. By 1982 Nigeria had 168 federal government-owned public enterprises, while Ghana and Kenya similarly own public sector enterprises.

In addition to these economic enterprises, some African governments including those of Kenya, Ghana and Nigeria have taken over control of education. In Nigeria government has taken control over education at all levels, thus bringing educational institutions and research institutes under the umbrella, more or less, of the civil service.

Given this widespread and deep involvement of African governments, not only in the state machinery but also in economic ventures and educational institutions, it is difficult if not impossible to insulate these organisations from being politicised. And one of the ways by which this is done is through the appointment and control of the key personnel in these organisations.

The creation of personnel policies and practices that would properly reflect the objectives of these diverse organisations is one of the Herculean challenges of public personnel management in most African nations. This has necessitated reforms and commissions of enquiry over the years. The 1988 Civil Service reform in Nigeria is the tenth of its type since 1946.

Personnel management in the private sector

Except in the socialist countries like Tanzania, Algeria, etc., the private sectors of the economies of African capitalist nations are dominated by the multinational companies, mostly from the West and, more recently, from Third World countries, mainly from Asia.

In spite of what may be said about the multinational companies in terms of their economic impact, the fact remains that the personnel policies and practices of the large ones tend, by and large, to command respect and, therefore, are better able to attract and retain more qualified employees.

In a study of personnel activities carried out in a sample of ten organisations, seven of which are predominantly expatriate, Ekpo-Ufot (1986) found that these organisations 'did very well' in the areas of compensation and discipline, management – labour union relations, training and development, whereas they were 'inadequate' in the areas of quality of work life, work motivation and productivity, prepartion of organisational context and personnel engagement (see Table 10.1). Also, as Table 10.1 shows, the organisations under study seem to attach no significance to quality of work life, little significance to preparation of organisational context, personnel engagement, work motivation and labour productivity and personnel research. On the other hand, they tend to attach 'moderate significance' to training and development, compensation and discipline and management – labour relations.

The importance attached to these personnel functions is related to the size of the organisations, where large firms tend to professionalise their personnel management but only in three functional areas. The dominance of compensation, management – labour union relations and training and development over the

Table 10.1 Mean personnel departments' activity ratio and mean function significance indices for defined personnel function areas in ten case organisations

Personnel function areas	Activity ratios (maximum value = 100)	Mean functional significance (as % of maximum values)
1. Preparation of organisational context	36.67	43
2. Personnel engagement	45.56	33
3. Traning and development	65.63	59
4. Compensation and discipline	91.25	66
5. Quality of work life	23.33	17
6. Management–labour union relations	75.00	62
7. Work motivation and labour productivity	30.00	29
8. Personnel research	53.33	37
9. All function areas combined	57.50	49

Source: Ekpo-Ufot (1986), pp. 301 and 302

traditional personnel engagement functions is interesting when one remembers that this position is the reverse of what obtains in developed countries like the USA. In the Nigerian context personnel functions' practices have resulted from the history of the development of personnel services starting with concerns about staff welfare and industrial relations. They have also resulted from the influences of the government in various ways, for example the support given for training through the Industrial Training Fund and other governmental agencies that promote training, such as the Centre for Management Development and Administrative Staff College in Nigeria, the Nigerian Institute of Management, and their counterparts in Ghana and Kenya.

While what is said above may reflect the conditions among the large multinational organisations, the personnel practices in the medium and small ones are as poor as in the vast majority of indigenous organisations that practise what may be called management paternalism. This is a management style that is largely or exclusively authoritarian and is normally associated with the traditional master – servant relationship and with a social system that gives workers a low social status and demands from them unquestioning personal allegiance to the employer or manager and their complete subservience to his will and judgement. Although proper documentation of these practices is difficult to find in the literature, workers in these organisations when pushed to the wall often cry out and make sensational news. These practices are most common in multinational companies from the Third World and also in predominantly one-man businesses, which characterise most of the indigenous African organisations.

In these circumstances, therefore, employees, especially at the lower levels, suffer a great deal of alienation and exploitation which they have to endure due to the scarcity of job opportunities. This experience is widespread in Africa and has been reported by Blunt (1984) in Kenya, Ogionwo (1971) in Nigeria and by Peil (1972) among Ghanaian workers.

Contemporary issues in personnel management in Africa

Personnel management in Africa is confronted with unique problems arising from factors internal and external to organisations, private or public. Some of the important external factors include the nature of the society, culture, the state of the economy, government and technology. Internal factors include organisational climate, inter-group conflict and rivalry, and the integrity and professionalism of managers. All these cause personnel problems such as the use of particularist criteria, politicisation of personnel functions, especially public sector institutions, and inefficient management of human resources, resulting in problems of low morale, inability to attract and retain qualified candidates and low productivity. To appreciate the seriousness of these problems, we shall examine some of them in detail.

Use of particularism versus universalism

One of the problems that bedevil the personnel function in Africa is the use of particularist as opposed to universalist criteria in making important personnel decisions. The notions of particularism and universalism are derived from Parsons (1951). They refer to different means of interpersonal control and interaction. In particularist exchanges, interaction is governed by the personal relationships of the participants, such as ethnic affiliations, while universalist behaviour takes no account of personal relationships and concentrates instead on other aspects of the individual such as his or her formal qualifications or expertise, or ability to perform effectively in a particular job.

The pervasive tendency to act in a particularist manner in selection, performance appraisal, promotion and discipline, etc. is part of the general malaise of corruption that is very rampant in African society and organisational life. One need not look far to find the reason for particularist behaviour in the personnel functions in Africa. As Blunt and Popoola (1985) remarked:

In Africa . . . personnel managers are preoccupied with selection and placement . . . But if anything, selection and placement attract more interest and attention, generally among decision makers in African organisations than in Western ones. Reasons for this are not difficult to find. In settings where paid work is scarce, and where there are strong pressures to allocate jobs in a particularistic fashion, the selection process constitutes a prime means of fulfilling one's obligations to kin and other personal contacts. Moreover, in many African societies, this behaviour is virtually regarded as compulsory.

(Blunt and Popoola, 1985, p. 51)

The more successful or influential the manager is, be he or she a civil servant, politican or personnel manager, the more he or she is expected to share his or her good fortune with kin and to behave in a particularist manner, thus creating severe role conflicts and stress for most African managers.

The practice of particularism has given rise to vociferous accusations of ethnicity, favouritism, godfatherism, nepotism and the like in selection, placement, promotion, transfers, training opportunities and many other areas of personnel administration. The result is that people tend to lose confidence in the system and instead place their reliance on fate or curry the favour of bosses (Oloko, 1977). Further deleterious effects of particularism are the placing of 'square pegs' in 'round holes' and, of course, the ethnic rivalry and jealousies that the practice generates.

It is to forestall this that the federal character clause was inserted into the Nigerian Constitution (1979) as part of the efforts to make governmental organisations responsive to the needs of the larger society. Section 13(3) of the 1979 Constitution stipulates that:

> The composition of the Government of the Federation or any of its agencies and the conduct of its affairs shall be carried out in such manner as to reflect the federal character of Nigeria and the need to promote national unity, and also to command national loyalty thereby ensuring that there shall be no predominance of persons from a few states or from a few ethnic or other sectional groups in that government or in any of its agencies.

Though noble in its intention, the federal character has in practice had the tendency to undermine the merit principle in employment as positions cannot be filled, either because there are no qualified candidates from the states or because they are filled by inexperienced and less qualified candidates. Whatever the case may be, the federal character has a generally demoralising effect on serving officers. In any case, it has created more challenges for personnel officers in public organisations.

Inefficient management of human resources

Although the economy of African nations is labour-intensive, the management of human resources leaves much to be desired. This partly explains the low productivity of labour in Africa. Kilby (1969) asserts that the African worker is not inherently lazy as was believed but that the problem militating against his or her performance is the poor organisational structure, supervision and incentive system under which he or she is operating.

Earlier, we noted the low significance given to quality of work life, preparation of organisational context (i.e. organisational planning and design, job analysis, design and evaluation and human resource planning), work motivation, labour productivity and personnel research even in large multinational organisations in Africa. This implies that staffing matters are often unrelated to corporate objectives and usually there is a lack of objective criteria for personnel selection and placement. Also, jobs are hardly analysed and evaluated and so the wage structures in most organisatons are haphazard and constitute a source of dissatisfaction and conflict (Oye-Igbimo, 1987).

Also, we noted in the previous section the prevalent use of particularism in personnel selection, placement, appraisal and promotion. This, together with politicisation of key positions, especially in public enterprises, meant that unsuitable and mediocre candidates are employed, thus sowing the seeds of inefficiency. The faulty postings and frequent transfers, especially in the public service, tend to breed inefficiency and frustration.

Even though training has been stepped up, following programmes of Africanisation at independence, much still remains to be done as training is still focused more on senior management to the neglect of lower-level cadres where serious attitudinal problems exist. Moreover, the dearth of professional trainers, lack of local teaching materials and the indiscriminate adoption of foreign theories and concepts tend to reduce the impact of training (Akinnusi, 1983; Ejiofor, 1985).

Although the open reporting system has replaced the confidential system in most organisations, there is still a considerable amount of false reporting due to fear of exposure on the part of supervisors who have weaknesses to hide, or due to social pressures, blackmail or physical attacks. This is in addition to the use of particularist criteria in appraisal which we have talked about.

Finally, a major contributor to inefficient human resource management in Africa is supervisory incompetence. We have noted the prevalence of a paternalistic management style characterised by an authoritarian, master–servant relationship. Under this regime, the technological and motivational potential of African workers is bound to be under-utilised, as Damachi and Seibel (1986) found in their study of employees in some Nigerian organisations.

New challenges facing personnel functions in Africa today

As noted at the outset of this chapter, African nations are making desperate attempts to develop their economies. They are creating new institutions and bringing about technological and social changes. All this demands intelligent forecasting, diagnosis in policy-making and planning at the national as well as at the corporate level. Human resource managers in Africa will need to broaden their own knowledge and abilities to cope with these new realities. They will need to have a better knowledge and appreciation of general economic forces, the industry, government policies (finance, legal, etc.) and social phenomena and development which have a bearing on their organisations' objectives and roles.

The success of the personnel manager as a professional expert will be measured by the effectiveness with which he or she can demonstrate a degree of expertise in the systematic analysis of the social consequences of economic and technological decisions which other members of top management do not possess. This is the personnel manager's new role — as a change agent, a catalyst — to which all professional training should be geared.

Accompanying this trend is the need to focus attention on how to use current cultural revival to foster coexistence. This will mean the elimination of the use of ethnicity, tribalism and nepotism, as the basis for competition for jobs, promotions and other rewards. Inter-ethnic competition and tribalism, reinforced by differences in language and subculture, badly damage communications between socially mobilised persons. The result of poor inter-ethnic relations is a breakdown of trust between groups, which destroys the basis for co-operative endeavours within an organisational context. The responsibility of the personnel function to strive to eliminate discriminatory employment practices and infuse nationalistic values into African citizens cannot be overemphasised.

Moreover, the African labour force is becoming more enlightened, more diversified and more complex in terms of their needs and demands from the employer. The complexities may even increase in the coming years as social and economic conditions are deteriorating and trade unions are becoming better organised and more militant. The labour force will become more critical of conditions of work, living conditions and health and safety, and will seek improvements in training facilities, opportunities for advancement, protection from redundancy and sickness, retirement benefits and their individual rights as workers. These are challenges for personnel managers in Africa as they must bear all these in mind when they fashion their personnel policies and practices, so as to create and enhance a better quality of work life.

As the world moves towards increasing competition on the basis of quality of information, personnel managers in Africa must address themselves to the world of the computer. There is increasing computerisation of personnel and payroll records, recruitment, appraisal, training and development and information management. The personnel manager in Africa cannot ignore this trend without serious injury to his or her personal interests or effectiveness.

Thus, personnel management functions in Africa require men and women of high integrity, knowledge and, above all, courage to discharge their functions objectively. This, therefore, necessitates increased professionalism in personnel management, to which nations in Africa are addressing themselves through programmes of business education at universities and polytechnics, and other governmental and private initiatives.

Finally, a major challenge that faces personnel management in Africa is the urgent need to undertake research into personnel practices and their effects on employee motivation and productivity and organisational effectiveness. The need for this stems from three issues we have highlighted in this chapter: the rapid changes taking place in the environment of organisations in Africa; the problems that beset personnel management in both private and public organisations; and the need to develop indigenous approaches to such matters as selection tests, appraisal systems and training methods, most of which are at present foreign-based.

Summary and conclusions

In this chapter we have singled out the personnel function as a major constraint in the developmental efforts of African nations. In both private and public organisations we have identified personnel issues that must be addressed if the potential of the African labour force is to be released. It is a challenge to government, industry, managers and researchers. Above all, it is a formidable challenge to personnel managers.

In a way, this is a welcome development as it signals the rising importance of the personnel function, which has hitherto been the Cinderella among the other functional aspects of management.

References

Akinnusi, D. M. (1983) 'Management Training and Development Techniques in Nigeria Today', ASCON Journal of Management, Vol. 2, No. 1, pp. 5–16.

Banjoko, S. A. (1987) 'Personnel Management in the Nigerian Public Sector', in T. Fashoyin (Ed.) Collective Bargaining in the Public Sector in Nigeria, Macmillan Nigeria, Lagos, pp. 109–18.

Blunt, P. (1984) 'Work Alienation and Adaptation in Sub-Sahara Africa: Some Evidence from Kenya', Journal of Contemporary African Studies.

Blunt, P. and Popoola, O. (1985) Personnel Management in Africa, Longman, New York.

Damachi, U. G. and Seibel, D. H. (1986) 'Workers' Participation in Technological and Organizational Development: The Human Resources for a Suggestion Programme in Nigerian Industry', in U. G. Damachi and D. H. Seibel (Eds) Management Problems in Africa, Macmillan, London, pp. 69–85.

Ejiofor, P. N. O. (Ed.) (1985) Development of Management Education in Nigeria, Centre for Management Development, Ikeja.

Ekpo-Ufot, A. (1986) 'Personnel Functions, Practices and Productivity in Nigeria', in Damachi and Seibel (Eds) op. cit., pp. 292–314.

Enahoro, E. O., Longe, A. B. F., Imoisili, I. C. and Ikara, B. A. (1987) *Culture and Management in Nigeria*, Lantern Books, Lagos.

Harbison, F. H. (1973) *Human Resources as the Wealth of Nations*, Oxford University Press, New York.

Kilby, P. (1969) *Industrialization in an Open Economy – Nigeria, 1945–66*, Cambridge University Press.

Ogionwo, W. (1971) 'The Alienated Nigerian Worker: A Test of the Generalization Thesis', *Nigerian Journal of Economic and Social Studies*, Vol. 13, No. 3, pp. 267–84.

Oloko, O. (1977) 'Incentives and Rewards for Effort', *Management in Nigeria*, Vol. 15, No. 5, pp. 59–70.

Oye-Igbimo, D. O. (1987) *Job Evaluation As a Basis for Equitable Wage Structure*, unpublished M.Sc. thesis, Department of Industrial Relations and Personnel Management, University of Lagos.

Parsons, T. (1951) *The Social System*, Free Press, New York.

Peil, M. (1972) *The Ghanaian Factory Worker*, Cambridge University Press.

Part four

Comparisons of human resource policies – disputes and conciliation

The two chapters in this part address a specific aspect of human resource policies: that of the means of dispute resolution. Interestingly, both chapters compare countries which, at first glance, would appear to be culturally and industrially rather similar. And both find significant differences.

Haiven's chapter examines dispute resolution in Canada and Great Britain. It considers both national-level public policy and, significantly, the impact at the workplace. Haiven draws attention to the similarities between Canada and Britain, particularly in industrial relations. However, he also points out the greater degree of formalism and legal constraints that characterise Canada, as opposed to the indeterminacy and vagueness of the British system.

Once Haiven begins to examine the outcomes of the systems, however, he is able to show that disputes develop into industrial action far more often in Canada than in the UK. He examines, and rejects, several of the explanations that have been offered previously. What is needed is a detailed, analytical consideration of the key substantive issues where conflict is generated: at the workplace.

Such an analysis, presented in the chapter, leads to the conclusion that the greater formalism and legality of the Canadian system actually encourage industrial action by reducing the power of localised union groups, and decreasing the ability of unions and managements at the partial work-group level to 'fudge' resolution.

Haiven is bold enough to make predictions based on his analysis. He argues that an extension of informality would assist the working of the Canadian system and points to changes in British industry which are weakening the power of the work-group unit of the union: requiring perhaps the 'floor of protections' which Canadian workers and unions have. It is in this context that the British trade union movement's recent espousal of the European Community's Social Charter should be viewed. The Haiven analysis has obviously been accepted at that level, at least.

One final, parenthetical, point about this chapter which gratifies the editors is its disaggregation of the 'North American' or even 'Anglo-Saxon' approach to industrial relations. It is, we believe, a mistake in international comparisons to drift too readily into grouping countries which, on closer examination, prove to be significantly different.

The chapter by Kirkbride, Lai and Leggett examines the same issue but presents an interesting contrast. Like Haiven, the authors argue for the value of detailed local evaluation of differences between two countries which have, superficially at least, much in common. They compare Hong Kong and Singapore: both small, highly successful Pacific city-states with British colonial backgrounds and a Chinese cultural foundation. Once again, they are able to contrast a highly formalised, legalistic and, in the case of Singapore, government-constrained system with a less regulated and more *ad hoc* approach.

The authors concentrate upon the process of conciliaton of industrial disputes by governmental officers, or conciliators appointed by the government. By means of surveys of the 'consumers' of such services and the conciliation officers themselves Kirkbride and his colleagues are able to draw conclusions about relevant attitudes to the process. They find, in broad terms, that there is considerable support in both countries for their own system of conciliation. They find that in Singapore and Hong Kong the two sides to the conciliation have substantial confidence in the conciliators. They also find, however, that the more formalised and perhaps constrained system in Singapore shows a greater uniformity of attitudes than they find in Hong Kong. In this latter country they identify noticeable differences in attitude between levels of the employee representatives (lay or full-time union officials) and also between the parties and the conciliators themselves. In Hong Kong the conciliators tended to prefer a proactive role, while the parties themselves were more inclined to prefer the neutral voluntary role, reflecting the more voluntaristic nature of the Hong Kong system.

Together, these two chapters indicate the value of detailed, country-level analysis and research which eschew the tendency to conglomerate apparently similar countries into international groupings. By taking specific issues for careful research, while locating them within an overall national context, the authors provide further evidence of the value of the comparative approach.

11

The generation and resolution of industrial conflict

Public policy, regulation and the workplace in Canada and Britain – a four-workplace study in the two countries

LARRY HAIVEN

Introduction

This chapter summarises a major research project on the generation and resolution of industrial conflict in Canada and Britain (Haiven, 1988). The project arises from the experience of the author as a trade union officer in Canada for 12 years. Working within the very rigid confines of Canada's industrial dispute resolution system brings the realisation that an effective critique of that system is needed. One practising Canadian labour lawyer described it as 'a system designed to make people mad'. He didn't explain which of the definitions of 'mad' he was using, perhaps both. Such a criticism coming from a lawyer makes it doubly interesting – because the Canadian system has been very good to lawyers.

But mounting a full-blown critique from within one country is most difficult. Only by comparing their system to those of other countries can one truly appreciate its disadvantages and its advantages. In fact, after a certain point, analysis of all aspects of employment relations become sterile unless a comparative exercise is undertaken.

In carrying out such an exercise, we have to choose carefully the countries to compare. Choose too many and we risk losing our grasp of detail; choose countries too disparate and we trivialise the exercise. Our best choice is a set of countries where there are sufficient similarities to make the differences worth explaining in research terms.

Canada and Britain: similarities

Canada and Britain provide a most interesting comparison. They have many similarities – in language, culture, political structure, legal foundations and business practices. In industrial relations there are more similarities than is commonly realised, especially when they are compared to other groups of countries.

Union density is roughly similar. Britain's is declining and Canada's is rising but the percentage of the workforce in trade unions in both countries is between 40–50 per cent, with a slightly larger proportion covered by collective agreements.

Although British trade unionists like to decry the 'business unionism' of North America, their outlook in international comparison is remarkably similar to their Canadian counterparts. They are fundamentally 'job conscious' rather than 'class conscious' in the sense of not being anti-capitalist, of having a strong social-democratic orientation. There is a strict division between industrial and political activity, with the emphasis being on the former.

Both Canada and Britain have a largely adversarial system, wherein trade unions and employers choose not to engage in extensive co-determination on the Northern European model. Rather, they choose to settle major differences by periodic contests of economic power.

Yet while the parties in both countries have hesitated to engage in co-management, they have co-operated in developing a kind of 'semi-constitutional' system (Gallie, 1978) where procedural rules are laid out in a fairly explicit, jointly accepted collective agreement.

Both countries have largely decentralised collective bargaining, taking place mostly at the workplace rather than industrially or nationally. Accordingly, central labour federations have little power in collective bargaining and hence little power to deliver industrial peace or strife of their own accord.

Finally, while there has been more Canadian state intervention in collective bargaining procedure, both the Canadian and British states have refrained from intervention in the substance or outcome of collective bargaining (except, that is, on the few occasions in the 1970s where incomes policies were imposed in both countries).

Canada and Britain: differences

The greatest divergence between the two countries comes in the procedure for resolving disputes. The list below compels us to an intuitive prediction that Britain would have a higher level of strike activity than Canada.

(a) Canadian unions can strike and employers lock out only after a collective agreement has expired. In Britain there is no such prohibition. British workers can strike at any time and on any issue related to the workplace.

(b) In Canada, in most jurisdictions, public employees above municipal level (including both government and fire, hospital and police employees) are barred entirely from striking. In Britain, for the most part, strikes by public employees are not barred by law.

(c) In Canada, collective agreements are legally binding. In Britain they are not. Only the desire of the parties to honour the collective agreement enforces it.

(*d*) Because of the above conditions, the distinction between rights and interests disputes is clear in Canada: interests disputes being those over the making of the actual contents of the agreement at its expiry and rights disputes being those over the interpretation or alleged violation of the agreement which arise during its term. In Britain, the distinction is not clear at all. Agreements do not really expire in the Canadian sense. So disputes that arise from day to day are often a combination of both rule setting and rule interpretation.

(*e*) In Canada the collective agreement is meant to circumscribe the disputable issues. That is, if it's not in the collective agreement, it's not disputable. In Britain all workplace issues are disputable whether they are in the collective agreement or not.

(*f*) The general rule in Canada is that if an issue is not covered in the collective agreement, management has the right to do as it wishes. Because of this, Canadian collective agreements tend to be quite precise and the scope for interpretation generally small. British collective agreements, on the other hand, tend to be quite indeterminate and very open to interpretation by the parties.

(*g*) In Britain the indeterminate collective agreement is supplemented by a body of 'custom and practice' which, especially in well-organised union shops, forms the real body of law governing the workplace. 'Custom and practice' is as much a function of power as it is of memory. In Canada, up to a decade ago, past practice was virtually irrelevant in formal dispute resolution. Even today, though liberal arbitrators have made some inroads using the doctrines of promissory estoppel and fairness, past practice is still marginal as compared to Britain.

(*h*) In Canada the issues that are disputable (which we know are those contained in the collective agreement) are handled mainly through a formal and well-defined grievance procedure. Informality is minimal in disputes handling. In Britain formal disputes procedures were a rarity before the 1970s. Even now that they are widespread, they are much vaguer than the Canadian ones. Both unions and management will bypass the procedure if it suits their purposes. While unions pay lip service to the concept of delaying strike action until due procedure is exhausted, they are under no obligation to do so and strikes often occur in the middle of or in the absence of proper procedure.

(*i*) In Canada those issues (of course, disputable ones) which have gone through procedure without settlement must be submitted to a third party for binding arbitration. There is a body of experienced arbitrators in all jurisdictions and an almost encyclopaedic body of arbitral jurisprudence covering nearly every conceivable issue. At least 2,000 arbitration cases are decided every year. In Britain, although arbitration is available, it is entirely voluntary and is not only seldom used but actively shunned by the parties. Both ACAS and the Central Arbitration Committee (CAC) deal with less than 200 cases a year.

(*j*) In Canada there are three key features of union control of the dispute resolution process which differ from Britain. It is the full-time officer external to the workplace who is the most important union representative in the Canadian process, even in many large workplaces with full-time shop stewards and chairman. The central union office at the district or regional level has a great amount of power in the Canadian system and plays a major role in policing the activities of members in the workplace. In Britain, on the other hand, real power lies with the workplace chairman and the shop stewards; the external organisers and the union central office play a relatively minor role, and definitely not a policing one. The full-time union officers interviewed in this research project had not visited some of their bargaining units for several years! That is a situation that would simply never occur in Canada.

Thus, all the above features in Canada bespeak procedural predictability, institutionalisation of conflict and order, while in Britain they bespeak procedural anarchy, the breeding of conflict and disorder. (What is more, in the minds of many Canadians, Britain – especially in the 1970s – was the model of a strike-prone country. When people discussed strikes in Canada, the question was whether Canada would catch the 'British disease'. When it is suggested to policy-makers that they apply deregulation to industrial relations, Britain is held up as the example of chaos that lack of regulation will bring.)

Strikes compared

Yet a look at the statistics in those years tells a different story. Before going into them, however, it must be said that this is not meant to be a quantitative exercise or a statistical study of strikes but, rather, shows how general patterns of industrial conflict in the two countries have been the impetus for the larger study.

It has long been known that Canada is a world leader in strike days lost. That is supposed to be because Canadian strikes are so long, which is certainly true, but British strikes involve more workers, as we can see in Table 11.1. So when we measure strike days lost in the two countries, we are not comparing apples and pears. The comparison is quite dramatic, as we can see in Table 11.1. Canada's volume of strike activity has regularly been between 75 and 150 per cent higher than Britain's. But what about the actual numbers or incidence of strikes? In Table 11.2 we see Canada just about equal and, for a few years, ahead of the UK.

One of the reasons commonly given for Canada's high strike activity is the inordinate reliance of the Canadian economy on industries subject to cyclical instability, such as unprocessed or semi-processed natural resources (Jamieson, 1973; Lacroix, 1986), i.e. the primary sector, especially in comparison to Britain. But we can correct for this somewhat by comparing strikes in the two countries

Table 11.1 Indicators of strike activity for various countries, 1948–81

Country	% of workers affected				Days lost per worker			
	'48–'57	'58–'67	'68–'77	'78–'81	'48–'57	'58–'67	'68–'77	'78–'81
Belgium	7	2	2	1.5	0.6	0.1	0.2	0.16
Denmark	1	1	4	3.4	0.1	0.2	0.2	0.12
France	19	14	12	3.0	0.5	0.2	0.2	b
Italy	19	19	56	57.5	0.5	0.8	1.5	0.79
Netherlands	1	1	1	a	b	b	b	b
Norway	1	1	a	a	0.2	b	b	b
Sweden	a	a	a	a	b	b	b	b
W. Germany	1	a	1	1.3	0.1	b	b	b
US	5	3	3	1.4	0.7	0.4	0.5	0.33
UK	3	5	7	8.2	0.1	0.2	0.5	0.56
Canada	2	3	6	3.9	0.4	0.4	0.9	0.78

Note: a. Less than 1 per cent   b. Less than one-tenth of one day.
Source: Lacroix, R. (1986), p. 188

Table 11.2 Number of strikes per thousand workers, various countries, 1970–81

Country	1970–75	1976–81	1970–81
Belgium	52.5	56 (a)	54.1(b)
Denmark	45.5	87.8	66.6
France	174.9	146.7	160.8
W. Germany	–	–	–
Italy	237.9	123.4	180.6
Netherlands	6.2	6.3	6.2
Norway	9.1	11.3	10.9
Sweden	19.4	27.7	23.3
US	65.0	46.8	55.9
UK	114.1	81.6	97.8
Canada	93.2	98.8	96.1

Note: a. 1976–80   b. 1970–80
Source: Lacroix, R. (1986).

in manufacturing only. In Table 11.3 we see Canada actually ahead in both strike volume and incidence in this sector.

Another reason given for greater Canadian strike activity is that despite the ban on strikes during collective agreements, Canadians more than make up for it in strikes when they are over. This is undoubtedly true, but for the last 20 years, approximately 20 per cent of all strikes each year have been illegal mid-term strikes. Geoffrey England (1983) says that the high rate of wildcat strikes in a system that prohibits them reveals the reality of the system, in all its disorderliness.

Given the intuitive predictions we would have made about the levels of conflict in the two countries and the actual evidence, how do we go about explaining the phenomenon?

There are two major sets of theories on cross-national variations in industrial conflict: the institutional approaches and the political economy approaches.

Table 11.3 Strikes in manufacturing, Canada and Britain

	CANADA					BRITAIN				
	No. of strikes	Wkg days lost (000's)	000's of manufacturing workers	No. of strikes /worker	Wkg days lost /worker	No. of strikes	Wkg days lost (000's)	000's of manufacturing workers	No. of strikes /worker	Wkg days lost /worker
1985	357	1586	1981	.18	.80	388	912	5728	.07	.16
1984	343	2356	1968	.17	1.20	699	2658	5715	.12	.47
1983	311	1385	1886	.17	.73	610	1776	5749	.11	.31
1982	292	1691	1930	.15	.88	711	1919	6040	.12	.32
1981	423	4638	2122	.20	2.19	660	2292	6365	.10	.36
1980	402	3161	2111	.19	1.50	612	10896	7085	.09	1.54
1979	511	3129	2071	.25	1.51	1276	22552	7403	.17	3.05
1978	459	2527	1956	.23	1.29	1518	7678	7437	.20	1.03
1977	342	1665	1888	.18	.88	1719	8057	7473	.23	1.08
1976	457	4493	1921	.24	2.34	1118	2308	7425	.15	.31
1975	523	5340	1890	.28	2.83	1474	5002	7629	.19	.65
1974	685	4815	2024	.34	2.38	1946	7498	7994	.24	.94
1973	384	3376	1968	.20	1.72	1857	5701	7953	.23	.72
1972	290	2042	1857	.16	1.10	1671	7876	7906	.21	1.00
1971	278	1541	1795	.15	.86	1465	6577	8179	.18	.81
1970	263	3631	1790	.15	2.03	2588	6495	8462	.31	.77
Avg. 70–79				.22	1.69				.21	1.04

Source: International Labour Office Yearbook of Labour Statistics, relevant years.

Institutional approaches

The institutional approaches go back some way, to Ross and Hartman (1960), Kerr *et al.* (1960) and Kassalow (1969). But perhaps the most sophisticated presentation comes from Hugh Clegg (1976). The institutional approach sees conflict between labour and capital as inevitable but as being resolved through various institutions of accommodation between the two – such as trade unions, employers' associations, state regulation and law, collective bargaining and disputes procedures. This approach is also the engine driving public policy reform in most industrialised countries. If the machinery isn't working, you tinker with the machine.

Clegg presents his comparison of countries by making a detailed breakdown of collective bargaining into several dimensions such as extent, level, depth, union security arrangements, degree of control of collective bargaining and its scope. He also looks at the efficiency of disputes procedures.

Yet Clegg's analysis doesn't explain and in fact is often contradicted by the Canada–Britain comparison. The institutional approaches have some other problems too. They ignore macro-political developments at the level of the state and the involvement of the labour movement in governments. They assume that institutions prescribed at a public policy level will necessarily operate in a certain fashion in the workplace and that institutions that seem similar actually operate the same way in different countries.

Like many overarching theories, they risk missing much of the detail which can be very important in comparing countries. Not the least of the problems is that they conflate Canada into a 'North American' model though Canada and the USA have diverged substantially in union strength and conflict patterns.

Political economy approaches

A second group of theoretical approaches can be called the 'political economy' school, with major contributors being Shorter and Tilly (1974), Hibbs (1976, 1978), Pizzorno (1978), Korpi and Shalev (1979), Shalev (1980, 1983), Snyder (1975) and Cameron (1984). This approach sees the institutions we have just discussed as merely intervening variables between levels of industrial conflict, on the one hand, and the real source, on the other; the real source being the organisational and political power of the working classes of different countries.

These authors postulate that at a certain point in the history of the working classes of industrialised countries, a shift in the locus of the struggle for equality and distribution takes place, from the industrial to the political sphere, in a process which Pizzorno (1978) called 'political exchange'.

According to Korpi and Shalev (1979), a high level of union power as manifested in the gaining of political office by labour parties is seen to result in a lower level of industrial conflict. This is borne out when you compare, for example, Sweden and the USA, the former with a social democratic government, the latter without even such a party, the former with a low level of industrial conflict, the latter with a high level.

Cameron (1984) improves the theory somewhat, suggesting that it is not the mere access to political power by labour parties but rather two things: first, the ability of a labour movement to co-ordinate its efforts at a central level to bring its industrial power to bear; second, the actual pay-offs that a labour party is able to bring about while it is in office, the most important being low unemployment and a high social wage. If workers and unions perceive these pay-offs, then there will be a trade-off against industrial militancy.

The political economy approaches do explain a lot of things that institutional approaches do not. They deal squarely with macro-political developments and better explain why northern European countries have less industrial conflict and they shed light on strike patterns in France and Italy. But they are still quite unable to explain the variation in conflict in countries like Canada and Britain, which both have low levels of working-class political power, little central bargaining power and where the workplace is still the primary locus of struggle. In both Canada and Britain the labour parties have tasted political power but have never been able to erect an abiding social contract and most certainly have never been able to achieve the pay-offs mentioned above.

The political economy approaches concentrate too much on trade unions, however, and not enough on employers, for instance on the attitude of employers in different countries to the production process, such as the fabled ignorance of British managers about what workers are doing. Likewise, the political economy approaches fail to see the state as a relatively autonomous actor. They also ignore the micro or workplace politics of production. Like the institutional approaches, they conflate Canada and the USA into a 'North American' model. And again, the overarching scope of the approaches misses much.

A 'politics of production' approach

Macro-theorisation in the field of comparative industrial relations seems to have sailed into a dead calm. New wind needs to be blown into the sails before we can have another try at grand theory: a somewhat new way of looking at the problem, which could be called the politics of production approach. First, let us step back from overarching views, narrowing the field to interesting pairs or triplets of countries and examining them more carefully. Second, let us explore an area that has received scant attention in comparative studies – the workplace. That means we need good comprehensive case studies in different countries. Let us see how the institutions really work and how they operate in the workplace, where it counts. Third, let us try to link developments at the level of the state to developments in the workplace, rather than assuming the relationship. And fourth, let us concentrate on the generation and resolution of so-called 'day-to-day' conflict as well as the set-piece battles between labour and management. We concentrate too much on the pay issues, probably because they lend themselves so well to quantification. We concentrate too little on the struggles for control at the workplace. Such disputes may hold a hitherto-neglected power to explain differing patterns of industrial conflict.

The theoretical point of departure for this approach is the work of Burawoy (1979, 1985) and Edwards (1986). Burawoy has explored how different production regimes have worked to generate consent from workers. He suggests that the history of capitalism is one of movement from despotic production regimes to what he calls 'hegemonic' regimes, wherein management fiat decreases and workers' participation in their exploitation increases. He contends that the state has intervened along two dimensions in employment relations. First, it has intervened in the 'constitution of the social wage', that is, in protecting workers from absolute reliance on the employer for their subsistence, by providing such things as unemployment insurance, medicare, welfare, etc. Second the state has intervened directly in the workplace to limit managerial discretion, by, for instance, limiting the employer's ability to avoid unions, to discharge at will, to make workers redundant or to operate without regard to workers' safety. Burawoy theorises that the form and content of state intervention affect what he calls the 'political apparatuses of production', that is, those institutions that regulate and shape struggles in the workplace.

Edwards (1986) makes the argument subtler by suggesting that managers and groups of workers differentially generate both co-operation and conflict in a complex amalgam.

Working from this, let us look at exactly how conflict is generated and resolved at the workplace in different countries. This means we must look not only at the procedure (formal and informal) that the parties use to interact with each other but also how the procedure articulates with various substantive issues.

In Canada and Britain there are three key loci of workplace struggle between management and labour, where both consent and conflict are differentially generated, and the outcome of these struggles in a very large way determines the resulting levels of conflict across many workplaces.

The three key substantive issues are *discipline, regulation* of the internal labour market and *job control*.

Discipline

The power to discipline employees is essential to employers. But increasing complexity of work organisation and division of labour and the increasing power of trade unions and state intervention in managerial discretion make it counter-productive for employers to use this tool arbitrarily. So employers have developed work rules and negotiated disciplinary procedures to interpret those rules, thereby legitimising them. Moving from the days when employers relied on common law rights of dismissal, employers now have an arsenal of calibrated punishments to draw upon and are no longer forced to rely on whatever industrial muscle they have to obtain equity. Now employees take part in their own discipline. Arbitrary discipline has been displaced by arbitrated discipline, by a system that promises equity and due process. But it is an imperfect system and does not always 'deliver'. So it is most interesting to observe the generation and resolution of conflict around this key issue in the two countries.

The system of arbitral review of discipline would seem to be the jewel in the crown of North American dispute resolution (Collins, 1982) compared to the industrial tribunal system in Britain. It is a far more sensitive and finely tuned instrument with a comprehensive body of jurisprudence. So we might be excused for thinking it to be much more effective at venting worker frustration than the system in Britain. But here is a perfect instance of how looking at institutions at a national level can be misleading. What counts is how they play themselves out in the workplace.

We must look at how employers and unions actually deal with discipline. And we find that in many ways the Canadian system may generate more conflict than the British. While British tribunals are not used much by unions or workers, they have had a large impact on the workplace. In response to the imposition of disciplinary tribunals, British employers have moved in recent years to elaborate in-house disciplinary procedures to protect themselves (Millward and Stevens, 1986). But British employers also generally do more suspending and dismissing than their Canadian counterparts. British unions are much more effective than Canadian ones at deciding which cases need fighting and which do not, at 'sorting their members out' and deciding the ground on which they will fight. The British workplace has its own, quite effective methods of mollifying conflict on this issue while the Canadian workplace system can be quite effective in doing the opposite (Glasbeek, 1984).

Regulation of the internal labour market

The second substantive issue is regulation of the internal labour market. For many firms, especially those in the monopoly sector, there are positive efficiencies in having at least part of their workforce in a system of job allocation, training, pricing and promotion that is internal to the firm and also in having another part of the workforce in a more precarious position, subject to the icy winds of the external market (Doeringer and Piore, 1971; Gordon, Edwards and Reich, 1982). But these efficiencies are not strictly economic. Several commentators (Gordon, Edwards and Reich, 1982; Burawoy, 1979) have suggested that the internal labour market is a way of securing commitment from employees and of draining potentially dysfunctional conflict away from the workplace.

Like discipline, the ability to move employees about the workplace, and out the door in bad times, is an essential tool for employers. But because of the rise of trade unions and because states have intervened in the construction of the social wage, the employer's ability to use the whip of the market is considerably weaker than it used to be. So certain rules and procedures have come into being to regulate conflict in this area. Canada and Britain differ considerably in this area.

The key operative concept in North America, and quite unique to it, is seniority. Next to arbitral review of discipline, the seniority system would seem to be the second jewel in the crown of North American dispute resolution. It seems fair, predictable, easy to administer, and except in those workplaces where there are huge differentials in employee skill requirements, not particularly disadvantageous to the employer.

It would also seem that the highly structured job ladder, including elaborate job-bidding systems in the case of promotion and bumping systems in the case of redundancy or lay-off, would do much to reduce conflict and generate commitment.

In Britain the regulation of internal labour markets is not nearly so well developed. Seniority is a marginal concept and the grid of job differentiation is much flatter than in Canada. It would seem that the potential for the politicisation of job allocation is much greater in Britain. But, as with discipline, here is another area where a cursory look at national institutions is misleading: for the British workplace actually has quite efficient methods of dealing with problems arising in this area.

Let us look at redundancy as one example. The concept of voluntary redundancy whereby older workers accept sometimes large lump sum payments and early retirement bonuses in return for leaving before the age of 65, in fact works much more effectively to depoliticise redundancy, especially when it is on a large scale. It also results in a much younger average workforce remaining. On the other hand, the Canadian seniority system has many built-in defects for both management and labour and especially breaks down under large-scale redundancy, as the research study reveals. In this and other areas conflict in the British workplace over the regulation of the internal labour market is resolved more efficiently than in Canada.

Job control

The third area around which conflict centres is job control. This is probably the most contentious area in both countries, the area in which management is least willing to surrender its authority. But the essential dialectic of control is that wherever management requires workers to be more than mere automatons, actually to offer freely their skill and intellectual initiative, it must, in the words of Alan Flanders, 'regain control by sharing it'.

Aspects of job control include effort bargaining, the pace of work, the design of jobs and manning. It is the issue where the divergence between Canada and Britain is most dramatic. While there are still areas that British management holds sacred and defends vigorously, job control has long been a legitimate forum of negotiation in Britain. In fact, it has been said that British trade unions may have concentrated on it to the exclusion of economic advancement (Edwards, 1986). In Canada virtually no formal mechanism for its regulation exists.

In Canada job control (except in the area of health and safety) is the realm of exclusive management rights. And yet this does not mean it is not an area of great concern to workers and that they do not attempt to and sometimes succeed in negotiating aspects of job control. What is missing entirely, however, is the sense that joint regulation in this area is in any way a legitimate preoccupation of unions.

Conflict over these issues certainly arises in the British workplace, but as we shall see presently, the very fact that they are negotiable at one level contributes much to the resolution of conflict at another. In Canada, forced underground, conflict over job control manifests itself indirectly in three ways: first, some of it surfaces with all the rest of the residual irritants at contract expiry; second, some of it emerges in the wildcat strikes; third, some of it is displaced to the forum of discipline, emerging as the most common cause of discipline in Canada: insubordination. If the Canadian shop floor is not a debating society it is still often a battlefield.

The case study workplaces

The case studies were undertaken at aluminium fabricating plants and breweries in Britain and Canada. They were chosen because they were in well-established, fairly stable industries which have not undergone drastic changes in technology, product markets and labour markets or labour force in the past ten years. Records and interviews covered the dispute resolution process over that period.

The workplaces had between 350 and 500 employees, somewhat smaller than those in much of the academic literature. Yet these are more 'representative' of medium workplace size in the two countries, especially in light of the trend of the last two decades. Also, studying workplaces at this size level allows unique insight into the critical threshold where the size factor can mean a quantitative leap in union organisation and power.

All the plants were unionised and had been for many years, with active union–management relations and a discernible history of dispute resolution, providing rich data. The Canadian plants had a single union, as is the norm in that country. In the British plants there was a single union or one overwhelmingly dominant union.

In all the plants members of management, mainly personnel and industrial relations officers at plant level, and workers, but mainly chief stewards, plant chairmen or conveners, were interviewed.

As well as the interviews, documents in all the workplaces on disputes, discipline, grievances, arbitrations and other relevant items were examined.

While one must be very cautious in attributing 'typicality' to four case studies, they all compare well to patterns of industrial relations and personnel management in their industries, sectors and countries. In other words, none of the four can in any way be considered 'atypical'. The pairs of workplaces in the same industry match well in terms of technology employed, methods of work organisation and external labour markets. While the structure of the product markets in the British and Canadian breweries differs slightly, general trends in beer consumption and product market pressures are remarkably similar.

Patterns of industrial relations in the workplaces

In so far as industrial conflict is concerned, typically, neither British workplace has had a major (everybody out) strike lasting more than a few days over the last decade or more, while both Canadian workplaces have had everybody out in wars of attrition lasting several weeks or months as well as several angry wildcat strikes. In fact, one of the Canadian plants had just ended a marathon four-month strike a few weeks before the study began.

The parties in both British workplaces avoided third-party intervention (that is, by union and management 'outsiders' and conciliators and arbitrators). Where they did accept conciliation, it was with mixed feelings. And they definitely shunned anything more binding. At the one plant that had experienced arbitration, both union and management rejected the award and thenceforth swore never to use it again.

Yet despite this, disputes were never solved by full-blown strikes. In fact, a British personnel manager insisted that his plant hadn't had a strike in years. Challenged with evidence of several sectional work stoppages within recent memory, he replied: 'Those weren't strikes. A strike is a work stoppage that seriously impairs our ability to trade.' Disputes are more often resolved by processes which might be called 'massaging', 'fudging', and 'consensualising'. Formal and informal systems of dispute resolution operated side by side and the parties slipped comfortably between them according to their needs. Sectional agreements of varying degrees of formality and 'custom and practice' of varying degrees of clarity supplemented thin collective agreements.

While the union in the British aluminium fabricating plant was fairly weak, it was stubborn, unpredictable and volatile and management took pains to ensure that the union was on board for changes in working practices. The union in the brewery was more powerful, such that little happened on the shop floor which the union had not in some way vetted. Yet for all this, the British workplaces were neither inefficient nor unbusinesslike. Both were quite successful at what they do and were meeting the challenges of the 1980s well.

By contrast, both parties in the Canadian workplaces, and especially the brewery, worked from almost encyclopaedic collective agreements. Disputes not over the application, interpretation or alleged violation of the collective agreement seldom saw the light of day. The parties either actively shunned or uneasily toyed with informal methods of dispute resolution, preferring to commit disputes to writing early and advance them up the formal grievance procedure. While a certain amount of negotiation went on within the grievance procedure, it was almost negligible. The parties would seldom if ever openly reach agreement within this procedure. In fact the Canadian dispute resolution system itself often was a source of conflict or a catalyst to conflict. We will return to this theme presently.

From the earliest stages, both parties in the Canadian workplaces consulted the arbitral jurisprudence and used it as a basis for action. We have seen before the marginality of 'past practice' in Canadian arbitral jurisprudence. Nevertheless, it has had an effect. Sophisticated unions are invoking it more and more. But the response of sophisticated employers has been to track down common shopfloor practices, divide them into those they want to keep and those they do not and then codify the former, and give notice to the union to eliminate the latter.

At the final stages of procedure, and certainly in arbitration, the parties sometimes use and often consult lawyers. The entire process, then, has become highly legalised and very constraining.

In one sense, management in the Canadian workplaces was able to introduce changes in working practices and work organisation much more easily than in the British. There is no formal requirement for bargaining on day-to-day changes and the twin iron rules of Canadian arbitration hold sway: 'work now, grieve later' and 'the industrial plant is not a debating society'. In the British plant, although management is not in any way prevented from introducing changes, they are forced to consider carefully the consequences of their actions. The best personnel and production managers have a finely honed sense of what will carry on the shop floor and what won't, and if something needs to be done in the face of worker or union resistance they have a much clearer idea of how to do it. In this sense, Canadian managers are much more easily lulled into a false sense of security about the long-term effects of their actions and are commonly 'caught by surprise' by the intensity of workers' and union opposition and bloody-mindedness at the bargaining table when it is often too late to avoid industrial conflict.

Some conclusions

The following are some tentative conclusions drawn from the study.

A key concept when talking about conflict is that of levels of conflict. Quite definitely, certain work groups in the British workplace, by dint of their skills or strategic position in the production chain and because of a payment-by-results system, have developed power bases and sectional leverage that do not exist to anywhere near the same extent in Canada. Much of the conflict and work stoppage in British plants occurs at this level.

Yet this work group control was not necessarily as injurious to the employer as it was to the union's overall site power. As Kuhn (1961) points out, fractional bargaining poses a more fundamental challenge to the union than to management. So much so that when one of the British employers finally took on one work group in a two-week strike over a much abused incentive scheme, it was the union more than the company that emerged as the long-term beneficiary when the scheme was amended to decrease the power of the sectional group.

While this situation seems to provide an opportunity for a greater degree of localised conflict, in a way it reduces the probability of more generalised conflict, first by giving otherwise churlish worker groups a tough bone to chew (as a robber might give to a big guard dog), second, by dividing and weakening the integrity of the site-wide union. In Canada, on the other hand, the very centralisation of power and the absence of sectionalised conflict may lead to a more concentrated type of conflict.

The workforce size of the case studies affords an interesting insight into the effect of this dimension on union and management power. At about 350 to 800 blue-collar employees, key differences in the Canadian and British systems reveal themselves more fully than at larger workplaces. For this is the area in which organised shop steward committees and full-time conveners begin to emerge. Other variables such as technology, labour markets, perishability of the product, strategic location of workers and history of union militancy may interact with the size factor to determine exactly where the threshold lies. Nevertheless, in these case studies there is a distinct demarcation in union power between the breweries and the aluminium plants. In the latter there are no full-time conveners or well-organised steward committees. In the former there are. In the latter the union is much weaker than in the former.

Thus it was possible to observe that where union power is potentially high, the British system allows the union much greater exercise of that power. The relative informality and tractability of procedure and relative absence of the dampening effect of the union hierarchy put fewer limits on the ability of the British workplace union to assert itself. As mentioned before, this does not necessarily lead to more conflict at a higher level.

In Canada, though, there are definite upper bounds on the degree to which even the most powerful union can 'throw its weight around'. There is, first, more authority in the trade union hierarchy and the full-time officer than in the work groups; second, the tradition of relying on the collective agreement rather than shopfloor bargaining to settle disputes; third, strict limitations on the issues the collective agreement will handle; and, fourth, a well-defined arbitral jurisprudence on how those issues can be handled.

But when union power in Britain is potentially low, the union is at a great disadvantage. Where is cannot mount a regular, organised and coherent challenge to management, it may be trampled. In Canada the very same factors that limit union power also provide a minimum floor of rights and equity available to even the smallest groups of unionised workers.

Closely allied to the above point: the British system, because of its informality and tractability, depends on constant mobilisation by both union and employer. This can consume a tremendous amount of energy on both sides unless the size factor allows it to be institutionalised. This is especially crucial to the application of custom and practice to disputes. The study revealed that custom and practice relies at least as much on the mobilisation of power as on memory. So where the British union has a full-time convener, strong stewards and a certain momentum, it can effectively establish and maintain a body of custom and practice. Where the union is weak, however, it must continually reinvent the wheel, attempting to mobilise discontent every time a dispute arises. But it encounters tremendous inertia. By the same token, management can and does counter-mobilise for acquiescence.

In Canada mobilisation is far less important because work regulation is so highly codified. While this can make for less victimisation of workers where unions are weak, it also lulls potentially strong unions into complacency and makes them singularly vulnerable in times of crisis when a threat not covered in the collective agreement, such as technological change or mass redundancy, occurs.

To sum up somewhat glibly: at the workplace strong British unions are stronger than strong Canadian ones and weak British unions are weaker than weak Canadian ones.

It may well be that industrial conflict in the two countries is generally of two different types. In Britain it tends to be more focused, more strategic, more purposive; or what might be called instrumental conflict. In Canada it tends to be more diffuse, more undirected, more desperate; what might be called reactive conflict. Canadian workplace unions with potential power are like sorcerer's apprentices, unable to harness and direct but able to do much damage.

In Britain there are two aspects of disputes procedure which lend themselves better to the attenuation of conflict than to its generation. First, there is the dual system of formal and informal procedure which ensures that the parties can avoid being 'locked in' to a dispute irretrievably. There are many ways of withdrawing and times to withdraw for both parties without losing face or setting dangerous precedents, ways of blurring the issues if they wish, i.e. fudging, if they feel this is in their best interests. But they can also bring an issue to a head and open conflict if they wish.

Perhaps because of this tractability, British unions are more willing to 'sort their members out', i.e. decide which issues to pursue and which not. There is no duty of fair representation in Britain.

The second aspect of dispute procedure is the fact that the formal rounds of bargaining, usually every year, are restricted to a very few items, mostly of pay and benefits. Other, perhaps more contentious issues can be left either to separate spells of site-wide bargaining outside the annual round or to sectional bargaining. It is interesting that in neither British plant studied has there been a strike on an annual pay round within living memory.

In Canada, on the other hand, the vacuum cleaner of grievance procedure sweeps very low, sucking up even the most trivial disagreement into the formal arena of confrontation. Once into the lower levels, there is great resistance from lower supervisors to concede; once into the higher levels, there is great reluctance by the union to do so. Canadian unions are much less willing than British to 'kick ass', partly because of the fear of unfair representation and partly because the political costs of putting the members in their place are high. The grievance procedure is like a conveyor belt with a life of its own, separate from the real interests of the parties and in constant state of overload. This gives rise to bad feeling and frustration, when, almost inevitably, grievances are abandoned or lost.

In Canada, also, the formal rounds of interest bargaining at contract expiry are seldom annual and creak under the weight of a multiplicity of issues, not the least of which may be unresolved grievances. Because the whole process of interest bargaining is so highly formal it also tends to take on a life of its own, especially after third parties have intervened. It is said that interest arbitration is subject to a 'chilling effect' and a 'narcotic effect', but so are interest bargaining and grievance arbitration. It is small wonder, then, that both the Canadian workplaces observed, and the aggregate, engage in such long, bitter battles of attrition at regular intervals.

These, then, are some of the tentative conclusions drawn from the study. To conclude, a look to the future. It would be impractical for Canada to adopt a more British type of system. But there is much to learn from that system, especially for those who, as Canadian industrial conflict continues at its high level, believe that formal regulation is the answer. On the British side, there is much to learn from the Canadian situation. As the nature of British industry changes, as the average workplace size shrinks, as the typical work group moves from masses of blue-collar workers to small crews of white-collar workers then the old British model will start to disappear. Unless it can be replaced with a floor of protections such as exist in Canada, British unions and British workers will be in big trouble.

References

Burawoy, M. (1979) *The Politics of Production*, Verso, London.

Burawoy, M. (1985) *Manufacturing Consent: Changes in the Labor Process under Monopoly Capitalism*, University of Chicago Press.

Cameron, D. R. (1984) 'Social Democracy, Corporatism, Labour Quiescence and the Representation of Economic Interest in Advanced Capitalist Society', in J. H. Goldthorpe (Ed.) *Order and Conflict in Contemporary Capitalism*, Clarendon, Oxford, pp. 143–78.

Clegg, H. (1976) *Trade Unionism under Collective Bargaining*, Blackwell, Oxford.

Collins, H. (1982) 'Capitalist Discipline and Corporatist Law', *The Industrial Law Journal*, Vol. 11, p. 170.

Doeringer, P. and Piore, M. (1971) *Internal Labor Markets and Manpower Analysis*, D. C. Heath, Lexington, Mass.

Edwards, P. K. (1986) *Conflict at Work*, Blackwell, Oxford.

England, G. (1983) 'Some Observations on Selected Strike Laws', in K. P. Swan and K. E. Swinton (Eds) *Studies in Labour Law*, Butterworth, Toronto.

Gallie, D. (1978) *In Search of the New Working Class*, Cambridge University Press.

Glasbeek, H. (1984) 'The Utility of Model-Building – Collins' Capitalist Discipline and Corporatist Law', *The Industrial Law Journal*, Vol. 13, No. 3, pp. 133–52.

Gordon, D. M., Edwards, R. and Reich, M. (1982) *Segmented Work, Divided Workers: The Historical Transformation of Labor in the United States*, Cambridge University Press.

Haiven, L. (1988) *The Political Apparatuses of Production: Generation and Resolution of Industrial Conflict in Canada and Britain*, Ph.D. thesis, University of Warwick.

Hibbs, D. A. (1976) 'On the Political Economy of Long-Run Trends in Strike Activity', *British Journal of Political Science*, Vol. 8.

Hibbs, D. A. (1978) 'Industrial Conflict in Advanced Industrial Societies', *American Political Science Review*, Vol. 70.

Jamieson, S. (1973) *Industrial Relations in Canada*, 2nd Edition, St Martins Press, New York.

Kassalow, E. M. (1969) *Trade Unions and Industrial Relations: An International Comparison*, Random House, New York.

Kerr, Clark, Dunlop, J. T., Harbison, F. and Myers, C. A. (1960) *Industrialism and Industrial Management*, Penguin, Harmondsworth.

Korpi, W. and Shalev, M. (1979) 'Strikes, Industrial Relations and Class Conflict in Capitalist Societies', *British Journal of Sociology*, Vol. 30, pp. 164–87.

Kuhn, J. W. (1961) *Bargaining in Grievance Settlement: The Power of Industrial Work Groups*, Columbia University Press, New York.

Lacroix, R. (1986) 'Strike Activity in Canada', in Craig Riddell (Ed.) *Canadian Labour Relations*, University of Toronto Press.

Millward, N. and Stevens, M. (1986) *British Workplace Industrial Relations 1980–84*, Gower, Aldershot.

Phelps-Brown, H. (1986) *The Origins of Trade Union Power*, Oxford University Press.

Pizzorno, A. (1978) 'Political Exchange and Collective Identity in Industrial Conflict', in C. Crouch and A. Pizzorno (Eds) *The Resurgence of Class Conflict in Europe Since 1968, Vol. 2, Comparative Studies*, Macmillan, Lonodn.

Ross, A. M. and Hartman, P. T. (1960) *Changing Patterns of Industrial Conflict*, John Wiley, New York.

Shalev, M. (1980) 'Industrial Relations Theory and the Comparative Study of Industrial Relations and Industrial Conflict', *British Journal of Industrial Relations*, Vol. 18, pp. 26–43.

Shalev, M. (1983) 'Strikes and the Crisis: Industrial Conflict and Unemployment in the Western Nations', *Economic and Industrial Democracy*, Vol. 4, pp. 417–60.

Shorter, E. and Tilly, C. (1974) *Strikes in France: 1830–1968*, Cambridge University Press.

Snyder, D. (1975) 'Institutional Setting and Industrial Conflict: Comparative Analyses of France, Italy and the United States', *American Sociological Review*, Vol. 40.

12

Perceptions of labour conciliation in Hong Kong and Singapore

A comparative replication

PAUL KIRKBRIDE, ANDY LAI and CHRIS LEGGETT

Conciliation has been officially acknowledged as 'one of the key institutions of today's industrial relations systems' and as having 'displaced other dispute settlement procedures as the main government instrument for maintaining industrial peace' (ILO, 1983, p. 1). In Hong Kong conciliation developed in an *ad hoc* fashion without legal underpinning. However, with the passing of the Labour Relations Ordinance in 1975, this changed and conciliation has become both a legally regulated and formally structured procedure. At the end of the 1970s England and Rear (1981, p. 321) noted that in Hong Kong 'ordinary conciliation remains the essential and most heavily used method for resolving disputes' and as such represents 'the central role now played by the Labour Department in Hong Kong's system of industrial relations'; a development consistent with the International Labour Office's observation of a worldwide trend. Defined as 'a procedure for the settlement of labour disputes which is aimed at helping the parties to the dispute to reduce their differences and achieve agreement' (ILO, 1983, p. 1), 'conciliation' as surveyed in the studies of both Singapore and Hong Kong reported here includes 'mediation', whereby the third party may advance new proposals for the disputants to consider rather than simply facilitate reconciliation with the existing ones.

Given the current centrality of conciliation in Hong Kong and the increasing interest in comparative studies of industrial relations, the authors sought to examine the separate perceptions of Hong Kong's conciliation service by disputants and the Labour Department's conciliators and compare the results with a similar survey made in Singapore in 1984 (Krislov and Leggett, 1985). Of particular interest were: (1) the general level of acceptance of conciliation by the parties, (2) the possible differences in perception among the parties to the conciliation process, (3) the degree of confidence in the conciliators felt by labour and by employers. With these focuses the survey constituted an audit of the Hong Kong Labour Department's conciliation service, as had the earlier survey of the Singapore Ministry of Labour's service.

Country studies of conciliation accumulated during the 1970s and there have been some attempts at comparative analyses, mostly initiated by Professor Joseph Krislov of the University of Kentucky (Goodman and Krislov, 1974; Krislov and Galin, 1979; Krislov and Leggett, 1985). While these studies have dealt mainly with European conciliation services, comparative studies of conciliation among the Asian countries of the Asia-Pacific region are unknown to the authors. Consequently, it was apposite for them to compare perceptions of conciliation in Singapore with those in Hong Kong, city-states with sufficient socio-economic similarities to make the exercise academically justifiable.

Some environmental features of industrial relations in Hong Kong and Singapore

Both city-states, the sovereign Singapore and the British dependent territory of Hong Kong, are commonly linked by observers with Taiwan and South Korea as the newly industrialised countries (NICs) of East Asia and distinguished from Thailand, Malaysia, the Philippines and Indonesia by the extent of their industrialisation and economic development. Of the 'gang of four' (Harris, 1987), as they are sometimes waggishly called, only Singapore's independent political status remains unchallenged, and Hong Kong is destined to become a 'Special Administrative Zone' of the People's Republic of China (PRC) in 1997, albeit with a pledged capitalist economy for 50 years.

With 1,071 square kilometres of land and 5.7 million persons, Hong Kong's population at 5,322 per square kilometre is substantially denser than Singapore's, with 4,193 per square kilometre (land area 620 square kilometres and population 2.6 million), and even denser than the figures indicate because of the greater extent of the former's usable land. Singapore's and Hong Kong's workforce participation rates at 46 and 47 per cent respectively compare, but are distributed differently by sectors: Singapore's commerce and services employ 58 per cent of the workforce compared with Hong Kong's 40 per cent, but both record 35 per cent in manufacturing. Surprisingly, given the different political ideologies of the two governments, but significantly for industrial relations, Hong Kong and Singapore respectively employ 7 and 6 per cent of their workforces in government and public authorities. However, Hong Kong, with more than twice Singapore's population, in 1986 recorded public expenditure of US$5.12 billion as against Singapore's US$7.4 billion. In 1987 per capita income was US$8,292 in Hong Kong and US$7,325 in Singapore, surpassed only by Japan (substantially, with US$20,833) and Australia (marginally, with US$9,188) in the Asia-Pacific region (Far Eastern Economic Review, 1988, 1989).

Ethnically Singapore is less homogeneous than Hong Kong, with the latter's population of 98 per cent Chinese being substantially Cantonese. Singapore's 76 per cent Chinese are divided by dialects, although the government has had some success in promoting Mandarin as the national Chinese language. Fifteen per cent of Singaporeans are Malays and 6.4 per cent Indians, mostly Tamils.

In each state the population is mostly of immigrant origin – substantially from post-Second World War migrations in Hong Kong. In spite of Singapore's ethnic heterogeneity, all of the 'gang of four' have inherited Confucianist cultural milieux, a fact acknowledged by the Singapore government's selective immigration policy, its requirement for genetic quality and racial balance in procreation and its secondary schools' moral education syllabus (Wilkinson and Leggett, 1985).

Whereas Hong Kong has come close to the neo-classical model of an economy with only minimal state intervention, Singapore's economy and society have been substantially state-directed, some claim even engineered (Wilkinson, 1988). While it is easy to understate the role of government in Hong Kong and to overstate it in Singapore, the Hong Kong government's self-styled 'positive non-intervention' and political analysts' classification of Singapore as an 'administrative state' (Chee, 1981) signal the contrast, and beg the question of its pertinence to the quality of industrial relations in each state.

Industrial relations in Hong Kong and Singapore

Independent observers are virtually unanimous in emphasising the dominant role of the People's Action Party (PAP) government in shaping, maintaining and developing the character of Singapore's industrial relations after the PAP's creation of the National Trades Union Congress (NTUC) in 1962 to rival the 'leftist' Singapore Association of Trade Unions (SATU). Already, a legal framework for the orderly management of industrial conflict had been established by the 1960 Industrial Relations Act with its provisions for compulsory, judicial arbitration by Industrial Arbitration Courts (IACs) and for conciliation by the Ministry of Labour, and in 1968 the potential for confrontational industrial relations was reduced by the curtailment of collective bargaining, procedurally and substantively, by the combined effects of the Industrial Relations (Amendment) Act and the Employment Act. The former legally sanctioned the exercise of managerial prerogatives and made the minimum terms and conditions of employment laid down in the latter the mandatory maximum for the bulk of the workforce.

Although the curtailment of collective bargaining depressed trade union membership in Singapore, the tripartite constitution of the authoritative National Wages Council (NWC) on which there is representation of both national and multinational employers' associations which was established in 1973 to set annual pay settlement guidelines restored the credibility of the NTUC until membership peaked in 1979. Corporatist controls and proscriptions in the Trade Disputes Act and the Criminal Law (Temporary Provisions) Act ensured the orderly resolution of disputes and Singapore remained strike-free between 1977 and 1986. In 1986, however, the NTUC did endorse an affiliate's strike over employer victimization, but the intention was to signal to employers not to act independently at a time when unions were being required to forgo pay rises among a package of government cost-cutting measures to deal with a temporary recession. Such unions as might have been tempted to deviate from public policy had only to recall the deregistration in 1980 of the non-NTUC Singapore Airline Pilots Association for illegally working to rule and the ignominy meted out to leaders of NTUC affiliates who had recently carped at the prospect of restructuring their unions along house lines in compliance with an official policy of emulation of Japanese practice (Leggett 1984, 1988). Singapore's trade unions had already been required to amend their constitutions and reregister under the Trade Unions (Amendment) Act of 1982, which redefined the objects of trade unions to include the promotion of productivity and 'good' human relations. Significantly, and in contrast to Hong Kong, Singapore's Registrar of Trade Unions is a civil servant in the Labour Ministry accountable to the Minister.

In spite of the legal and corporatist constraints, including NWC guidelines, collective bargaining in Singapore remains an integral part of a highly regulated industrial relations system. Collective agreements are monitored and registered by the IAC and, with few exceptions, an employer is required by law to recognise and bargain in good faith with a registered trade union which has the support of a majority of eligible employees. The process is simplified by the intentional avoidance of multi-unionism – through the rules governing union registration and the NTUC's authority over its affiliates. Declining union membership was once again reversed in the mid-1980s as worker complacency was shaken by the prospect of retrenchments and negotiable redundancy payments, and as the pressures to Japanise employment relations were relaxed.

In contrast to Singapore, industrial relations in Hong Kong are characterised by the limited role of government. As Turner et al. (1980) have noted:

> Perhaps the most distinctive peculiarity of Hong Kong however, considering it as an industrial rather than an 'under-developed' economy – and one which distinguishes it from its twin-city state of Singapore (which is otherwise marked by not totally dissimilar features of high growth, uneven development, a Chinese cultural foundation overlaid by ethnic diversity, and so on) – is that the socio-political development which has generally accompanied industrialisation in non-communist societies is much less apparent.
>
> (Turner et al., 1980, p. 6)

Indeed, the self-styled 'positive non-intervention' approach of the Hong Kong government generally contrasts with the highly regulatory role of the Singapore government. For industrial relations England and Rear (1981, p. 321) have interpreted 'positive non-intervention' to mean 'the absence of a tight legal framework for the determination of wages and conditions of work and the reliance instead upon the provision of administrative machinery which facilitates agreement and assists in dispute settlement'. In other words, Hong Kong's industrial relations are characterised by a lack of legalism and are presented, at least by the government, as an expressed preference by the parties for the kind of voluntarism that was once said to typify British industrial relations (Flanders, 1970). Nevertheless, albeit cautiously, the Hong Kong government has, since the late 1960s, extended its limited role in the regulation of industrial relations.

A variety of factors have contributed to the Hong Kong government's modification of its non-interventionist strategy with regard to industrial relations. These have included the changing expectations of the workforce for a better lifestyle as Hong Kong has economically developed, criticism of labour standards in Hong Kong from overseas, and, probably, a slight ideological shift by the government itself. Thus, the 1972 Labour Tribunal Ordinance provides for the adjudication of rights disputes under a contract of employment and the 1975 Labour Relations Ordinance extended the government's role in the regulation of collective relations by providing for special conciliation, arbitration and commissions of enquiry. However, there is no provision for compelling employers either to recognise or bargain in good faith with a trade union which can demonstrate it has a mandate from employees to act as their bargaining agent. Consequently, formal collective bargaining, although it exists, is not characteristic of industrial relations in Hong Kong.

Conciliation in Singapore

Collective bargaining and dispute settlement in Singapore operate in a climate described as 'non-adversarial' or 'congenial' (Anantaraman, 1984; Krislov and Leggett,1984). Wilkinson (1986, p. 111) has observed that 'open industrial conflict has been all but eliminated with the help of the NTUC leadership "closely aligned" with the ruling PAP government since its rise to power in the late 1950s'. Although industrial disputes are defined (as trade disputes) by the Trade Disputes Act and conciliated by the Labour Relations Division of the Ministry of Labour and, much less often, adjudicated by the IAC, the NTUC's Industrial Relations Secretariat vets its affiliates' disputes before deciding to give a go-ahead to use the official machinery. Likewise the Labour Relations Division through its Labour Information Service practises 'preventive mediation', whereby its specialised officers anticipate and head off disputes. As the NTUC Secretary-General and Second Deputy Prime Minister put it in 1984 to an NTUC delegates' conference:

> Although conciliation and arbitration is [sic] less disruptive [than a strike], it is already a sad state of affairs when workers and their employers have to iron out their difference by arguing it out before a third party. Even though

the conciliation and arbitration machinery is intended for settling disputes in a non-disruptive manner, a need to make use of this machinery indicates an unhealthy relation between the workers and their employers.

(Krislov and Leggett, 1985; p. 179)

In addition to the climate of congeniality the non-disruptive quality of Singapore's collective bargaining may be attributed to amendments to the Industrial Relations Act in 1968, referred to above, which substantially restricted the scope of collective bargaining by specifying that in new industrial undertakings after 1968 no collective agreement could contain provisions with regard to terms and conditions of service that were more favourable to employees than those minima contained in Part IV of the Employment Act of 1968 and the sanctioning of managerial prerogatives by making it illegal for a trade union to raise matters for collective bargaining concerning the hiring, placement, promotion, non-detrimental transfer, retrenchment, dismissal and reinstatement of an employee.

Singapore's labour legislation distinguishes unionised from non-unionised dispute procedures. The Employment Act, although not confined to this, regulates how non-unionised disputes are to be settled by the Ministry of Labour while the Industrial Relations Act regulates collective bargaining procedures. The Ministry of Labour – in effect the Labour Relations Division – is empowered to arrange for the services of a conciliation officer where negotiation has failed to produce an agreement. Should voluntary conciliation fail, the Minister of Labour may then call a compulsory conference of the parties, at which they may be represented by professionals (including lawyers).

In spite of the official sentiment and the legal constraints on the scope of collective bargaining, the Labour Relations Division of the Ministry of Labour has continued to play a significant role in collective bargaining and dispute settlement, although the number of trade disputes declined in the 1980s. During the decade 1978 to 1987 the conciliation caseload of the Labour Relations Division averaged 551 and declined from 947 in 1979 to 347 in 1987, while the settlement success rate averaged 79 per cent, the rest either being withdrawn or in a few cases referred to the IAC. By far the largest number of cases each year concerned wage increases, the others being disputes over retrenchment benefits, bonuses and non-classified matters (Ministry of Labour, 1976–87).

Conciliation in Hong Kong

Hong Kong's 1975 Labour Relations Ordinance interprets conciliation as 'a discussion or action initiated or undertaken by a conciliation officer to assist the parties to a trade dispute to reach a settlement of the trade dispute', thus allowing for 'mediation'. It may be argued that conciliation is a culturally preferred mode of conflict resolution in Chinese societies (Tang and Kirkbride, 1986; Kirkbride, Tang and Westwood, 1988). A common traditional practice in China was for a respected village elder to 'arbitrate' (or conciliate) local disputes in remote districts far from access to formal judicial authority. While arbitration and conciliation are different processes they both require the intervention of a respected third party perceived by the disputants as able fairly to resolve or assist in the resolution of a dispute.

Officers of Hong Kong's Labour Department practised conciliation before there was a statutory requirement for them to do so and developed it into 'a procedure which although without any legal standing had grown over the years to be an accepted part of the service provided by the Department . . . not available however unless asked for by one of the parties in dispute, and not workable unless accepted by the other' (England and Rear, 1981, p. 321). With the Labour Department before 1967 being likened to a 'casualty department', from 1967 conciliation officers began to take on more preventive roles, initiating contacts with disputants rather than waiting for invitations. Rather than simply firefighting the conciliation officers began to arrange meetings, conduct investigations, explain the law and generally facilitate the achievement of agreement. Nevertheless, such activities required at least the tacit consent of the parties in dispute. However, observers of industrial relations in Hong Kong in the late 1970s suggested that the conciliators were performing a distinctly mediatory function. They reported that:

> Advice offered by the Labour Relations Service (of the Labour Department) in cases of industrial disagreements has certainly gone beyond information on the legal position of the parties, and arranging meetings (itself often a difficult business, involving telling workers how to appoint representatives and persuading managers or employers to meet them on a basis of formal equality), or acting as a go-between and neutral chairman. It has extended to suggesting possible terms of settlement, to insisting that they be recorded in some written form, and to consistently attempting to attach agreement on future grievance procedure to the reconciliation of the immediate issues in the conflict.
>
> (Turner *et al.*, 1980, p. 6)

Conciliation may be undertaken by a single third party or by a number of conciliators, the latter to be distinguished in Hong Kong from the exceptional boards of enquiry into disputes referred by the Governor-in-Council. Virtually all labour conciliation in Hong Kong is conducted by individual officers of the Labour Department. This mode of conciliation is recommended by the International Labour Organisation because of the flexibility it offers the conciliator and the disputants. In summary, conciliation in Hong Kong is characterised by voluntary participation, informal proceedings, the use of individual conciliators and non-legally binding agreements. The contrast with

Singapore lies with that country's provision for compulsory conciliation and legally enforceable agreements which must comply in content with certain substantive prescriptions in the labour legislation.

A trade dispute in Hong Kong is defined in the 1975 Labour Relations Ordinance, and there are two types which may be referred to the Labour Department. One, termed 'dispute', is when the conflict involves many employees and there is the possibility of industrial action. Such disputes are not numerous – for example, 205 in 1986 involving 16,813 employees – and are often dealt with by the conciliation officer taking the initiative. The other disputes, which are numerous (21,608 in 1986), are termed 'claims' and comprise small-scale conflicts both over rights and interests. Claimants are individuals who seek the intervention of the Labour Department to conciliate their grievances. Most cases (61 per cent in 1986) are settled by Labour Department conciliation but a substantial number (24 per cent in 1986) may be referred to a Labour Tribunal (Department of Labour, 1986).

The distinction is similar to that between unionised and non-unionised disputes in Singapore. However, the procedural arrangements for each are clearly prescribed, separately administered and reflect the greater parts played by trade unions and collective bargaining in the industrial relations of Singapore.

The Hong Kong survey

Modifications to suit the Hong Kong context were made to the questionnaire used in the earlier Singapore survey. As with the Singapore questionnaire, the Hong Kong questionnaire comprised three sections of forced-choice statements with which the respondents were asked to 'agree', 'disagree' or indicate that they were 'undecided' (see Appendix 12.1).

The first sections contained ten statements and one question concerned with general attitudes towards conciliation, the statements being taken from the same section in the Singapore survey. The added question was of the appropriateness of compulsory conciliation. The second section contained the same ten statements as in the second section of the Singapore questionnaire and which were intended to elicit views on specific conciliation techniques. The third section, not administered to the conciliation officers, sought disputing parties' perceptions of the performance of the conciliation officers. It comprised 12 statements of which eight were from the same section of the Singapore questionnaire. To them were added four statements concerning the benefits of avoiding negotiation, the time-saving benefits of conciliation, satisfaction with the results of conciliation, and the prospect of using the conciliation service again.

In the Singapore survey questionnaires were mailed to union and employer spokesmen who had been involved in cases during the fiscal year 1982–3 and distributed to all 11 conciliation officers in the service at the time. Usable responses were received from 141 union representatives, 100 employer representatives and all 11 conciliation officers. A replication of this process in Hong Kong was not possible due to the need to maintain confidentiality and not identify parties to 'claims'. Instead, after discussions with the Labour Department, it was decided to administer the questionnaire to the disputants and conciliation officers at the point and time of the conciliation.

Between 9 and 27 March 1987 student assistants from the City Polytechnic of Hong Kong were stationed at six of the nine branch offices of the Department of Labour's Labour Relations Service – at Kwun Tong, Kwai Hing, Kowloon West, Kowloon South, Hong Kong East and Hong Kong West – selected to cover all Hong Kong and for being the busiest offices. The questionnaires were administered only after the completion of the conciliation, when both parties to the claim were present and when both gave their consent. A total of 365 usable responses were collected from employee representatives and 209 from employer representatives, the difference being accounted for by there sometimes being more than one employee representative per claim.

In addition, it was decided to mail the questionnaires to trade unions who often represent individual workers in cases handled by the Labour Relations Service. Of the 448 trade unions in Hong Kong 199 were excluded as they were either civil service unions (154), employers' associations (30) or mixed associations of employees and employers (15). Thus questionnaires were sent to the remaining 249 unions for completion. Ninety-six usable questionnaires were returned, representing a response rate of 38.5 per cent. These responses can be loosely included in the worker side, leading to a total of 461 responses for each question, divided into 'worker respondents' and 'trade union respondents' categories. Employer respondents are categorised by size of firm, measured by number of employees, from 'less than 50' to '51 – 200' and '200 plus'.

Conciliators are defined as officers of the Labour Relations Division of the Labour Department authorised by the Commissioner for Labour to initiate or undertake conciliation. As it is the practice that all officers in the Labour Officer (LO) grade are posted at least once in their careers to the Labour Relations Division, it was decided not to confine the survey to the then current staff of the Labour Relations Service. At the time of the survey the Labour Department included 57 labour officers (LOs) and 114 assistant labour officers on its staff. Thus 171 questionnaires were mailed to these officers with experience of conciliation duties. A total of 61 valid responses were returned representing a response rate of 35.7 per cent.

Analysis of the results

Attitudes towards conciliation

Interest here is with how the contrasts and similarities between Singapore and Hong Kong may be reflected in the general attitudes towards conciliation. Table 12.1 represents the responses from both the Hong Kong and the Singapore surveys.

Table 12.1 Attitudes towards conciliation in Hong Kong (HK) and Singapore (S)

Statement/ question		Labour/employers/conciliators (%)			
		Agree	Undecided	Disagree	N.R.
1.1	HK	55/44/1	17/12/9	28/44/90	
	S	45/26/0	3/3/0	52/71/100	
1.2	HK	40/21/5	18/25/5	42/54/90	
	S	13/17/0	7/7/0	79/76/100	
1.3	HK	37/83/72	33/3/5	30/14/23	
	S	75/79/73	11/8/0	14/13/27	
1.4	HK	77/54/94	13/27/0	10/19/6	
	S	91/69/82	7/18/0	2/11/18	0/2/0
1.5	HK	48/47/51	28/28/10	24/25/39	
	S	31/18/0	4/20/9	65/62/91	
1.6	HK	38/33/16	41/38/24	21/29/60	
	S	25/16/0	15/26/9	60/56/91	0/2/0
1.7	HK	77/75/89	11/14/0	12/11/11	
	S	85/86/91	4/11/0	11/3/9	
1.8	HK	25/24/0	17/20/6	58/56/94	
	S	23/29/0	9/19/0	67/52/100	
1.9	HK	33/44/2	29/31/11	38/25/87	
	S	1/5/0	5/11/0	98/84/94	
1.10	HK	48/44/41	36/41/21	16/15/38	
	S	94/75/80	6/16/10	0/9/10	

Number of respondents	Hong Kong	Singapore
Labour	461	141
Employers	209	100
Conciliators	61	11

Note: Singapore data from Krislov and Leggett (1985)

From the data for some statements (1.2, 1.5, 1.6, 1.9 and 1.10) there appear to be distinct differences in the pattern of responses, while for other statements (1.4, 1.7 and 1.8) the responses are almost the same.

The responses to statement 1.4 show that in both countries a high percentage of conciliators and labour representatives see the labour side in a dispute as generally accepting the services of a conciliator. Equally, in both countries, employers are rather more sceptical but still positive (Krislov and Leggett, 1985).

Similarly, in relation to statement 1.7 there is an overwhelming agreement by all parties in both countries that the conciliation service has reduced the number of cases referred for arbitration to either the Industrial Arbitration Court (Singapore) or the Labour Tribunal (Hong Kong). Finally, there is general agreement that the conciliation process actually achieves results and has a positive effect on outcomes (1.8). Not surprisingly, in both countries this is the view of the conciliators themselves. However, there is a sizeable minority of both labour and employer respondents in both countries who feel that conciliation has little or no effect.

For statements 1.1 and 1.3 there are only slight differences. In both Hong Kong and Singapore virtually all conciliators disagreed with the statement that the need for a conciliator is a sign of immaturity on the part of management or labour. However, in Singapore there was also very high disagreement from employer respondents, whereas in Hong Kong employer respondents were divided. In Hong Kong the majority of labour respondents agreed with the statement, whereas in Singapore there was an almost equal division with a slight leaning towards disagreement. In general this seems to signal a greater perception in Hong Kong of the labour relations systems as 'immature' and 'under-developed'. The one difference concerns the labour respondents: Hong Kong labour respondents were divided, but generally sceptical, whereas in Singapore they were as positive as the conciliators and the employers.

There were some major differences in responses to statement 1.2. In Singapore there was a strong feeling among both labour and employer respondents that the stronger party in a dispute would co-operate with conciliation. However, in Hong Kong employers were not so convinced and labour respondents were relatively unconvinced. The implication of this could be that in Singapore, as Krislov and Leggett (1985) note, conciliation is preferred to direct confrontation, perhaps as a result of the 'congenial' industrial relations system. In the *laissez-faire* system of Hong Kong there is less pressure on companies to be 'non-confrontational' and thus a greater tendency to attempt to resolve labour matters by managerial fiat and a greater incidence of rejection of conciliation.

In Hong Kong a small majority of respondents held that conciliation works best for small companies or unions, whereas in Singapore the general view was the opposite. This divergence of view is particularly marked in the case of conciliators, with 51 per cent in Hong Kong agreeing with the statement (1.5) and in Singapore 91 per cent disagreeing. Krislov and Leggett (1985) suggest the Singapore response is perhaps not so surprising in view of the fact that the alternative of industrial action by a union against a large company is unlikely to be allowed by either the government or the National Trades Union Congress. Stronger support for the statement in Hong Kong may be explained by the predominance of small firms and the acceptance of government authority. Small firms may feel compelled to participate in government-sponsored conciliation even though it is supposed to be 'voluntary'. Larger firms may be more willing to encourage confrontation and resist conciliation, especially in view of the general weakness of trade unions in Hong Kong.

In Singapore, where multinational companies are typically the larger employers, the pattern of responses to statement 1.6 paralleled those to the previous statement. However, the responses in Hong Kong were much more mixed (esepcially from labour and employer respondents) with a high percentage of respondents undecided. This could perhaps be a result of the lower exposure of many of the respondents to multinationals and the different response pattern of the conciliators could reflect their greater exposure.

The Singapore parties were virtually unanimous in arguing that the Industrial Arbitration Court did not discourage collective bargaining and conciliation. This correlates with a similar response pattern to statement 1.7, Krislov and Legget (1985, p. 183) having remarked that: 'It would seem that the parties regard the Industrial Arbitration Court . . . as very much a last resort and share a strong faith in the efficiency of the official conciliation service.' In contrast to their common response to statement 1.7 the Hong Kong respondents were divided over the effect of the Labour Tribunal on collective bargaining and conciliation. There was strong support from the conciliators for the statement that the Labour Tribunal did not discourage collective bargaining and conciliation, but the labour and employer respondents were almost evenly divided. The reason for this is explained by the different nature of the two bodies in question. In Singapore the IAC is a permanent arbitration mechanism adjudicating on disputes referred to it by the parties or government, and the process is compulsory and the awards legally binding. It is headed by a president with the status of a High Court judge who, depending on the nature of the case, sits either alone or with representatives of employers and unions. The IAC's role includes resolving key disputes and monitoring and certifying all collective agreements. In Hong Kong the Labour Tribunal provides a procedurally informal mechanism for the resolution of claims arising out of employment and is confined to hearing claims for sums of money, mostly for wages in lieu of notice.

It would seem that many Hong Kong respondents view the Labour Tribunal as an efficient mechanism for the settlement of claims and as preferable to collective bargaining or conciliation. Both parties are quite happy to resort to the Tribunal, perhaps because of its easy, informal, non-legalistic style. However, England and Rear (1981) have observed that the Tribunal over time has become more formal in its approach and has substituted a courtroom for its conference table format. They further point out that the previous style

> appeared to foster the misconception among many litigants that the tribunal was a section of the Labour Department and that they had come along for further negotiations. This impression was strengthened by the name of the Tribunal in Chinese – *Loo Chee Sum Choi Chu* – which bore similarities

to the name of the Department — known as *Loo Chee Kwan Hai For*. Despite the increased formality the tribunal is still reasonably relaxed and informal in the way it goes about its business.

(England and Rear, 1981, p. 321)

Statement 1.10 was included in the Singapore questionnaire because, unlike 'conciliation services in other countries which focus almost entirely on the voluntary resolution of collective bargaining disputes, the conciliation service in Singapore is required to perform other tasks . . . [which] . . . include the settlement of "dismissal without just cause" allegations, union recognition claims, and "refusal to negotiate" disputes' (Krislov and Leggett, 1985). The researchers considered leaving out this question because such disputes are extremely rare in Hong Kong and the conciliation service and its legal context are different from Singapore. In the end it was decided to keep it in for comparative purposes. The responses show a lack of agreement with this type of intervention by the conciliators, perhaps as a result of lack of expertise of such cases or because they are seen as outside the normal scope of conciliation. Some respondents from both sides did, however, accept such a potential role for the Labour Relations Service.

Views on conciliation techniques

Table 12.2 presents the responses to the section of the questionnaire concerned with the parties' views on conciliation techniques.

In both Hong Kong and Singapore labour and employer respondents to statement 2.5 agreed that conciliation should be restricted to issues raised by themselves as opposed to issues raised by the conciliator. However, in Singapore conciliators appear to take a more 'proactive' view than their Hong Kong counterparts, although the difference is small. Similarly, both the parties in Hong Kong and Singapore were generally supportive of the notion that a conciliator should gain approval from both parties prior to making suggestions at a joint negotiating session (2.6). This support was rather more pronounced in Singapore than in Hong Kong but both countries' conciliators were divided, with the Hong Kong respondents just supporting the view. Both sets of conciliators rejected the view that they should act as a simple 'conduit' or as an intermediate negotiator for the parties. However, it appears that both labour and employer respondents preferred the conciliators in this role. Consistently, then, for statements 2.5, 2.6 and 2.10 there is little difference between the two countries, but for statements 2.1, 2.2, 2.3, 2.4 and 2.9 differences emerge.

Both labour and employer respondents in Hong Kong were more convinced that conciliation techniques could easily be learned than their counterparts were in Singapore, while conciliators in Singapore were much more dismissive than those in Hong Kong (2.1). In Hong Kong conciliators were strongly convinced

Table 12.2 Views on conciliation techniques in Hong Kong (HK) and Singapore (S)

Statement/ question		Agree	Labour/employers/conciliators (%) Undecided	Disagree	N.R.
2.1	HK	83/82/35	12/10/8	5/8/57	
	S	52/52/18	10/15/0	38/30/82	0/3/0
2.2	HK	24/28/5	31/26/5	45/46/90	
	S	63/25/27	2/13/9	35/61/64	0/1/0
2.3	HK	44/38/21	15/18/6	41/44/73	
	S	30/34/0	5/7/18	65/58/82	0/1/0
2.4	HK	45/33/74	26/23/13	29/44/13	
	S	82/63/73	0/19/27	18/17/0	0/1/0
2.5	HK	74/75/49	9/10/10	16/15/41	
	S	68/86/36	4/2/0	28/11/64	0/1/0
2.6	HK	54/59/57	12/7/5	34/34/38	
	S	70/67/45	4/2/9	26/30/45	0/1/0
2.7	HK	39/31/11	17/13/9	44/56/80	
	S	72/46/63	7/11/9	21/41/27	0/2/0
2.8	HK	33/27/54	20/18/11	47/55/35·	
	S	71/64/82	16/11/0	13/23/18	0/2/0
2.9	HK	52/52/48	15/14/3	33/34/49	
	S	67/49/18	3/16/0	30/31/82	0/4/0
2.10	HK	54/49/10	20/29/11	26/22/79	
	S	74/49/18	2/5/9	23/44/73	0/2/0

Number of respondents	Hong Kong	Singapore
Labour	461	141
Employers	209	100
Conciliators	61	11

Note: Singapore data from Krislov and Leggett (1985)

that their skills could be taught and the conciliators in Singapore agreed but with less conviction. The other major difference on this statement (2.2) was that the labour respondents in Singapore were more convinced that the skills could not be taught than were their Hong Kong counterparts. Interesting differences on statement 2.3 were the generally higher levels of disagreement by labour and employer respondents in Singapore and the total rejection of the statement by the Singapore conciliators, demonstrating that the Hong Kong respondents were generally more willing to view the simple presence of a conciliator as an aid to agreement. Concerning the degree of force to be used by the conciliator (2.4), the labour respondents in Singapore were more inclined to the view that the conciliator should be forceful than were the Hong Kong labour respondents. While Singapore employers generally supported a forceful role for the conciliator the Hong Kong employers generally rejected it. Finally, with statement 2.9 the higher level of Singapore conciliator disagreement is noted. They almost all seemed to feel that a conciliator should not hesitate to call for a separation of the parties even if the possibility of agreement was not high. The conciliators in Hong Kong were equally divided, with 48 per cent preferring to hesitate.

On two statements, 2.7 and 2.8, there is a clear divergence in the response patterns between the two countries. Eighty per cent of Hong Kong conciliators believed that they should not aggressively support the position of one or other of the parties. Thus they preferred an 'even-handed' neutral role. In contrast, only 27 per cent of the Singapore respondents preferred this approach, with 63 per cent taking a more partisan aggressive approach. This view was mirrored by the labour and employer respondents in Singapore. A similar pattern emerged in response to statement 2.8, where the Singaporeans generally preferred a more vigorous approach. This was rejected by the labour and employer respondents in Hong Kong and only moderately supported by the Hong Kong conciliators.

It appears, then, that the general Hong Kong view of the conciliation process is a preference for a more restrained, neutral and non-directive approach in contradistinction to the Singaporean preference for an aggressive and interventionist style. These differences reflect the different styles of the governments, with the Singapore government being more directive and the Hong Kong government being more *laissez-faire* and non-interventionist. Perhaps as a consequence of these perceptions the parties in Hong Kong tended to have a lower regard for the skills of the conciliators.

Views of the conciliators

Responses by labour and management to statements about the conciliator are presented in Table 12.3.

Here there is only one statement (3.1) where the responses show major differences in views between the two countries. The Hong Kong respondents were almost unanimous in saying that the conciliator pressed them for a solution to the issue. This, of course, does not match their preferred styles of conciliation, characterised above as neutral and non-directive. To a certain extent this response could signal differences in expectations between the conciliators and the parties. On the other hand, it could be a question of perception. As the Hong Kong parties prefer and expect a neutral conciliator, they might tend to view any active role by the conciliator as strong pressure. The Singapore respondents, who prefer and expect a more assertive style, are more likely to perceive the same level of pressure as less assertive. This conjecture seems to be supported by the Singapore data.

There were also some minor differences among the responses to statements 3.3 and 3.6. Hong Kong respondents strongly agreed that the conciliator helped them to understand the other party's position while much greater numbers of the Singapore respondents (34 per cent labour and 26 per cent employers) did not agree with the statement. Both countries' employer respondents claimed that the conciliator had a wealth of knowledge of conciliation. However, support

Table 12.3 Views of the conciliator: Hong Kong (HK) and Singapore (S)

Statement/ question		Labour/employers (%)			
		Agree	Undecided	Disagree	N.R.
3.1	HK	84/86	9/7	7/7	
	S	47/43	3/6	50/44	0/7
3.2	HK	81/89	12/10	7/1	
	S	82/74	6/6	11/12	0/8
3.3	HK	77/85	14/9	9/6	
	S	60/57	6/9	34/26	0/8
3.4	HK	49/49	27/28	24/23	
	S	57/34	6/18	37/38	0/10
3.5	HK	68/64	21/26	11/10	
	S	73/76	16/8	10/9	0/7
3.6	HK	70/61	23/24	7/5	
	S	47/58	29/28	23/6	0/8
3.7	HK	74/75	16/15	10/10	
	S	71/72	25/14	4/8	0/6
3.8	HK	74/80	13/12	13/8	
	S	70/76	15/11	14/8	0/5

Number of respondents	Hong Kong	Singapore
Labour	461	141
Employers	209	100

Note: Singapore data from Krislov and Leggett (1985)

for this statement was much stronger from Hong Kong labour respondents (70 per cent) than for Singapore (47 per cent), and a large number of Singapore respondents (23 per cent) actually disagreed.

For statements 3.2, 3.4, 3.5, 3.7 and 3.8 responses were almost identical in Hong Kong and Singapore. Both parties in both countries saw the conciliator as making constructive suggestions (3.2), as understanding the complexity of the issue (3.5), as showing no favouritism (3.7) and as preventing the referral of the dispute to the Labour Tribunal/Industrial Arbitration Court (3.8). Neither country's respondents were convinced that the conciliator helped them to retreat from a difficult position (3.4), perhaps reflecting the key salience of 'face' in the dynamics of Chinese conflict and negotiation. In summary, both sets of respondents had very positive views towards their conciliator and the process of the conciliation process.

Conclusion

From the above analysis of the response data it is possible briefly to summarise the main findings. To do so it is necessary to return to the central issues raised at the start of this chapter. Of interest here is the general acceptance of the conciliation process in Hong Kong. On the basis of the data, especially with regard to the first part of the questionnaire, it can be fairly said that there is demonstrated general support for the voluntarist and non-compulsory system of conciliation. However, this general acceptance does preclude some differences between the parties and the process. On the whole there were few differences between labour and employer respondents. There were marked differences between worker representatives and trade union officials, with the latter less supportive of the system but concerned to maintain their role in the process. Not surprisingly the views of the conciliators themselves were often at odds with the disputing parties. They were naturally very supportive of the general system, had a high regard for their own skills and seemed to prefer an active role to one of passivity. The general support for the system is reflected in the high degree of confidence in the conciliators expressed by the parties. The acid test of any system or service is its repeated use and it was interesting to note the high levels of willingness to use the Hong Kong conciliation provisions. Against this, however, has to be set the realisation that, given the weakness of collective bargaining, for many claimants there is no viable alternative.

A potential difference between the 'pure' notion of conciliation and the more active role identified in Hong Kong by Turner et al. (1980) was noted above. Unfortunately the response data does not seem able to resolve this question. There is evidence of preferences for a 'neutral' minimalist approach in terms of opposition to compulsion (1.11), restriction of issues to ones suggested by the parties (2.5), the need for conciliators to seek approval before making suggestions (2.6) and rejection of vigorous conciliator support for one side (2.8). However, there is also evidence of preference for a more active role in terms of the conciliator acting as a spokesman for one side (2.10). It can, nevertheless, be seen that differences exist between the disputing parties and the conciliators, with the conciliators more in favour of an active approach. They rejected the passive catalyst approach (2.3), supported a forceful role (2.4), and favoured vigorous support for the position of one of the parties (2.8).

Turning to the perceptions of the actual behaviour of the conciliator by the parties, again a mixed picture emerges. There is evidence that the conciliators tended to be neutral (3.7) but also evidence that they were forceful (3.1) and made suggestions of a mediating kind (3.2). Overall it may be argued that while on balance the disputing parties appear to prefer the traditional neutral, passive and voluntary role, the conciliators, for whatever reason, tended to prefer a more active role and this would support the comment made by Turner et al. (1980).

In their overview of Singapore's labour relations context Krislov and Leggett (1985) generated three hypotheses concerning conciliation: 'first, there should be a considerable acceptance of conciliation. Second, all three parties, that is, labour, management and conciliators, should share basically similar attitudes to conciliation. Third, labour and management should indicate substantial confidence in the competence of the conciliators.' In relation to Hong Kong the authors feel able to accept the first and the last of these hypotheses, but, in terms of attitudes, note a wider degree of variation between the parties, especially between the disputants and the conciliation officers.

From their results Krislov and Leggett (1985) were able to claim that all their three hypotheses were basically supported. Similarly, it has been seen that in Hong Kong there is a high level of support for conciliation, some differences in attitudes/perceptions between the disputants and the conciliators and strong confidence in the competence of the Conciliation Service. Thus the major difference between the two countries is in terms of variability of perceptions. It can be seen from the responses that there is a greater uniformity of view among the Singaporean conciliation officers than among their Hong Kong counterparts. There are also some marked differences between the views of these conciliators and the disputing parties. However, the overwhelming impression from the responses is one of general similarity despite the very different conciliation and industrial relations systems. One tentative explanation of this phenomenon could be located at the level of culture. The majority of the respondents in both systems are Chinese and it has been suggested that the conciliation process may be a culturally preferred mode of conflict resolution (Tang and Kirkbride, 1986; Leung, 1987). This is, however, a complex area and further work needs to be done before this assertion can be conclusively demonstrated.

Appendix 12.1
A survey on perceptions of conciliation in Hong Kong

Conciliation is an important process whereby a third party tries to help labour and management disputants reach a settlement. In order to have an understanding of how people involved in the process perceive conciliation, the Human Resource Management Subject Team of the Department of Business and Management at the City Polytechnic of Hong Kong, with the assistance of the Labour Relations Service of the Labour Department, requests your help in completing this questionnaire. Your answers will be treated in the strictest confidence and used only in combination with those of others to form a statistical profile.

When you fill in the questionnaire, please bear in mind your own recent experience of conciliation.

We would be grateful if you could return your completed questionnaire to the staff of the LRS branch offices. In case of doubt, you may turn to them for assistance. If you require any further information you may call the researchers at the City Polytechnic . . .

[*Note*: in the three sections that follow, only the questions/statements have been reproduced. In each case respondents were asked to indicate, by a tick, 'agree', 'undecided' or 'disagree'.]

Part I: *Please [indicate] your choice to reflect your attitude towards conciliation*

1.1 The need for conciliation is a sign of immaturity on the part of management or labour.

1.2 The stronger party in a dispute will not request conciliation or co-operate in conciliation.

1.3 Management representatives generally accept the services of a conciliator.

1.4 Labour representatives generally accept the services of a conciliator.

1.5 Conciliation works best for small companies or small unions.

1.6 Conciliation works best for multinational companies.

1.7 Without conciliation by the Labour Department the number of disputes referred to the Labour Tribunal would increase significantly.

1.8 Without conciliation by the Labour Department most disputes would still turn out about the same.

1.9 The existence of the Labour Tribunal discourages collective bargaining and conciliation.

1.10 It is quite appropriate for conciliators to intervene in union recognition claims and refusal to negotiate disputes.

1.11 It is appropriate for the conciliation process to be made compulsory.

Part II: *Please [indicate] your choice to reflect your views towards techniques of conciliation*

2.1 Conciliation techniques are easily learned by experience.

2.2 The ability of conciliators to work effectively with labour – management people cannot be taught.

2.3 Even if a conciliator does nothing but sit in on a meeting, he acts as a catalyst to encourage agreement.

2.4 It is better for a conciliator to be *too* forceful than *too* timid.

2.5 Conciliation should be restricted to those issues suggested by the parties.

2.6 A conciliator should gain approval from both parties before he makes *suggestions* at a joint negotiating session.

2.7 Sometimes in joint conferences the conciliator should aggressively support the position of one side or the other on important issues.

2.8 When meeting separately with one of the parties, it is acceptable for a conciliator to vigorously support the position of the other party on an important issue.

2.9   The conciliator should hesitate to call for a separation of the parties unless there is a real possibility of achieving some agreement.

2.10 When a conciliator carries a position of one party to the other, he must exert the same degree of pressure that the parties would exert on each other if they were face to face.

Part III: Please [indicate] your choice to reflect your views of the conciliator in handling your case. Please be assured that your views will be treated anonymously and not revealed directly to the conciliator

3.1   The conciliator pressed the parties for a solution to the issue.

3;2   The conciliator made constructive suggestions to resolve issues.

3.3   The conciliator helped me understand the other party's position.

3.4   The conciliator helped me retreat from a difficult position.

3.5   The conciliator understood the complexities of the issues.

3.6   The conciliator had a wealth of knowledge about conciliation.

3.7   The conciliator showed no favouritism towards either of the parties.

3.8   The conciliation process prevented the referral of the dispute to the Labour Tribunal.

3.9   The conciliation process saves me from arguing with the other party.

3.10 Without the conciliation process, it is likely the case would drag on.

3.11 I am satisfied with the result of the conciliation.

3.12 I would continue to use the service of conciliation should disputes with my employer/employees occur again.

References

Anantaraman, V. (1984) 'Significance of Non-Adversary Union – Management Relationship in Singapore', *Singapore Management Review*, Vol. 6, No. 1, pp. 35 – 50.

Chee, C. H. (1981) 'The Emerging Administrative State', in S. H. Saw and R. S. Bhathal (Eds), *Singapore Towards the Year 2000*, Singapore University Press, pp. 10 – 14.

Department of Labour (1986) *Annual Departmental Report*, Government Printer, Hong Kong.

England, J. and Rear, J. (1981) *Industrial Relations and Law in Hong Kong*, Oxford University Press, Hong Kong.

Far Eastern Economic Review (1988) *Asia Yearbook 1988*, Review Publishing Company, Hong Kong.

Far Eastern Economic Review (1989) *Asia Yearbook 1989*, Review Publishing Company, Hong Kong.

Flanders, A. (1970) *Management and Unions*, Faber and Faber, London.

Goodman, J. F. B. and Krislov, J. (1974) 'Conciliation in Industrial Disputes in Great Britain: A Survey of the Attitudes of the Parties', *British Journal of Industrial Relations*, Vol. 12, pp. 327–51.

Harris, N. (1987) *The End of the Third World*, Penguin, Harmondsworth.

International Labour Office (1983) *Conciliation Services: Structures, Functions and Techniques*, International Labour Organisation, Geneva.

Kirkbride, P. S., Tang, S. F. Y. and Westwood, R. I. (1988) 'Chinese Bargaining and Negotiation Behaviour: The Cultural Effects', Working Paper No. 23, Department of Business and Management, City Polytechnic of Hong Kong.

Krislov, J. and Galin, A. (1979) 'Evaluating the Israeli Mediation Service', *International Labour Review*, Vol. 118, pp. 487–97.

Krislov, J. and Leggett, C. (1984) 'The Impact of Singapore's Congenial Labour Relations Ethic on its Conciliation Service', *Singapore Management Review*, Vol. 6, No. 2, pp. 95–106.

Krislov, J. and Leggett, C. (1985) 'Perceptions of Conciliation in Singapore: A Tripartite Survey', *Journal of Industrial Relations*, Vol. 2, pp. 172–90.

Leggett, C. (1984) 'Airline Pilots and Public Industrial Relations', *Indian Journal of Industrial Relations*, Vol. 20, No. 1, pp. 27–43.

Leggett, C. (1988) 'Industrial Relations and Enterprise Unionism in Singapore', *Labour and Industry*, Vol. 1, No. 2, pp. 242–57.

Leung, K. (1987) 'Some Determinants of Reactions to Procedural Models of Conflict Resolution: A Cross-National Study', *Journal of Personality and Social Psychology*, Vol. 53, No. 5, pp. 898–908.

Ministry of Labour (1976–87) *Annual Report*, Government Printer, Singapore.

Tang, S. F. Y. and Kirkbride, P. S. (1986) 'Developing Conflict Management Skills in Hong Kong: An Analysis of Some Cross-Cultural Implications', *Management Education and Development*, Vol. 17, No. 3, pp. 287–301.

Turner, H. A., Fosh, P., Gardner, M., Hart, K., Morris, R., Ng, S. H., Quinlan, M. and Yerbury, D. (1980) *The Last Colony: But Whose?* Cambridge University Press.

Wilkinson, B. (1986) 'Human Resources in Singapore's Second Industrial Revolution', *Industrial Relations Journal*, Vol. 17, No. 2, p. 111.

Wilkinson, B. (1988) 'Social Engineering in Singapore', *Journal of Contemporary Asia*, Vol. 2, pp. 165–88.

Wilkinson, B. and Leggett, C. (1985) 'Human and Industrial Relations in Singapore: The Management of Compliance', *Euro-Asia Business Review*, Vol. 3, pp. 9–15.

Part five

Comparisons of human resource policies – management occupations and development

Managers tend to be the most mobile of employees. One might expect to see in this occupation the most powerful impact of different cultures and the strongest tendency to convergence. Managers are also usually seen as an expensive and important resource in most organisations, with a leadership role that accords them a special status in human resource policies.

The chapters in this final part represent three aspects to the enquiry about the management of this most vital resource. Myron Roomkin discusses the way the status of managers as employees is affected by the social, economic and technological environments where they work. His broad overview shows how the separation between ownership and control resulted in the emergence of a distinct managerial status in most industrialised societies. Taking the convergence thesis as his implicit starting point, Roomkin goes on to consider how the status of managers has developed in West Germany, New Zealand, Australia, Britain, France, Italy, Sweden, the USA and Japan. He believes that although similar patterns have emerged, especially in the way managers are utilised by their employers, significant differences are explained by cultural variations in these societies.

By contrast, Andrew Kakabadse reports on his research into the characteristics of senior managers in 32 European organisations. He takes a case study approach and describes the common competencies among senior executives in North America, Britain, Iceland, France and Greece. From his research he found considerable commonality between managers; the key differences were explicable in terms of their drives, values, skills in implementing appropriate organisation structures, their communication skills, personal maturity and interpersonal skills. These major competencies were seen to be more significant determinants of managerial performance than national cultures.

The final chapter, by Frank Bournois and Pat Metcalfe, reports on research into the structures and policies used by companies towards their executives, from a study conducted throughout the European Community. Here we find that although organisation structures were not the prime causes of policies used to manage executives, policies were influenced by nationality, industry sector, the company/group structure, and by the size of company.

This result helps to explain the apparent discrepancy between Roomkin's and Kakabadse's positions. By taking a contingency perspective we can explain differences in management policies by showing that national culture is one variable among several. These chapters therefore call into question a simple version of the convergence thesis. Instead we may see a convergence in certain of the variables which influence managerial work, so managerial competencies are not culture-specific. However, aspects of the way executives are managed may be subject to more cultural influence, according to the mixture of variables such as company size and industry.

13

The changing characteristics of managers and managerial employment in the 1980s

MYRON J. ROOMKIN

It is often overlooked, but a manager is also an employee or worker. To some, the concept of managers as employees is a contradiction. They would argue that a manager is an owner of the enterprise or an agent of the owner, not an employee. Although this is sometimes true, most managers participate in an employment relationship that, in many countries, implies a specific legal status involving entitlements, duties, obligations and responsibilities. From a practical point of view, however, managers are in fact employees because they assume the role of employees in organisations: they take orders, not just give them; they are compensated for doing specific jobs or fulfilling responsibilities; and they may be dismissed for inadequate or unsatisfactory performance. In short, managers are employees because they exchange services for pay.

This recognition prompted a group of researchers in the early 1980s in nine developed countries – Britain, the USA, Australia, New Zealand, Japan, France, Sweden, West Germany and Italy – to question how the status of managers as employees might be affected by significant developments in the social, economic and technological environments (Berting, 1982). Among these developments are economic recessions and periods of inflation, the oil shocks of 1973 and 1978, the internationalisation of business and foreign competition, changing workforce demographics such as increased feminisation and ageing, business restructurings, changes in the technology of white-collar work, and shifting patterns of regulation and deregulation. The existence of such worldwide changes gives us the opportunity to test once again the validity of the well-known 'convergence hypothesis', which claims that social systems will respond to common stimuli in similar ways.

When the group began this project, it did not foresee that the 1980s would be a time of tremendous upheaval in managerial employment. No one in the group had an inkling that the world would experience its most severe postwar recession. Nor did any of us anticipate the dramatic rise in the social status and acceptability of managers and managerial careers. In retrospect, it is possible to suggest that these two developments were related. Drucker (1974) once referred to the 'managerial boom' that began after the Second World War and ended in the 1970s, during which industrial society recognised the enormous benefits of adapting basic managerial techniques to the administration of social and private enterprises. By the 1970s societies had become disillusioned with government's inability to solve social problems and again turned to the private sector to manage their way out of their problems. Thus, the project was a study in 'real time' — forcing us to draw conclusions as trends were developing and before definitive data could be gathered.

This chapter summarises the findings of the nine studies and identifies several issues for further study.

Defining managerial workers

From the planning stages, the researchers understood that it is very difficult to define a managerial worker. Managerial jobs and occupational interests vary across levels of the organisations and across different industries or sectors. Likewise, many groups of professional employees, even though they lack responsibilites for management or administration, share interests and values with those who actually perform those tasks.

In the end the research accepted the concept of a 'managerial and professional staff' as the focus of the study. As defined by the International Labour Office, the managerial and professional staff are those persons who:

(*a*) are employed by organisations for a salary;

(*b*) have achieved a higher level of education and training or recognised experience in a scientific, technical, or administrative field;

(*c*) perform functions of a predominantly intellectual character involving a high degree of judgement and initiative;

(*d*) may have been delegated by the employer with responsibility for planning, managing, controlling and co-ordinating the activities of the organisation or portion of the organisation; and

(*e*) do not occupy positions as either first-line supervisors, foremen or top-level executives.

The definition covers persons employed in the public, private and not-for-profit sectors.

There is evidence that a precise definition may be growing more rather than less difficult to fashion. First, technology has blurred the lines of distinction between managerial tasks and the work of other occupations. Second, as firms substitute temporary or short-term professionals for permanent employees, many of the workers doing professional tasks will lose their identification with other professionals in the firm and be excluded from the career-promotion systems of the company.

Patterns of stability and change

Considerable diversity exists in the characteristics of managerial employment among the studied countries. In some, managers work under formal, written and individually tailored contracts of employment, while in others, written contracts are not commonly used. Also, there are the well-documented differences in the components and level of compensation. In a few countries managers have unionised; in others, where co-determination is practised, managers are represented on different governing boards. There are also differences in the ways people obtain access to managerial occupations, advance professionally and retire.

At the same time, there are broad similarities among these countries. Perhaps the strongest is that despite problems of definition, managers are recognised as a distinct group of employees by the law, collectively bargained agreements and employers' practices. Their distinctiveness is established by company policies, the growing professionalisation of the occupation, changing educational requirements and identifiable career patterns. Moreover, managers tend to have different but not necessarily more desirable terms and conditions of employment. In several countries specialised agencies play an important role in the way managers are treated with regard to retirement benefits, unemployment insurance, salary setting and job seeking.

Developments in studied countries

Among the major changes in the treatment of managers in studied countries are the following developments.

In West Germany there has been a decline in the motivation among middle managers, a condition that has perhaps been brought about by the great success of West German business and rising living standards. At the same time, however, we are told that young people entering the market today could face diminished opportunities for advancement in business, suggesting that the problem of motivation may solve itself.

In New Zealand the dominant experience has been that of a country poorer than others, with a severe shortage of managers. Under such circumstances little momentum for change has developed to modify personnel practices toward managers or to increase the state's role in shaping their employment conditions.

Australia, which has drained away many of New Zealand's managers, especially among younger workers, has been experiencing a greater need for managers because of growth in the economy. Companies have adopted more aggressive policies and practices toward this group of employees.

New personnel practices dealing with managers are also a dominant theme in Britain. Prompted by British industries' lack of competitiveness, there is a trend toward increasing the skill of managers. This has led to a greater awareness that managerial education and training are important, and an increased willingness of employers to emphasise merit and ability rather than economic class in the development of managerial human resources.

In France managers have experienced a process of continued professionalisation but declining job security. Education seems to be playing a greater role in the preparation of managers, and family background is becoming less of a barrier to a managerial career. Worsening job security and pay status relative to others have not yet produced a broad-based social protest movement, perhaps because the conditions of employment for managers still remain quite good.

Italian managers, especially those in the middle and lower levels, have become an important interest group in Italy. Their dissatisfaction with worsening conditions of employment has made them the focus of attention from both unions and the government.

Swedish companies have begun efforts to improve the productivity of their managers or, as they have labelled it, to revitalise management. Unfortunately, the high degree of managerial unionisation and the standardised conditions of employment are making it extremely difficult for companies to reward managers who have outperformed others.

The major theme in US managerial relationships has been the decline of stable employment in the larger organisations and the demise of highly bureaucratic personnel practices and traditions dealing with managers. These developments are the product of several long-term and recent trends that came together in the mid-1980s but have not yet yielded a new dominant model of employment. They have, however, created a great deal of career uncertainty and competition for advancement, which in turn has resulted in making management education and training much more popular.

In comparison, the changes in Japanese employment practices towards managers have been more subtle. Due to the ageing of Japan's workforce and the oversupply of middle-level managers, Japanese firms long ago began rewarding managerial employees on the basis of merit, thereby deviating from the so-called traditional practices of lifelong employment and seniority-based reward systems. In the 1980s, however, companies began pursuing merit much more explicitly and visibly, enlarging the gap between those who were successful and those who were not.

Analytically, the major issue is whether or not any common themes emerge in these developments. The answer appears to be yes, but the amount of change, even though it has varied among the countries, has not been strong enough to remove cultural differences in the ways managers are treated. Moreover, contrary to popular belief, these developments did not start suddenly in the 1980s but began as long as 20 years ago.

Three interrelated themes appear in these changes. First, employers have been trying to utilise managerial employees more aggressively and efficiently. Second, patterns of employment and mobility are becoming more varied. Third, most of the surveyed countries have recently passed laws against discrimination of women for managerial positions, although much progress remains to be made.

New practices

Employers are taking a much more active role in influencing the terms and conditions of managers' employment. Through a process I have called marginalisation – that is, matching labour costs with actual productivity.

Marginalisation is a significant change in the economic and cultural logic on which the managerial employment relationship is based. Although it may not be as important a development as Taylorism was to the way employers conceptualised blue-collar employment, marginalisation represents a greater concern for the utilisation of managers as human resources.

This new emphasis has resulted in the growth of several practices that have achieved different degrees of popularity. In the area of compensation practices, employers have tried to increase the role of economic variables such as performance or productivity and diminish the importance of other factors. Efforts to assess managerial performance also have become more commonplace.

Perhaps the simplest way to control labour costs is to reduce headcounts. Not surprisingly, therefore, reductions in the number of managers employed and increases in the rate of unemployment among managers were reported in several countries. Nevertheless, the level of managerial unemployment relative to the rate of other groups has remained low. Managers still enjoy a privileged place in the employment queue.

Reliance on temporary, part-time and project workers as managers and professional staffs is a new, but rather modest, development in Britain and the USA. However, in Japan these staffing practices have been more widely used for several years. It is difficult to say whether such arrangements will ultimately represent a substantial portion of employment in countries other than Japan. Judging from the limited experience of American companies, which probably have the greatest potential for such flexibility, these staffing arrangements do possess significant problems of design and implementation.

To students of American personnel management, the developments discussed in this overview appear rather uncontroversial and quite commonplace; however, they are comparatively novel in the other societies to which they have spread. At least one researcher in our study identified the role of US multinational firms in taking these techniques abroad, although the demand for expertise in personnel matters has grown beyond multinational companies.

Careers and mobility

Patterns of labour mobility and career paths are changing in many of the countries surveyed. Access to the occupation is more open in Britain and France as socio-economic background has declined in importance and education in management is easier to obtain. A college degree in business or management is now a popular route for those wishing to enter the profession. Ironically, however, in the USA where enrolment in management programmes has become ubiquitous, businesspeople and educators are starting to question the efficacy of this education (Porter and McKibbin, 1988).

Change is also apparent in the amount of inter-firm mobility for managers. Managers in Britain, Australia, the USA, and New Zealand are reported to be changing employers more often. Even in Japan, where the practices of stable employment are probably most deeply entrenched, there has been an increase, albeit a small one, in the number of persons changing jobs. More significant, however, is the much larger number of managers who, when surveyed, expressed an interest in changing employers during their working life.

Clearly, one of the causes of such mobility has been the new personnel practices described above, which have increased the incidence of involuntary unemployment and made managers more concerned about employment security. At the same time, however, there is evidence of greater voluntary mobility, as managers seek out more desirable positions. In some places the propensity towards mobility has been fuelled by the development of managerial job opportunities in either small and medium-sized enterprises or in emerging sectors of the economy. Also important has been the willingness of employers to hire experienced managers rather than to develop them internally.

Some authors mentioned the growth of managerial careers through self-employment or small business ownership and a corresponding interest in entrepreneurship. While there appears to have been an increase in new entrepreneurs and owner–operators, their relatively small numbers should not be a threat to the continued professionalisation of the occupation. However, the more important significance of this development may be ideological, in so far as it reinforces managers' association with the values of economic growth and the business community.

Another type of mobility is the experience managers receive in different types of jobs during their careers. American managers, especially those in emerging companies, and Japanese managers have the most experience with cross-functional job changes, although the practice of broadening their experience is becoming more popular where promotion opportunities have lessened.

Despite the continued internationalisation of business, our research revealed very little mobility of managers across borders; the exception, of course, is the common labour market between Australia and New Zealand. However, apart from those senior managers and professionals who are sent abroad to work in foreign-owned subsidiaries (a common practice in Japanese firms), there is relatively little mobility of managers from one country to another in pursuit of employment. Apparently, significant economic and political barriers remain to international job seeking and recruitment, even in Europe where geographic distances are comparatively small.

Women managers

The underutilisation of women in management is a problem common to all the countries under consideration. Even in egalitarian Sweden women hold a modest proportion of entry and mid-level management positions, but virtually none in senior management. Women have made the greatest degree of progress in the USA in entry and mid-level positions, but now seem to be facing greater obstacles in reaching senior executive ranks. Moreover, much of this limited success has been in jobs traditionally held by females or in the public sector.

The responsibility for increasing women's representation in management is now acknowledged by all societies. Some have passed laws to increase access to employment and punish employers for discriminating. The Japanese anti-discrimination law, by comparison, establishes a social obligation not to discriminate but provides no punishment for those who break the law.

Looking to the future, greater representation of women at all levels of the managerial hierarchy could be a side benefit of the new mobility in managerial careers, giving women options they have not had before. Likewise, discrimination may become harder to disguise as employers introduce compensation and reward systems based on demonstrated performance. Ironically, the Japanese have been the most resistant to equal opportunity employment for women, but as the Japanese economy passes from its current labour surplus into a period of labour shortage during the next few decades, these prejudices may receive direct and severe testing.

The reactions of managers

Complaints of managers involve the traditional economic concerns of salary and job security as well as a desire to participate more actively in the decisions of the organisation. Economic concerns have been made more salient because of wage compression, greater uncertainty about careers and promotions, and the aggressive personnel practices previously described. The desire to participate in decision-making stems from a loss of authority that can be traced to, among other things, growth of employee involvement and increased regulation of business.

Managers' reactions to these developments have been consistent within each country's industrial relations and political system. In countries with strong labour movements managers channelled their reactions through the collective bargaining system.

The prospects for the growth of unionisation among managers are not strong, even though their employment problems may be growing. At a minimum, traditional obstacles to unionisation remain: managers themselves are not convinced of the legitimacy of managers' unions and may not be willing to co-operate with unionised non-managerial employees; at the same time, employers' resistance to the concept remains strong. In addition, it is difficult to imagine unions having greater success organising managers when union membership among traditional groups is on the decline.

Unions, however, understand that managers and professionals are a group they can not overlook. As the study found, and as confirmed more recently (FIET, 1987), the labour movements in Western economies are trying to organise these employees, frequently by resorting to special tactics and through separate or free-standing organisational units.

With regard to political activism, several researchers reported early indications of greater cohesiveness among managers to achieve legal protections already given to other employees and to compete more effectively for political spoils. However, these developments fall far short of convincing us that managers have become a so-called 'third force' in society between employers and unions. Even if they are more active politically, it appears that managers are generally politically conservative and tend to support the position of business interests.

Issues for further research

Although it is difficult to predict how managerial employment will change in the future, this comparative study points to several issues for further investigation. The following are some that I find especially interesting:

(a) *What will be the long-term impact of marginalisation on the relationship between managers and their employers?* Marginalisation represents more than just change; it is the type of change that should strain the traditional relationship between manager and employer. It represents a major challenge to the continued professionalisation of the occupation.

The case studies were not able to draw detailed distinctions among the ways different types of firms were engaging in marginalisation. In the analysis, however, there was a strong hint that the spread of such practices was linked in no small way to the activities of the multinational company. It would be interesting to determine how such innovations were introduced in countries and how the practices diffused to other companies.

(b) *Is there a role for labour market policies and programmes for professional and managerial employees?* On the basis of equity alone, society will have a hard time justifying the use of public funds to assist unemployed and underemployed managers. Still, several countries already have special public organisations dedicated to providing services to this class of employees in such areas as pensions, labour standards and job seeking. How effective are these organisations and what aspects of their successful operation could be beneficially adopted elsewhere?

(c) *What implications are there for managerial employment in the changing demand for managerial workers in the 1990s?* First, apart from inter-industry shifts in the demand, the growth of employment in small and medium-sized firms should have a major impact on managers and what they do. While some smaller companies are not tied to old ways and are very innovative, others (and I suspect the majority of such firms) are just the opposite. Second, if other nations follow America's experience, the demand for managers will spread to atypical settings, not just business and industry. Mobility between the public and private sectors has been difficult in most countries for managers. Will comparable difficulties arise among other sectors of the economy as they take on more managers?

(d) *Is it feasible to think in terms of a truly internationalised labour market for managers and professionals?* At the present time, the dominant international flow of workers at this level consists of employees being reassigned by their employer. Here, again, the multinational corporation is playing a major role. This topic seems well suited for study by the International Labour Office.

(e) *Will company-provided training become the major form of training, displacing formal, classroom training in degree-granting institutions?* Even though there has been a sudden expansion in degree programmes in management, the signs are that employers would prefer to control the curriculum of management education.

(f) *Will public policy achieve greater opportunities for women in managerial jobs?* Countries with an Anglo-Saxon judicial heritage stand the best chance of increasing female participation in managerial jobs at the entry level. However, the obstacles preventing participation in higher-ranking positions are more subtle and perhaps are less amenable to legal remedies.

[This chapter has drawn heavily on the book edited by the author, *Managers as Employees: An International Comparison of the Changing Conditions of Managerial Employment*, Oxford University Press, 1989. The author is indebted to the colleagues who participated in the writing of this book.]

References

Berting, J. (1982) 'Why Compare in International Research? Theoretical and Practical Limitations of International Research', in M. Niessen and J. Peschar (Eds) *International Comparative Research: Problems of theory, methodology, and organization in Eastern and Western Europe*, Pergamon Press, New York, pp. 5 – 16.

Drucker, P. F. (1974) *Management: Tasks, Responsibilities, Practice*, Harper & Row, New York.

FIET (1987) *Organizing for Tomorrow*, International Federation of Commercial, Clerical, Professional and Technical Employees, Geneva.

Porter, L. W. and McKibbin, L. E. (1988) *Management Education and Development: Drift or Thrust into the 21st Century*, McGraw-Hill, New York.

14

Effectiveness at the top
Preliminary analysis of 32 European organisations

ANDREW KAKABADSE

The attitudes, qualities and behaviours of the members of the senior executive of an enterprise are of crucial concern when considering the future growth and prosperity of the organisation. These personal characteristics of leaders need to be perceived as holding levels of importance comparable to issues of policy, strategy and organisation structure. So-called objective data highlighting external, market and internal organisational conditions can form the cornerstone of policy and structural decisions. However, subjective concerns such as the interpretation of external and internal data, especially in relation to one's own vision of the future, feelings concerning colleagues and one's own position in the organisation and the placement and development of executives in key and sensitive roles in the structure, are of equal importance to the management of an enterprise.

An examination of the literature on policy, decision-making and top executives indicates a plethora of terminologies and findings, at times overlapping in meanings and conclusions. A recently completed literature review (Alderson and Kakabadse, 1989) highlights the different conceptual categories underpinning executive performance and development, which range from identifying the elements of performance (Hackman, 1984; Garfield, 1986), performance appraisal (Ilgen and Faulro, 1985), vision performance and success (Hunsicker, 1986; Quinn, 1985), personal effectiveness (Reddin, 1970; Morse and Wagner, 1978; Steiner, 1983), successful attainment of role and continuing success in role (Margerison and Kakabadse, 1984; Mardique and Hayes, 1985), managerial competence (Byrd, 1987; Powers, 1987), managerial behaviour (Leontiades, 1982; Hambrick and Mason, 1984), personality characteristics (Taggart and Robey, 1981; Kets de Vries and Miller, 1986), managerial work (Mintzberg, 1980), leadership (Karmel, 1978; Vecchio, 1979; Bolt, 1985; Heller, 1985), decision-making (Shirley, 1982; Ford and Hegarty, 1984; Shrivastava and Mitroff, 1984) and organisational form and culture (Brown and Agnew, 1982; Ohmae, 1982; Smith, Mitchell and Summer, 1985; Chaffee, 1985).

As can be seen, the range of conceptual categories examining the role and attributes of senior executives is considerable. With such breadth of perspective and lack of guidance as to which perspective would benefit from greater focus of examination, it was decided to undertake a 'start again' philosophy by adopting a case study approach, utilising an action research methodology, to identify the competencies required of senior executives for them to perform effectively in their role. The depth of involvement of the researchers in each case would vary according to the nature of the contract negotiated. Thirty-two case studies were undertaken with organisations from North America, Britain, Ireland, France and Greece, from both the private and public sectors. This chapter outlines the findings from action research.

Currently, a more comprehensive questionnaire-based survey is under way, contrasting the competencies and job-related behaviours of European, American and Japanese executives.

The competencies

One characteristic common to all senior level executives, in both the private and public sectors, is discretion in role, namely the *choice potential* which, if utilised, allows the individual to identify and pursue the policies, strategies and directions he or she deems appropriate. Yet, identifying the boundaries to choice, the processes of making and implementing decisions and the pursuit of policy are as much influenced by issues of objectivity as by personal preferences, the quality of relationships among key executives and by needing to account actively for the different interpretations of other influential executives as to ways forward, for not to do so could damage not only the policies but the fabric of the organisation. The capacity to manage discretion within the context of the circumstances in which the executive finds himself or herself has been observed as key to the practice of the competencies identified below.

Through the application of discretion, six competency areas are identified: two are termed 'drives', and four 'skills of implementation'.

The drives

What drives executives to do what they do?

What stimulates individuals in roles of responsibility to pursue the course(s) of action they deem appropriate?

The drives of *shaping the future* and *executive values* have been observed to provide for the stimulus for success. These two in combination shape the attitudes, behaviours and perceptions of each key executive in determining what he or she wants to do, the people he or she employs, and how his or her ideas are implemented.

Shaping the future

Once appointed to a role which requires the application of considerable discretion, each executive needs to hold a view concerning the future of the organisation and likely trends in the marketplace. Not to do so would leave the organisation, function or unit for which the executive is accountable vulnerable. Some executives may foresee considerable changes. Others may wish to preserve the status quo, perceiving that the organisation is able to meet challenges, in structural, financial, product and human resource terms.

It is important that a consistent and coherent view is obtained, not only from each senior executive, but also from the top executive team concerning the future of the business. Vision, that is the clarity concerning the future and how to shape the organisation, and each executive's expectations concerning the future, is identified by each individual's ability to express that view in detail.

However, foreseeing is not enough. Displaying the confidence to foretell what will happen, and consequently what the organisation needs to do, is crucial in terms of allocating resources and building trust and commitment from the levels below.

Realistically appraising the future and recognising the necessary steps to take to enhance the fortunes of the organisation depend on having intimate knowledge of the markets in which the organisation operates. The particular nature of these markets in terms of the expectations of customers, the behaviour of suppliers and competitors, the time it takes to stimulate appropriate levels of sales, the likely life-cycle of products, and the degree of after-sales service desired and expected, all influence the way in which the company should be structured, its positioning in the market and the overhead to be carried in order for the company to function appropriately.

With that number of variables, differences of opinion may emerge concerning positioning in the market, the level of overhead and the likely organisation structural configuration necessary to focus resources to achieve particular goals.

In addition, it should not be assumed that all senior executives hold similar knowledge and insights concerning the market or the internal functioning of the organisation. Executives with limited knowledge of their markets may be placed as heads of key functions or units. Responding appropriately to requests and demands of customers, suppliers or competitors is unlikely to happen consistently; acting upon relevant advice may occur patchily; possessing the confidence to pursue particular strategies may be unlikely. Under such circumstances a great deal will depend on the individual's presentation skills to compensate for lack of market knowledge and to promote the confidence of others in him or her. Multinationals and organisations with multiple products, services or markets are particularly prone to the situation where their executives may not fully appreciate the finer points of the markets in which they operate, hence having a negative impact on the business.

Newly appointed executives will be pressured to 'learn' quickly about the particular nature of their markets and their organisation's capacity to respond. Depending on the nature of the deeply held values and beliefs in the organisation, learning from mistakes may or may not be tolerated. Equally, the individual may be more dependent on his or her direct reports than would normally the the case. Generating high-quality executive relationships, in which open conversation and a high degree of trust become the norm, is desired. However, an executive who may feel he or she is not in full command of the situation may respond defensively by not generating a team climate, but by imposing his or her own requirements, react negatively to questioning and focus on immediate, short-term activities rather than address the overall situation.

Hence, differences of view as to how to shape the future may occur due to intimate insights concerning the overall market or due to ignorance. Either way, the result may be the same. Problems can arise due to differences of vision which emerge from members of the top team. Some of the worst 'in-fighting' can occur among the senior members of the executive due to differences of vision.

It should be pointed out that gaining knowledge of the market(s) and insights as to the underlying dynamics in the organisation is a skill – a skill which can be learned. A great deal depends on each individual's capacity to nurture relevant relationships so that others can assist the individual to become accustomed to 'operating' in a new environment. Learning from and gaining the trust and confidence of others motivates individuals; they are driven to perform; they know they are good and they feel good.

Executives occupying roles involving considerable discretion are likely to be required to provide identity and clarity as to where they are taking the organisation. It is the combination of market and organisational knowledge, and a personal view concerning future direction, that provides the stimulus and motivation (drive) to shape the future.

Executive values

Executive values are those fundamental views each executive holds concerning how the organisation should be managed, how people should be handled, how resources should be allocated, how the individual concerned prefers to be managed, and with which other executives the individual more easily identifies. Each executive's values are the key to generating positive and healthy relationships among senior executives, which allows for open discussion of important issues – a process crucial to the success of the organisation. It is possible to ascertain whether policies will be consistently pursued by examining whether the members of the management team identify with one another and the strategies they generate. Coherence of expression of policy and consistency of direction of strategy are strongly influenced by the personal values held by each of the members of the executive. The skill is to manage others and adjust one's own performance to suite the circumstances. Reading the situation and nurturing key relationships in a manner that is of benefit to the business requires considerable forethought and sensitivity so as to effectively manage people and the business together.

Six key values have been identified.

External orientation

Externally orientated executives place emphasis on performing effectively external to the organisation in the markets, being sensitive to customer needs, improvements in revenues and customer satisfaction. Externally orientated executives are often characterised by high energy and drive. Individuals with externally orientated values readily identify others external to the organisation such as customers, suppliers and distributors, but tend to pay little attention to internal administration and internal organisation issues.

Organisational orientation

Organisation-orientated executives display respect for role boundaries and organisational structure. The individual is disciplined, administration-orientated, identifies readily with concepts of efficiency and is likely to be competent at follow-through, i.e. ensuring that decisions made and commitments given are implemented by regularly meeting and talking to the people concerned. Effective follow-through depends on the following factors:

(*a*) a mental capacity to recognise organisational relationships and linkages between departments/units/divisions;

(*b*) a personal application towards negotiating positive organisation relationships and linkages so that other role holders identify with the individual's requirements;

(*c*) that the organisation structure and discretion in the manager's role allows for effective negotiation on follow-through and establishing linkages across the organisation.

Being too organisationally orientated can mean the individual becomes out of touch with marketplace developments, can be inflexible to changes in markets and may be sufficiently conscious of status so as to respond negatively when status concerns are not respected.

Interpersonal orientation

Interpersonally orientated individuals judge other people by their manner, interpersonal skills and overall interpersonal conduct. Bosses, colleagues and subordinates may be judged by whether they appear to be optimistic or pleasant and not pessimistic or negative. Sensitive interpersonal forms of communication can give the appearance of an effective team through displays of harmony – such an appearance may be deceptive.

A more sensitive individual can fall into the trap of judging others simply on the nature of interpersonal interactions. Those interactions with others perceived as supportive are viewed positively and could become a primary criterion for rewarding or responding positively to those persons. Interactions perceived as negative are treated as threats, and the people whom the individual has to relate to on this basis are likely to be rejected, disregarded or put to one side.

Any senior executive who is too interpersonally orientated is likely to allow his or her emotions to cloud his or her appreciation of function and role and may find it difficult to distinguish between the demands, challenges, constraints and functional requirements of the role and the personal performance of the incumbents. Individuals who find themselves in a role which exposes them to considerable ambiguity may in turn be seen as responding negatively by others, especially so by the interpersonally orientated executive, who because of his or her personal discomfort may perceive the person as performing poorly.

Individuals who are too interpersonally orientated may externalise, i.e. blame others. Another response is to internalise, i.e. view other people's problems, complaints or misfortunes as your fault or responsibility. People who face problems and respond emotionally easily become angry, and the less mature wish to find a target on whom to direct their anger. Alternatively, anyone so sensitive and with a capacity for internalisation targets himself or herself, and others, for undue self-blame. After a time, the individual experiencing considerably negative emotions performs below par and substantially demotivates others.

Because of the intensity of emotions, all those involved may respond defensively in order to shield themselves from being blamed or simply feeling guilty.

Independence orientation
Independence-orientated individuals value doing their own thing in their own way. The need for considerable personal space and for the expression of one's own views and needs is a predominant concern. Perceived encroachment on one's own personal space is viewed negatively, which may stimulate the individual to enter into conflict with others. It is difficult to apply a team-orientated philosophy if a number of key executives identify with independence-orientated values.

Expertise orientation
Expertise-orientated executives identify with the values of a profession, discipline or technical expertise. Effective communication is more likely to occur with people who hold similar professional or expert orientation (i.e. talk the same language) but communication blocks may arise with people who do not identify or understand the values of that profession. Those individuals who exhibit the values of being an expert tend to apply high standards, acceptable in a professional sense, but which may be inappropriate for discussions among a group of general managers. In a sense, expertise-orientated executives lose their general management orientation through exposure to training and development

in one sphere of work. People with expertise orientated values, under negative circumstances, are unlikely to identify with their employing organisation.

Integration orientation
Integration-orientated executives are sensitive to the demands of the market and to the issues, problems and needs which face the team members and their subordinates. The aim of the integration-orientated person is to work with bosses, colleagues and subordinates for them to master the challenges that face them, help them identify with the organisation and its structure and move forward as a cohesive team. The integrator works closely with and through people, and is realistic and clear as to how long it would take, and what is needed, to develop an effective team. An integrator is able to appreciate and operationalise the desired short-, medium- and long-term policies through the key executive relationships he or she manages. In essence, the integrator is able to bring the people, the structure and market demands together, to enable the business to progress effectively.

Implementation skills

Appropriate application of organisation structure

Organisation structure is a means to an end. It is the means by which people and resources are focused to achieve particular objectives. However, identifying and applying appropriate organisation structure involves considerable conceptual ability. The executive needs to recognise market opportunities, to be capable of understanding the strengths and weaknesses of the organisation, and by combining market opportunities with perceived internal strengths and weaknesses, be able to visualise a structural configuration that realistically suits the company's circumstances. Having identified a blueprint of structure, which focuses people's energy and resources to pursuing particular goals, two further issues need to be considered.

First, executives need to respect the structure, the role boundaries, and administrative and organisational procedures. In effect, colleagues who should be involved or consulted are not by-passed and procedures are not disregarded. To do so can create considerable disarray and a feeling of lack of ownership in the structure. 'If top management are not bothering to stick to the rules, why should we?' – a sentiment which can undermine the fabric of the organisation.

Second, driving policies through the organisation and *following through* on commitments made are important to ensure that tasks and activities are addressed as desired. Negotiating effective follow-through in a manner deemed legitimate and in accordance with the distribution of responsibilites in the structure helps establish a culture of discipline among the managers in the organisation. Hitting targets, meeting deadlines and controlling costs, while maintaining identity with corporate direction, are positive organisational attitudes which emanate from disciplined behaviour. The senior executive needs to set an example for good discipline through the application of follow-through.

Communicating a coherent set of beliefs and values about the business

Communicating beliefs and values down the line has been identified not only as a stimulus to motivation but, further, as a mechanism for assisting individuals to identify with the purposes and practices of the organisation: in effect, a mechanism for establishing ownership. In the case studies few senior executives made the effort to identify the core values of their organisations. Of the few that attempted to identify and understand their core values, even fewer attempted to communicate these fundamental beliefs and values down through the organisation.

Of those that did communicate key beliefs, values or a sense of mission, particular practices were identified. Some senior managements organised a series of presentations to middle/lower management and staff over a planned period of time, explaining the work of the organisation, its future prospects, the measures being used to address current and future concerns and the fundamental principles that need to be internalised, respected and utilised as guidance in determining future action. If the presentation skills of senior management are professional and the levels of trust within the organisation are sufficiently positive, such a strategy of communication can be a positive mechanism for the transmission of ideas, policies and activities as well as the process in itself being identified as a positive and meaningful experience by the staff of the organisation, for they feel a part of an interesting enterprise.

Similarly, the strategy of 'walkabout' can attain similar ends. Walkabout involves senior management informally making themselves acquainted with the staff of the organisation by seemingly casually walking about the corridors, offices and units of that enterprise. By meeting people informally and entering into a dialogue with them, ideas can be exchanged and key messages and values clearly communicated and confirmed through informal discussion. If walkabout is well planned and key opinion holders and representatives of each level are met, such a process of information transmission can be as much a motivating experience as a strategy of more formal presentations. Under the right circumstances, walkabout is an effective means for communicating clearly those core values that bind the organisation together.

However, effective application of planned presentations or a series of well-timed walkabouts as mechanisms for communication requires that the levels of trust in the organisation be sufficiently high, so that people can believe what is being said, even if they disagree with the content of the message. To enter into two such strategies without a certain degree of trust invites aggravation. A particularly distressing experience for any senior team would be to call an internal management conference, prepare well the series of presentations on the company, its future and the commitment and behaviours required from its management, only to discover the presentations greeted with mistrust, even derision. Improving the standard of presentation is unlikely to help, for the problem is one of improving the levels of trust in order to attempt to communicate.

In the case studies it became apparent that the example set by the members of the senior executive, in terms of the attitudes and behaviour displayed, is considerably influential in terms of communicating certain beliefs and values about the organisation. Senior management represent, in their daily interactions, the core values of that enterprise. If, for example, the spoken values are 'people count' but senior management are seen to behave repeatedly in a non-consultative, over-directive and perhaps insensitive manner, those lower down in the organisation would not identify with the values of 'people count' as their experience would indicate the opposite. If a substantial gap exists between what is said and what is practised by senior management, core values are communicated down the structure, that is, the values are *those practised*! If others witness the top behaving in a cold, directive, out of touch, insensitive manner, then those become the core organisational values, strongly influencing the behaviour of most in that entity. In effect, some middle and lower level management would emulate and practise such values, others may become demotivated, while yet others leave.

In all organisations communicating a set of values and beliefs about the organisation is done on a daily basis, through the structure, in terms of the interactions with one's direct reports on a one-to-one or group basis. Senior executives need to be conscious of the impact they have on others through the attitudes they exhibit and behaviour they adopt. In order consciously to send the 'right' messages down the line, they have to recognise the example they set. It is of advantage to have nurtured a suitably robust relationship with senior colleagues, allowing one another the freedom to offer feedback on the impact each individual makes on the structure and his or her role.

Personal discipline and a willingness to listen to others are considered the cornerstones of effectively communicating a coherent set of beliefs and values supportive of the organisation.

Personal maturity

Performing effectively in a senior executive role involves comfortably managing considerable ambiguity, contradiction and paradox, which may mean renegotiating understandings or agreements with others, which could cause friction, while sustaining high-quality executive relationships. Concepts of trust and honesty need to be broadened to encompass concepts of change, and to do this it is imperative that the senior manager is able to read situations so that he or she can understand people's readiness to accept change.

Part of being able to manage stress, ambiguity and change is having an understanding of why other executives do or say the things they do. To come to terms with other people's actions or inactions, it is important to appreciate the opportunities, pressures and constraints they face in their role. The pressures of the role may, for example, leave the individual with little option but to adopt a conflict-orientated position or, alternatively, not to be forthcoming in declaring his or her intentions or future actions, or simply to distance himself or herself from the rest of his or her colleagues in the executive group. Such behaviour is likely to be interpreted as negative by other executives, who may in turn reject the lone executive and his or her policies. Tension, friction and lack of trust would, under such circumstances, easily arise and be sustained for considerable periods of time. To make matters worse, the lone executive could leave, but a similar situation could arise with the newly appointed executive, leaving other executives with the feeling that there exist few effective senior managers available in the market: a feeling of resignation which, unfortunately, can be quickly transmitted through the organisation, demotivating considerable numbers of subordinates.

Intimate knowledge of the organisation and the business, an overall experience of working in a senior management role, and an ability to extrapolate the problems likely to be faced by each executive in his or her role, are necessary in order to stimulate understanding of each other's job or role.

It would seem that such a process is largely cerebral in nature. In terms of analysing other people's problems in other organisations, that is not true. It is far easier to understand someone else's problems in another organisation largely because one is not involved. Considerable personal maturity is required, however, to distance oneself from one's own feelings concerning a fellow executive's behaviour, so that it is possible to analyse logically the problems faced by that person in his or her role.

Being able to analyse someone else's problems through his or her eyes, while at the same time controlling one's own feelings due to personal involvement in the situation, allows for a more positive discussion to take place. Instead of focusing on negative emotions, which are likely to hinder conversation and stimulate resentment, discussion centres on the problems being faced by each executive. The fact that such talking is taking place highlights an appreciation of each other's issues and although not necessarily agreeing with the actions of others, reduces the level of perceived threat which could bar such useful discourse.

In addition to taking a more relaxed and wider perspective on life, and in order to analyse and discuss each other's role problems, it is important that the executive responds positively to feedback. Receiving positive feedback is relatively easy to handle.

Giving feedback to others who do not wish to hear it could be problematic. Receiving negative feedback is far more difficult in that it can be personal and perceived as emotionally hurtful. To respond positively to such feedback, it is necessary that such data is presented in a depersonalised way, i.e. turned into an issue which can be reasonably comfortably discussed. People have to be helped to feel sufficiently comfortable to receive and consider feedback. The blocks to receiving feedback could be:

(a) the individual in his or her role and in the current structure has not been required to receive feedback, and hence is unaccustomed to such interaction;

(b) the individual has not in the past invited feedback, and thus the competence and confidence of others to offer feedback are low;

(c) it may be 'politically' inappropriate to request feedback as the quality of executive relationships is poor;

(d) all or most of the individuals involved have not appreciated the true source of the problem, focus on extraneous issues, offer feedback and then become disappointed or even angry when the executive in question cannot or will not act;

(e) appreciation of, and sensitivity to, managerial problems are low among bosses, colleagues and/or subordinates and hence nothing of value would emerge from requesting and receiving feedback: in fact, to do so may result in a considerably destructive outcome;

(f) the individual in his or her role may be unaccustomed or untrained in terms of receiving feedback and hence bars any information being offered concerning his or her performance;

(g) the individual may be threatened by the nature of the feedback and so not wish to listen.

Experience strongly indicates that the personal factors (i.e. items (d) and (e) – (g) predominate as reasons for poor or non-existent feedback. The message to senior executives is: 'Leave your ego at home.'

Interpersonal skills

It is important that executives are reasonably competent at interpersonal skills, as so much of their work involves influencing others. Presentation of self and ability to influence have been identified as key concerns.

Part of interpersonal skills concerns handling politics of managerial life. Politics does not arise for negative reasons. Differences of view, differences of vision, differences of executive values and differences in management style can lead to tensions and communication blocks. Such tensions and differences are natural. Each executive is still required to discharge his or her duties despite these frustrations. Hence, influencing people and managing interpersonal interactions in both an overt and covert manner are simply facts of life.

References

Alderson, S. and Kakabadse, A. P. (1989) *The Executive Competencies Research Programme Literature Review*, Cranfield Research Monograph Series No. 1, Cranfield School of Management, Bedford.

Bolt, J. F. (1985) 'Tailor Executive Development to Suit Strategy', *Harvard Business Review*, November–December, pp. 168–176.

Brown, J. L. and Agnew, N. McK. (1982) 'The Balance of Power in a Matrix Structure', *Business Horizons*, pp. 51–4.

Byrd, R. E. (1987) 'Corporate Leadership Skills: A New Synthesis', *Organisational Dynamics*, Vol. 16, Issue 1, pp. 34–43.

Chaffee, E. E. (1985) 'Three Models of Strategy', *Academy of Management Review*, Vol. 10, No. 1, pp. 89–98.

Ford, J. D. and Hegarty, W. H. (1984) 'Decision Makers' Beliefs about the Causes and Effects of Structure: An Exploratory Study', *Academy of Management Journal*, Vol. 27, No. 2, pp. 271–9.

Garfield, C. (1986) *Peak Performers − New Heroes in Business*, Hutchinson Business, London.

Hackman, J. R. (1984) 'Doing Research That Makes a Difference', *Yale University Papers*, March.

Hambrick, D. C. and Mason, P. A. (1984) 'Upper Echelons: The Organisation as a Reflection of its Top Managers', *Academy of Management Review*, Vol. 9, No. 2, pp. 193–206.

Heller, T. (1985) 'Changing Authority Patterns; A Cultural Perspective', *Academy of Management Review*, Vol. 10, No. 3, pp. 488–95.

Hunsicker, J. Q. (1986) 'Vision, Leadership and Europe's Business Future', *The McKinsey Quarterly*, Spring, pp. 22–39.

Ilgen, D. R. and Faulro, J. L. (1985) 'Limits in Generalisation from Psychological Research to Performance Appraisal Processes', *Academy of Management Review*, Vol. 10, No. 2, pp. 311–21.

Karmel, B. (1978) 'Leadership − A Challenge to Traditional Research Methods and Assumptions', *Academy of Management Review*, Vol. 3, No. 3, pp. 475–82.

Kets de Vries, M. F. R. and Miller, D. (1986) 'Personality, Culture and Organisation', *Academy of Management Review*, Vol. 11, No. 2, pp. 266–79.

Leontiades, M. (1982) 'Choosing the Right Manager to Fit the Strategy', *Journal of Business Strategy*, Vol. 3, No. 2, pp. 58–69.

Mardique, M. A. and Hayes, R. H. (1985) 'The Art of High Technology Management', *The McKinsey Quarterly*, Summer, pp. 23–34.

Margerison, C. and Kakabadse, A. P. (1984) *How American Chief Executives Succeed*, American Management Association Publication, AMA Survey Department, New York.

Mintzberg, H. (1980) *The Nature of Managerial Work*, Prentice-Hall, Englefield Cliffs, New Jersey.

Morse, J. J. and Wagner, F. R. (1978) 'Measuring the Process of Managerial Effectiveness', *Academy of Management Journal*, Vol. 21, No. 1, pp. 23–35.

Ohmae, K. (1982) *The Mind of the Strategist; The Art of Japanese Business*, McGraw-Hill, New York.

Powers, E. (1987) 'Enhancing Managerial Competence – The American Management Association Competency Programme', *Journal of Management Development*, Vol. 6, No. 4, pp. 7–18.

Quinn, J. B. (1985) 'Managing Innovation Controlled Chaos', *Harvard Business Review*, Vol. 63, No. 3, pp. 73–84.

Reddin, W. J. (1970) *Managerial Effectiveness*, McGraw-Hill, New York.

Shirley, R. C. (1982) 'Limiting the Scope of Strategy; A Decision Based Approach', *Academy of Management Review*, Vol. 7, No. 2, pp. 262–8.

Shrivastava, P. and Mitroff, I. I. (1984) 'Enhancing Organisational Research Utilisation: The Role of Decision Makers' Assumptions', *Academy of Management Review*, Vol. 9, No. 1, pp. 18–26.

Smith, K. G., Mitchell, T. R. and Summer, C. E. (1985) 'Top Level Management Priorities in Different Stages of the Organisational Life Cycle', *Academy of Management Journal*, Vol. 28, No. 4, pp. 46–57.

Steiner, G. A. (1983) *The New CEO*, Macmillan, New York.

Taggart, W. and Robey, D. (1981) 'Minds and Managers: On the Dual Nature of Human Information Processing', *Academy of Management Review*, Vol. 6, No. 2, pp. 96–105.

Vecchio, R. P. (1979) 'A Dyordic Interpretation of the Contingency Model of Leadership Effectiveness', *Academy of Management Journal*, Vol. 22, No. 3, pp. 590–600.

15

HR management of executives in Europe
Structures, policies and techniques

FRANK BOURNOIS and PATRICIA METCALFE

Introduction

The approach of 1992 continues inexorably. In its wake it brings an increasing necessity for organisations to rethink their strategic positions to take account of the challenges of this new international dimension. Whether the strategic choice involves proactive attack of foreign markets on their home ground, or defensive maintenance of a no-longer-captive domestic market, the principal agents of change on which the success of this choice will depend will be executives and managers. Human resource management issues as related to this group thus take on a new signficance to the survival of the organisation. If we really wish to see how organisations are shaping up to the Single Market challenge, it is their attitude to managing this key population which we need to examine.

This chapter aims to examine the HR management organisation structures, policies and techniques employed by large organisations in the managing of their executives as key resources across Europe, and to see both how these choices are interlinked, and which (if any) organisation characteristics are related to the choice. Our conclusions are based on the results of a statistical analysis of responses received from 107 large organisations across the European Community to a questionnaire enquiring into the organisation structure of their HR management function for executives, and the policies and techniques of HR management that they employ.

Problems related to Europeanisation

If widening the organisation's strategic focus beyond the confines of its own national boundaries to include the whole or even part of Europe can be considered a form of globalisation, many authors have stressed that in ensuring the success of such a challenge the human element is primordial.

Tex Smiley (1989) has argued that it is the human resource management function which has the most vital contribution to make in helping the organisation adapt to those 'movements' in the international business arena which are having most impact on the way in which companies are doing business. If, traditionally, so-called strategic planners have produced organisation structures and practices which programmed success in the medium to long term, it is nevertheless HR practitioners who can most aid the organisation in times of uncertainty and rapid change. Only this function can help to create new flexible structures which are adaptable to changing circumstances, and encourage new patterns of thought and enhanced adaptability in the minds of those who work for the organisation.

However, the process by which organisations are preparing for 1992 via people management strategies targeting the executive population is not without its problems, as we will see.

Harmonisation of practices across national boundaries

The drive to complete the European Single Market by the end of 1992 has resulted in a number of Community initiatives aimed at harmonising differing national legal frameworks. Not least of these is the so-called Social Charter, or by its full name the Community Charter of the Fundamental Social Rights of Workers. This is the main vehicle for the Commission's strategy so far as harmonising employment legislation is concerned, and aims to set down broad Community-wide standards on employment rights across all categories of employees.

What, however, are we referring to when we speak of harmonising the HR management of executives? There are essentially two aspects to the problem:

(*a*) harmonising strategies for managing senior-level human resources across different cultures;

(*b*) harmonising HR management policies and techniques for this staff category when the organisation functions across different national legal environments.

Cultural difficulties of harmonising HR management of executives
Clearly, if choosing appropriate methods of recruiting, retaining, training and motivating staff is essential to the success of the organisation, achieving the same level of success in different cultures must be an essential element in the globalisation or Europeanisation of its activities. Experts differ in their appreciation of the difficulty involved in this process.

According to those who support the so-called convergence hypothesis of management, cultural differences in managerial attitudes and methods will fade with time and exposure to different cultures (Kerr *et al.*, 1962); another aspect of this phenomenon is exemplified in the multinational corporation, whose strong organisational culture may well appear to supersede most national differences.

A number of studies have, however, revealed that such differences are much more deeply ingrained. One of the most influential of these, carried out by

Hofstede (1980), examined the attitudes of executives working in the same multinational on a number of issues relevant to management, and revealed that cultural differences did indeed persist over time. As Paul Evans, Professor of Organisational Behaviour at INSEAD, stated recently: 'There are profound differences between European countries, not just in markets and competencies, but in basic concepts of management' (Utley, 1990, p. 7).

If organisations are to adopt a successful strategy for retaining their best executives, it is clear that the process of career management is primordial to this success. Yet Schein (1984) has shown that the very notion of a career is culture-related. The requirements for fulfilling a given occupation, the degree of prestige relating to that occupation, the individual's own definition of professional success or failure, and even the degree of overt ambition which it is acceptable to display, are dependent on the constraints of a given culture. The very delicate process of managing an individual's rise in the organisation, so essential to the motivation and retention of key managers, can clearly be subject to gross mismanagement once national differences in expectations come into play.

A study by John Child and Alfred Kieser (1979), however, presented interesting results which indicate that a definite even if limited degree of adaptation is likely to take place when individuals are constantly exposed to the influence of other cultures. Managers' attitudes in the UK and West Germany were examined in relation to such questions as delegation, formalisation and hierarchy. It was found that for certain of these issues their attitudes and the managerial structures consequently adopted seemed unrelated to their cultures; the larger the company, for example, the greater the degree of formalisation. However, responses on the issues of delegation and decentralisation of power were consistently different, a result that has been replicated in Horowitz's (1978) study of firms in the UK, West Germany and France. This study found that firms in the UK preferred to maintain a flexible decentralised structure for the decision-making process, with few staff positions at headquarters, and co-ordination systems organised at all levels to make this level of delegation effective. But in West Germany, as in France, a much greater degree of centralisation in decision-making, with more reliance put on technical specialists at headquarters, resulted in a lower level of delegation.

Cultural differences in identifying and developing high-flyers
The very definition of what constitutes an exceptionally gifted executive can be seen to differ according to national expectations of managerial competence and leadership. When executives of different nationalities were asked whether a manager should be able to answer the majority of questions his subordinates should ask, the percentage of those in Latin countries answering in the affirmative was markedly higher than that of their counterparts further north (Laurent, 1986). Clearly, different cultures retain differing conceptions of the technical

knowledge-base required by a manager, as well as the degree of infallibility it is advisable for him or her to display!

This bias is also evident in the means employed both to identify and to manage the development of what Brooklyn Derr (1987) has baptised HIPOs, or high potentials, estimated to be capable of a rapid climb within the firm's hierarchy.

Companies are biased, on the one hand, towards identifying their HIPOs among those candidates who have undergone a particular form of initial training: in France engineers, in Germany technical specialists and functional generalists. Then, they differ in terms of the types of development and experience it is thought necessary for the company's future leaders to undergo in the course of their route to the top. Although experience outside the home country is given increasing weight, some nationalities are, as is confirmed by recruitment consultants, less geographically mobile than others; high in the mobility stakes are Belgians and Danes, low are Swedes (on account of the preponderance of dual-career families) and the British (Villard, 1989). Insisting on Europe-wide experience as a route to senior executive positions would conceivably be more difficult in such cultural environments.

Problems of determining salaries
Salary determination for executives expatriated abroad plays an important role in encouraging their geographical mobility. But if in the new European company employees of different nationalities will be hired to work alongside one another, harmonising salaries will be all the more complex because expectations of relative as well as absolute salary levels vary across national boundaries.

Quite apart from differences resulting from taxation systems and cost of living differentials, German and Swiss managers, for example, remain more expensive than their French equivalents; the latter are in turn more expensive than their British counterparts (Villard, 1989). The difficulty is compounded in the case of the genuinely globe-trotting executive who manages his or her strategic business unit across several national boundaries; in which currency and according to which national expectations should he or she be paid?

Legal difficulties
The legal constraints on creating HR policies for executives and managers in Europe would appear at first sight simple, as within the European Community there is no legislation specifically relating to this group. Essentially there are two reasons for this lack of legislation:

(a) *Defining the 'European executive'*   The very process of defining a 'European executive' presents difficulties in itself. First, what is understood by the concept of 'European'? Are we referring to the 12 million executives in the private sector in Europe, originating and working in member states of the EC, or the 70,000 'Euromanagers' (calculated from European Commission data on the migration of workers), executives who have undertaken a career which may span several countries, working for an organisation which operates far beyond the barriers of the country in which it was initially registered?

Then, the notion of 'executive' is defined differently in different countries; in some cultures, it is more closely linked to a notion of initial training and qualifications than others, in which it may be entirely dependent on the tasks carried out and/or the degree of authority over subordinates delegated by the employer. Imposing a Europe-wide legal framework on policies for managing a staff category which seems to defy cross-national definition would appear to be a hopeless task.

(*b*) *Desires of employers*   Second, senior managers and organisations themselves do not appear to wish the Commission to become involved in defining a legal framework for managing executives. As a member of UNICE, the European Employers' Association, stated recently, organisations have no desire to see their relations with executives, a group which is rarely problematic in industrial relations terms, restricted by a legal framework: 'We do not wish the Commission to interfere in this sort of problem.' Good practice has always been, and should continue to be, an initiative of companies themselves.

The fact that there is no European standardisation or even harmonisation of employment legislation relating to employees of *any* category means that harmonisation of policies and techniques of HR management across different European countries can be particularly difficult.

The problems faced by a European director in charge of managers are considerably complicated by the differing legislative environments in which he or she has to operate. If, for example, a French parent company aims to set up a management information system logging the skills and experience of its human resources across Europe, it will be severly hindered in West Germany, where national legislation (of 20 December 1988) makes it illegal to communicate to a third party any information related to an employee other than the minimal details on the payslip; the parent company abroad would be included under this definition of third party. It would thus be theoretically impossible for a foreign parent company to acquire reliable information allowing it to monitor its German executives.

An additional dilemma is presented by the question of retirement ages. If the executive population is to be geographically mobile and high-flyers are to acquire European experience, the fact that retirement ages differ across European countries will be a considerable hindrance to this process. If a 'Euromanager' of French nationality is sent abroad, for example to a country in which the legal retirement age is set at 65, and pays contributions in that country, problems will arise if he returns to his homeland to take retirement at the normal age of 60. His pension will be owed by the foreign power, yet there will be a gap of five years during which he will be considered as retired by the French, but still of working age and thus not pensionable by the country in which he paid contributions. Only by paying contributions in both countries could he prevent the problem arising; a manifestly undesirable situation.

Why the 'Euromanager'?

If there is indeed a reason for wishing to adopt HR policies for executives which can be applied on a Europe-wide scale, in spite of the many difficulties, one of its main aims must be to facilitate the development of a top management team with a truly European outlook. As we have seen, one of the increasingly important criteria for choosing top managers and for developing HIPOs is that of international experience; but few corporate headquarters can yet be said to be staffed by a genuinely multinational team (Villard, 1989). Nevertheless, the process of introducing foreign nationals into senior management teams has begun, if slowly, in an attempt to 'Europeanise' on the human resource front at the same time as on the marketing front.

This process may well take place in several steps: first, local managers take the place of expatriates at the head of foreign subsidiaries. Second, these locals themselves are expatriated to management positions in a third country. The third and final step is to bring such managers back to headquarters in very senior positions. As Roland Blain, manager in charge of international executives at Rhône-Poulenc, has stated, 'the only way to attract the best, regardless of nationality, is to offer them a career which spans the widest geographical area possible'. (Villard, 1989 p. 19). The French organisation Air Liquide predicts that in five years' time half the members of its board will be of nationalities other than French (*idem*). It is by giving the option of a career of Europe-wide dimensions that a company can ensure that sufficient openings will be available to its employees when their development requires them to move on.

If companies recognise that their future richness depends on seeking and retaining executive talent from beyond their borders (and some industry sectors, such as finance and banking, are already putting this recognition into practical effect), it is clear that organisations need to set up a framework of HR strategies for selecting these executives that avoids leaving the issue to luck or chance.

For those companies which have made moves in this direction, the first step is frequently to recruit on campuses across Europe, and increasingly to stress bilingualism as an essential prerequisite. Banque Paribas and ICL recruit on campuses beyond their own countries, and Rhône-Poulenc has set up a two-month induction course, available in English or in French, for its young executives. However, this latter strategy is not without its hiccups; in skill-shortage areas the company is at times obliged to relax its linguistic requirements, and as a consequence will find that not all employees from non-French and non-English-speaking countries can follow the programme.

The survey and its aims

As we have seen, the importance of the executive population, in terms of both its size (12 per cent of employees on average in European countries) and, more important, the significant role it plays as a major agent of change and progress within the organisation, cannot be denied. In view of this, many organisations have decided that HR policies adopted to manage this very valuable resource cannot be identical to those used to manage other staff categories.

To set up an effective system of HR management for executives on both a national and European level, organisations need to make a number of fundamental strategic choices. For these choices to be successfully implemented, they must subsequently be reflected in the choice of organisation structures and techniques of HR management. The objective of our study was to examine to what extent European companies are differentiated by their choice of HR organisation structures, and HR management policies and techniques. A framework was then created to demonstrate in what ways choices made by organisations on HR issues are interlinked.

Methodology

The sample
The findings were based on the results of a questionnaire distributed amongst human resource managers in large companies across the 12 EC member states in October 1988, and a follow-up sent to non-respondents in February 1989. The questionnaire was translated into the appropriate local language, i.e. English, French, German, Dutch, Italian, Greek, Spanish, Portuguese or Danish.

The companies targeted were among the first 80 (by number of employees) in each member state. We chose the number of employees as the principal criterion since it was clear that the larger the company, the more likely it would be to employ a large absolute number of executives. In addition, it was believed that organisations with a considerable number of executives would be more likely to have given thought to the problems inherent in defining suitable HR policies for managing them.

The HR director was asked to return the questionnaire if he or she believed that the organisation could be considered to have a Europe-wide HR strategy for its executives. We allowed the respondent to judge whether or not this was so; we had no objective means of verifying if it was indeed the case.

Of the 960 questionnaires sent, 107 responses were received. (Table 15.1 gives the country distribution.) The rate of response was higher in some countries than in others; this may have been related to the differing degrees of awareness of the issue across different countries. It must also be stressed that in choosing the 80 largest companies in each country we were not necessarily comparing companies of identical or sometimes even similar size; for example, the 80th German company was larger than the tenth Portuguese organisation.

Table 15.1 Response rates from each country

United Kingdom	22
France	21
West Germany	14
Denmark	11
Ireland	9
Netherlands	8
Spain	7
Portugal	6
Belgium	5
Italy	3
Luxembourg	1
Greece	0
Total	107

Hypotheses

Our first hypothesis was that the organisation structure used to manage executives was not positively correlated to the choice of specific HR management policies and techniques; for example, the fact that an organisation has centralised its HR management structure for executives at a European level does not determine whether that company would actually encourage a manager to acquire experience abroad (policy).

Our second hypothesis was that four characteristics (nationality, industry sector, membership of a larger group, company size by number of employees) all individually influence HR management policies for executives, in terms both of the organisation structures set up to manage them, and the HR management policies and techniques employed.

The accuracy of these hypotheses was tested by studying the correlations between responses to questions on structure, and their statistical significance. This allowed us to create a framework dividing companies into four groupings according to the way in which the section of the HR function concerned with the management of executives is structured.

Then, the correlations between responses relating to usage of specific HR management policies and techniques were examined, and a similar framework was created dividing companies into groupings according to their use of these policies and techniques.

Next, we established whether any correlation existed between the choice of certain organisation structures and that of specific management policies and techniques.

Finally, we examined the influence of organisation characteristics (nationality, size by number of employees, membership of a larger group, industry or service sector) on the usage of both HR management structures, and policies and techniques. In the ultimate stage of the analysis, we sought to find out if any of these characteristics were related to membership of a particular grouping.

A framework of HR management structures for managing executives

Links between HR management structures

The questionnaire aimed to establish which HR management structures were used to implement company strategy, and sought to clarify the following points to achieve this:

(a) whether or not there was a manager specifically responsible for HR issues relating to executives;

(b) if this person was a member of the board;

(c) if there was no specific position, who was responsible for such issues;

(d) to whom the manager in charge of HR issues for executives reported;

(e) at what level the function was centralised (international, European, national, and so on);

(f) how far in advance the person was made aware of corporate strategy (less than one year, one to three years, more than three years);

(g) which media were employed by the organisation to inform managers of future strategy (meetings, company magazine, forward plans, etc.);

(h) what was the degree of integration of human resource issues into corporate strategy.

A matrix of the correlations between the possible responses to these eight questions was drawn up, making it possible to establish the main links which existed between HR management structures for managing executives in large European companies.

The following were the most important results to emerge (at the 1 per cent level of significance).

(a) When there is no manager specifically in charge of HR management of executives, it is the HR director who takes charge of this activity; conversely, the HR director is not involved when a specific manager is in charge.

(b) When there is no one in charge of this function and the HR director supervises it directly, the HR director reports to the chairman.

(c) When HR management of executives is centrally organised, the person in charge has a place on the board. HR management of executives is then considered to be an essential issue in the formulation of corporate strategy, and this manager participates in board-level decision-making. If it is centralised at an international level, the manager is more likely to report directly to the chairman.

(*d*) The manager in charge of HR issues for executives who reports to the HR director is not a member of the board.

Company groupings of HR management structures for executives

In order to establish if any underlying trends existed, a principal components analysis was undertaken. This analysis was carried out on the responses to the structure questions as described above. The results distinguished four separate types of European organisation as far as organisation structures of HR management for executives were concerned.

Group I: 'Managing executives without structure'

In this group of companies, no separate structure has been set up for defining and implementing HR management policies for executives. There is no specific manager in charge; in this group HR directors will normally be responsible for HR policies relating to executives. They will most likely report directly to their chairmen on such questions; however, in spite of this, the function is very far from being centralised on a European level, being frequently planned on the site, and very short-term orientated.

Group II: The 'international' structure

This is the group of companies in which HR issues are best integrated into corporate strategy.

There is normally a manager in charge of HR management of executives, who is a member of the board and reports directly to the managing director. Policies tend to be centralised at an international level, and manpower planning is directed more frequently towards the long term than the short. The organisation prefers formal means such as written company plans to communicate its strategic intentions to executives rather than informal ones such as meetings.

Group III: The 'national' structure

In this group of organisations HR issues are the least well integrated into corporate strategy.

HR management policies for executives are centralised at a national level. The manager in charge of the function reports directly to the managing director; if there is no specific manager, the managing director himself takes charge of such questions. The planning horizon is relatively short term in this group of companies, and strategy is communicated mainly orally, in meetings.

Group IV: The 'forward-planning' organisation

In this group, the planning horizon for HR management issues relating to executives is very long term (well over three years). HR policies for executives are centralised at either a national or European level, and considered to be the job of specialists, never the managing director. Strategy is mainly communicated through company magazines and other written documents.

Apart from group IV, structures for HR management of senior staff can be principally differentiated according to their level of centralisation. No group has centralised its management of executives at a solely European level. This again poses the question whether it is relevant to distinguish between Europeanisation and internationalisation of HR policies.

A framework of HR management policies and techniques for managing executives

Links between HR management policies and techniques

As with HR management structures, the correlations between responses to the following questions relating to the use of HR management policies and techniques were calculated:

(*a*) Who is the prime mover in career management issues for executives: the executive, the executive's line manager, the HR director, or the managing director?

(*b*) Who is the secondary influence on this: the executive, the manager two levels above the executive, the director of the site?

(*c*) How does the company pay its young executives in relation to the competition?

(*d*) Are performance appraisal interviews carried out; if so, what is their purpose (to check on past objectives, determine pay, plan future career progress)?

(*e*) How does the company classify jobs?

(*f*) What are its policies on bonuses for executives?

(*g*) Is it a company which offers career-development possibilities and tends to retain its managers?

(*h*) Is the manpower planning horizon for executives short or long term?

(*i*) Does a definite policy of recruitment on a Europe-wide level exist?

(*j*) Has the organisation already started recruiting managers who are not nationals?

(*k*) Does it encourage its executives to be geographically mobile across Europe?

The most interesting correlations emerging from this at the 1 per cent level of significance were the following.

(*a*) If the prime mover in career terms is the HR director, the principal objective of performance appraisal interviews is career planning. Where the main concern of HR directors is career management, it is not surprising that they focus on this issue when they are in charge of the HR management of executives. If the prime mover in career terms is the line manager, there is a strong chance that few executives will remain loyal to the company in the long term by spending all or a large part of their career in the same company. This correlation reinforces the theory that an executive must be allowed some leeway in managing his or her own career; if HR management systems are too directive he or she will leave the organisation. If, however, the prime mover in career terms is the director of the site, there is little chance that the company will have already started Europe-wide recruitment of executives; decentralisation to this extent is clearly incompatible with a Europe-wide strategy.

(*b*) If the company pays its young executives less than the going rate, there is a strong chance that there will be no job classification system. It is also probable that Europe-wide recruitment will not yet have started in the organisation. This raises the important question whether it is necessary to be a top-paying organisation to enter the European recruitment market; our results are in keeping with comments from the specialised press on executive salaries. On the other hand, the organisation which has an established bonus system for executives tends to be an organisation which pays its executives above the market rate. There is also a significant correlation between offering the possibility of bonuses to the majority of executives and having already started Europe-wide recruitment.

(*c*) If there is no performance appraisal interview, the company is likely to have no job classification system either.

(*d*) The companies to which few managers remain loyal enough to develop a career in the long term tend to be companies in which recruitment is planned less than nine months in advance; the reverse is also true. This emphasises a harsh reality, i.e. that where the loyalty of key managers cannot be counted on, advance planning is extremely difficult for the HR manager.

(*e*) The company with a definite policy of recruiting executives across Europe usually has already started doing so. It also encourages its executives to be geographically mobile within Europe.

Company groupings of HR management policies and techniques for executives

By carrying out principal components analysis on the responses relating to HR management policies and techniques, it proved possible to establish a framework distinguishing four types of organisations.

Group I: The 'European HR management of executives' organisation

Companies in this grouping encourage managers to be geographically mobile within Europe; they have a strong policy commitment to recruiting executives who are nationals of other European countries, and have already started doing so.

They tend to pay executives higher than the industry average for the country, and offer the possibility of bonuses to most executives.

Manpower planning is practised. The managing director is usually the prime mover in the executive's career; the line manager plays an insignificant role.

Organisations in this grouping inspire a high level of company loyalty; a high proportion of their executives remain with the organisation in the long term.

Group II: The 'high remuneration' organisation

This type of organisation does not display a strong commitment to Europe-wide recruitment of managers. Manpower planning is not frequently practised, and many decisions concerning executives are short term.

The company pays its managers much more than the going rate, and sales executives are paid on a different scale.

Individual executives take the initiative in their own careers, but few executives remain with this type of organisation long enough to develop their careers in the long term.

Group III: The 'dependent on loyalty' organisation

The most significant characteristic of this type of organisation is to pay its executives relatively badly; it rarely offers the possibility of bonuses.

There is no performance appraisal interview. Career planning is short term and individual executives are the prime movers in their own careers.

In spite of this, company loyalty is very strong within the group; most managers remain within the organisation for a large part of their careers.

Group IV: The 'Europe uncertain' organisation

This organisation is characterised by its uncertainty in relation to Europe; the HR director is unable to say if it has a defined policy of recruitment across Europe, and it does not encourage geographical mobility in its executives.

The HR director plays a more significant role than in other groups in the career development of executives. The performance appraisal interview is a technique frequently employed, its main purpose being to determine the manager's pay. Bonuses are offered, and sales executives are paid on the same scale as the rest of the executive group.

Links between HR management structures and HR management policies and techniques

The next step in the analysis was to establish whether there was any correlation between the four HR structure groupings and the four HR management policies and techniques groupings; did companies which had an 'international' structure, for example, also tend to fall into the 'high remuneration' grouping in so far as HR management policies and techniques were concerned? The results of the two principal components analyses were used to determine these correlations.

This sample of 107 European organisations which claimed to have a Europe-wide strategy revealed *no statistically significant correlation between the type of structure chosen and the types of HR management policies and techniques employed by these companies to manage their executives.*

However, the results reveal some interesting cases of negative correlation: the 'national' or the 'managing managers without structure' organisations tend not to be 'Europe-wide management of managers' organisations.

The 'forward planning' organisation tends not to be a 'dependent on loyalty' organisation: not surprisingly, since for the latter manpower planning is short term. It also tends not to be a 'Europe uncertain' organisation; our interpretation is that the general uncertainty of the latter is inconsistent with the strong tendency towards formal planning of the former.

Influence of organisation characteristics on choice of HR management structure and HR management policies and techniques

The next step in the process was to examine whether any significant correlations existed between specific characteristics of organisations and the usage of specific HR management structure or HR management policies and techniques for executives.

The four organisation characteristics of nationality, industry sector (industrial or services), membership of a larger group and company size by number of employees were chosen to examine this question.

Given that the sample size was very small for some countries, it was decided to group countries together in geographical zones for the purpose of this exercise. Hofstede's (1987) country groupings as used to demonstrate cultural differences between executives from different zones were adopted.

Group I: Anglo-Saxon countries was composed of organisations in the UK, Eire and Denmark (42 companies in the sample).
Group II: Latin countries included organisations in Italy, France, Belgium, Luxembourg, Spain and Portugal (43 companies in the sample).

Group III: Germanic countries contained responses from Germany and the Netherlands (22 companies in the sample).

Companies were divided according to whether they were principally industrial or service organisations: the sample was composed of 61 of the former and 41 of the latter. Five could not be allocated.

The third significant characteristic was membership of a larger group: 59 companies in the sample were autonomous and 43 part of a group. Again, five could not be allocated.

Finally, size as expressed by number of employees was examined. Companies were divided into those with less than 1,000 employees (19) and those with more (88).

We sought to find out in relation to each of these four characteristics: first, whether there was any particular characteristic (size, nationality, etc.), which was closely linked to the usage of any specific HR management structures, policies or techniques. In other words, did responses from service companies tend to differ from those from industrial organisations on one or several questions relative to Europe-wide recruitment issues?

Second, whether any characteristic seemed to go hand in hand with membership of any particular grouping. For example, were service companies strongly differentiated from industrial ones by the number of them which fell into the grouping 'international structure'?

Links between organisation characteristics and the use of specific HR management structures, policies and techniques

HR structures

Neither industry sector, membership of a larger group nor size proved to have any influence on HR structures adopted by organisations for their executives.

Only nationality explained differences in structure. If there is no manager in charge of HR management of executives, then in Germanic and Latin countries it is usually the HR director and in Anglo-Saxon ones the managing director who is responsible. In the Anglo-Saxon grouping, the immediate superior of the manager in charge of executives is likely to be the managing director. These observations tend to support the notion that structures are flatter in Anglo-Saxon organisations.

HR management policies and techniques

Generally, industry sector and membership of a larger group played a minor role in influencing HR management policies and techniques for managing executives in our sample.

Nationality and size were the characteristics which significantly differentiated responses on almost half the questions. In Anglo-Saxon cultures executives rarely pursued an entire career within the same company; at the opposite end of the spectrum were Latin companies in which the majority of executives remained with the same organisation. Company size also explained much of the difference in response; the smaller the company, the fewer the managers who spend their entire career in the same organisation. One logical explanation of this is that a limited number of career opportunities exist in smaller companies. Latin and Anglo-Saxon companies also had shorter-term manpower planning and job creation/reduction cycles than Germanic ones.

Links between organisation characteristics and membership of a particular group

For five company groupings out of the eight in our two frameworks, it was found that *nationality was the significant characteristic associated with membership of a particular group.* For the other two groupings, membership was mainly linked to size ('forward planning' and 'high remuneration' companies).

We then sought to establish for each individual grouping in our two frameworks which characteristics (if any) explained the variance in responses.

HR structure groupings
Nationality was again significant. Anglo-Saxon companies were over-represented and Latin ones under-represented in the 'international structure' group. The 'national structure' group was also essentially made up of Anglo-Saxon companies, some Latin ones, but very few Germanic organisations.

Membership of the 'forward planning' group was dependent on two factors: nationality and size. Germanic and large organisations were over-represented in this category.

HR management policies and techniques groupings
Both nationality and size proved to be important. Large companies were over-represented in the 'European HR management of executives' grouping, confirming that it is necessary to have a certain number of managers to set up a complete system to manage them on a Europe-wide basis.

The 'high remuneration' grouping was composed mainly of Anglo-Saxon companies and those which were not members of a larger group. The 'dependent on loyalty' company was usually Latin rather than Germanic.

Conclusions

Our first working hypothesis proved true in so far as the structures of the HR management systems employed by our sample of 107 large companies across Europe were indeed unrelated to their choice of particular HR management policies and techniques, although in some cases instances of negative correlation were observed.

However, the second hypothesis, i.e. that all four characteristics of nationality, industry sector (service or industrial), membership of a larger group and company (size by number of employees) were each individually related to the choice of specific HR management structures, policies and techniques, was unconfirmed by this sample. Only nationality proved a significant factor related to choices of both structure and policies and techniques; size played a part in explaining the variance in some responses relating to the usage of specific policies and techniques. Nationality was also related to membership of particular groupings in our framework. In this sample, industry sector played no significant role.

Our results have significant implications for multinational corporations wishing to set up harmonised HR management systems for executive staff which span several cultures. This sample of 107 large European organisations reveals that, at present, the choice of HR strategies and the structures and techniques chosen to implement them are far more related to national expectations than any international framework.

References

Brooklyn Derr, C. (1987) Managing High Potentials in Europe: Some Cross-Cultural Findings', *European Management Journal*, Vol. 5, No. 2, pp. 72–80.

Child, J. and Kieser, A. (1979) 'Organizational and Managerial Roles in British and West Germany Companies: An Examination of the Culture Free Thesis', in C. J. Lammers and D. J. Hickson (Eds) *Organizations Like and Unlike*, Routledge, London, pp. 251–71.

Hofstede, G. (1980) *Culture's Consequences*, Sage, California.

Hofstede, G. (1987) 'Relativité culturelle des pratiques et théories de l'organisation', *Revue française de gestion*, September–October, pp. 10–21.

Horowitz, J. (1978) 'Allemagne, Grande Bretagne, France: Trois Styles de Management', *Revue française de gestion*, September–October, pp. 8–17.

Kerr, C., Dunlop, J. T., Harbison, F. H. and Myers, C. A. (1962) *Industrialism and Industrial Man*, Harvard University Press.

Laurent, A. (1986) 'The Cross-Cultural Puzzle of International Human Resource Management', *Human Resource Management*, Vol. 25, No. 1, pp. 91–102.

Schein, E. (1984) 'Culture as an Environmental Context for Careers', *Journal of Occupational Behaviour*, Vol. 5, pp. 71–81.

Smiley, T. (1989) 'A Challenge to the Human Resource and Organizational Function in International Firms', *European Management Journal*, Vol. 7, No. 2, pp. 189–97.

Utley, A. (1990) 'On yer vélo', *The Times Higher Educational Supplement*, 2 March, p. 7.

Villard, N. (1989) 'États-majors sans frontières', *L'Expansion*, May/June, pp. 19–22.

16

Conclusion: comparative studies and the development of human resource management

SHAUN TYSON and CHRIS BREWSTER

We began by commenting on the difficulties of comparative studies and the opportunities offered by research across cultures and geographical as well as organisational boundaries. While we do not wish to rehearse these arguments here, it is worth considering how far this collection of papers has advanced our understanding, and to ask where research efforts should next be concentrated.

The geographical coverage has been wide, ranging from research in Japan, Singapore, South Korea, India, the USA and Canada to European countries including the UK, France, Germany and Greece. Our approach has been to try a number of points of entry to comparative study. This has created interesting juxtapositions between different levels of analysis. By taking topics which range from industrial conflict to management development we have attempted to bring in a sufficient range of issues through which comparative study can enlighten our understanding of human resource management.

A number of clear messages emerge from the research described here. First, the notion that differences between societies can be explained by cultural patterns must be modified to consider the interaction between cultural norms and legal institutions and underlying economic factors. Second, as we might expect from contingency theory, the variables at the level of the organisation have a significant impact on human resource strategies and policies. These variables include management style, the personalities involved as well as the history of the organisation, its industrial relations traditions and the markets in which it trades.

While these two factors are important, the spread of common ideas about human resource management occurs because global information sharing is possible, and multinational companies promulgate common policies. There is a high degree of convergence, as evidenced by the acceptance of a common technical language, in such areas as job evaluation and employee appraisal and development. The papers here do reveal, however, that the human resource management agenda is reinterpreted locally; that different political, economic, social and cultural conditions impinge upon organisational variables, so that there are different models of human resource management in evidence.

One view on the issues raised here would be to conclude that in developing countries there are still vestiges of a normative role for the human resources department as a 'loyal opposition' or as a protector of the people, while a more sophisticated 'business consultant' model of human resources management is emerging in companies in the developed nations, in response to economic pressures and competition (Herman, 1968; Tyson and Fell, 1986).

The danger of attributing differences in human resource strategies to cultural differences rather than to differences between organisations is one reason why we must be cautious when interpreting comparative research results. Varying models of human resource management can be found within the same society, which should be an area for further study therefore.

Meanings are socially derived and context-bound, however. 'Skill' and 'utilisation' clearly have different connotations, for example, in different countries, and 'corporate cultures' may also have a profound behavioural effect; Laurent (1986, p. 93) points out that 'international human resource management may only be international in the eyes of the designers'.

If the possibilities promised under the banner of comparative international research are to be realised, a wider coverage of human resource policy areas is needed. There are gaps in our knowledge of recruitment, communication, appraisal and promotion policies, for example, which need to be filled within each country before we undertake a comparative analysis between countries.

As we write the final words of this book, we are conscious of the rapid changes taking place on the political map of Europe. Countries long avoided by researchers and by the general population of the West are assuming their new national characters. Change and adaptation are painful for countries such as Poland, Hungary and East Germany. We can sympathise with human resource staff in Germany who are now experiencing first hand the problems of different industrial relations systems and different strategies and policies, even where there is a common culture. For example, at the time of unification the average factory worker in East Germany earned around 1,000 Deutschmarks a month, whereas his West German counterpart receives around 4,000 a month. The economic union will lead to even more migration west unless the reward systems are redesigned. Any further comparative studies should include Eastern Europe, the Soviet Union and China. Our book has also not included any studies of South America, or of any of the many emerging nations such as Indonesia and Malaysia. Although we have a reasonably wide coverage of human resource issues and of different cultures, we are conscious that many more cultures should be researched, and that we have had to be highly selective in the comparisons chosen.

Not only do we need more data, we also need to develop a more comprehensive theory. There is some theory building in this text, but we believe there is need for more work showing the relationship between human resource strategies and the economic and legal frameworks which help to determine them, and for research into the strategies followed at the organisational level of analysis. These linkages between different levels of analysis are not easy to establish, but they are essential if we are to make progress. In practice, theory and data-gathering grow together, so our call for more theory is also a call for more data.

Successful organisations are often said to be those which are constantly changing (Kanter, 1983). The pace of human resource change is heightened by the social and economic pressures now finding expression through employees, pressure groups, governments, customers and competitors. This presents problems for all researchers in the social sciences, and is yet a further factor to be taken into account. However, we can at least see these changes as a constant test of the frameworks and methods of analysis deployed in comparative research. To be of value comparative research methods must be free of temporal limitations, since societies develop in different phases through different periods of time.

This is an argument for both macro-theories which focus on economic and political science as a basis for comparative studies in human resource management, and for micro-level theories which focus on behaviour and social action. Techniques, such as job evaluation or appraisal systems, may be interpreted purely as one manifestation of behaviour or as a part of the symbolic order in organisations. Human resource specialists operate at the interface between the symbolic order (organisation charts, job evaluation systems and similar formal expressions of authority) and behavioural realities (Tyson, 1987). This makes a comparative study of the occupation worthwhile sociologically.

We hope that this collection has helped to take further such a study and has provided scholars and practitioners with a broad overview of the relationships between the different levels of analysis, the significance of culture, and insights into issues which only comparative frameworks can offer. The papers here do show in our view that there are theories and processes of analysis which take the study of national cultures, human resource strategies, role and policies beyond journalistic description.

We are especially pleased that these papers were collected under the aegis of a conference jointly sponsored by the International Labour Office and Cranfield School of Management. It is through the collaboration between institutions at an international level that we believe international research will be taken forward, and the significant agenda of research into human resource management explored.

References

Herman, S. M. (1968) *The People Specialists*, Alfred Knopf, The Hague.

Kanter, R. M. (1983) *The Change Masters – Corporate Entrepreneurs at Work*, Allen and Unwin, London.

Laurent, A. (1986) 'The Cross-Cultural Puzzle of International Human Resource Management', *Human Resource Management*, Vol. 25, No. 1, pp. 91–102.

Tyson, S. (1987) 'The Management of the Personnel Function', *Journal of Management Studies*, Vol. 24, No. 5, pp. 523–32.

Tyson, S. and Fell, A. (1986) *Evaluating the Personnel Function*, Hutchinson, London.

Index